The Supremacist Syndrome

Of Related Interest

Peter Brandt
Indefensible
Adventures of a Farm Animal Protection Lawyer
244 pp, 978-1-59056-629-9

Aph Ko
Racism as Zoological Witchcraft
A Guide to Getting Out
168 pp, 978-1-59056-596-4

Alycee J. Lane
Nonviolence Now!
Living the 1963 Birmingham Campaign's Promise of Peace
216 pp, 978-1-59056-506-3

Jim Mason
An Unnatural Order
The Roots of Our Destruction of Nature
Fully Revised and Updated
256 pp, 978-1-59056-631-2

Charles Patterson
Eternal Treblinka
Our Treatment of Animals and the Holocaust
312 pp, 978-1-930051-99-7

Norm Phelps
The Longest Struggle
Animal Advocacy from Pythagoras to PETA
368 pp, 978-1-59056-106-5

Richard H. Schwartz, Ph.D.
Vegan Revolution
Saving Our World, Revitalizing Judaism
262 pp, 978-1-59056-627-5

THE SUPREMACIST SYNDROME

*How Domination Underpins Slavery,
Genocide, the Exploitation of Women, and
the Maltreatment of Animals*

Peter Marsh

Lantern Publishing & Media ● Brooklyn, NY

2021
Lantern Publishing & Media
128 Second Place
Brooklyn, NY 11231
www.lanternpm.org

Printed in the United States of America

Library of Congress Cataloging-in-Publication Data

Names: Marsh, Peter (Lawyer), author.
Title: The supremacist syndrome : how domination underpins slavery, genocide, the exploitation of women, and the maltreatment of animals / Peter Marsh.
Description: Brooklyn, NY : Lantern Publishing & Media, [2021] | Includes bibliographical references and index
Identifiers: LCCN 2020052723 (print) | LCCN 2020052724 (ebook) | ISBN 9781590566251 (paperback) | ISBN 9781590566268 (epub)
Subjects: LCSH: Power (Social sciences)—Case studies. | Oppression (Psychology)—Case studies. | Prejudices--Case studies. | White nationalism—Case studies. | Male domination (Social structure)—Case studies. | Ethnic relations—Case studies.
Classification: LCC HM1256 .M27 2021 (print) | LCC HM1256 (ebook) | DDC 303.3/85—dc23
LC record available at https://lccn.loc.gov/2020052723
LC ebook record available at https://lccn.loc.gov/2020052724

For Roxanne and our children, Moriah and Ethan

Contents

Illustrations, Charts, and Maps

Illustrations

Charts

Maps

Many thanks to the United States Holocaust Museum for generously granting permission to reprint the illustrations listed above.

Acknowledgments

Many thanks to Jim Mason, Peter Singer, Erik Marcus, Sue Stern, Merritt Clifton, João Graca, Kristof Dhont, and Charles Patterson for their generosity in reviewing all or parts of the manuscript and offering suggestions about how to improve it.

Thanks also to Mary Rostad for putting together the maps and to Bill Morris for editing the images.

Special thanks to Martin Rowe for the great care he took in editing the manuscript, and to Aaron and Doreen Baker of Mulberry Creek Imagery for taking my photograph.

Author's Note

This book discusses three different forms of supremacism—white supremacism, male supremacism, and anti-Semitic nationalist supremacism—to determine whether various supremacist ideologies have common elements that we can use to better understand how these ideologies work and how we can overcome them. Then it considers whether the way we commonly treat other animals has the same core features and is as wrong as other forms of supremacism.

I know some people may be offended by any comparison of human suffering to suffering undergone by nonhumans. I have avoided making such comparisons because they risk elevating concern for one type of suffering at the expense of concern for others, and *all* suffering matters.

Even if you believe that every human's well-being is far more important than that of any other animal, it turns out that people working to reduce human suffering can benefit from considering the suffering endured by nonhumans. Recent studies have found that different forms of prejudice are related—that people who are racists are more likely to be sexists too, and they're more likely to condone the exploitation of animals and the natural world. Attempts to overcome different forms of inequality are related too. For instance, studies have found that humane education programs can broaden a person's concern for the well-being of other people as well as for that of other animals.

Some people may also object to the idea of me, a white non-Jewish male, writing about domination. I understand that Jewish people rightfully consider the Holocaust especially hurtful and worry that any comparison to harms suffered by others will reduce its moral significance. I know, too, that Black people may be concerned that a white man cannot fairly discuss the oppression they have endured; I know that women may feel the same about their exploitation by men. I understand these concerns and will do my best to be fair to everyone.

While we members of a privileged group haven't suffered the pain of oppression, this shouldn't prevent us from doing what we can to help oppressed people gain full equality. The book's three case studies tell how a Swedish Lutheran helped rescue Jews living in Hungary, Europeans worked to free Africans from the clutches of a rapacious European king, and male members of Parliament convinced their colleagues to let women vote.

Introduction

Each group nourishes its own pride and vanity, boasts itself superior, exalts its own divinities, and looks with contempt on outsiders. Each group thinks its own folkways the only right ones, and if it observes that other groups have other folkways, these excite its scorn.
—William Graham Sumner[1]

Heinrich Himmler was a stickler for decent behavior. The Reichsführer insisted that SS soldiers carry out their work honestly and without brutality.[2] Above all, he repeatedly demanded one thing from his men—decency.[3]

In July of 1941, Himmler reinforced the mobile killing squads operating on the Eastern Front with SS cavalry units and police battalions to keep up with the work that would result from a new policy. From then on, he ordered, Jewish women and children would no longer be left to starve after the men in their community had been killed. Now, they, too, would be murdered.

He often visited the killing fields and delivered the new orders to death squad commanders personally.[4] On an inspection tour in Minsk, he once asked to see a mass shooting. An officer who traveled with him told later how the victims had been forced to dig an open grave. Then some were made to lie face down in it. After they were shot, others were forced to lie on top of them and were shot from the top of the pit. Himmler went right up to the edge to get a good look and became queasy when a victim's brains splashed on his immaculate gray field uniform. The officer jumped forward and steadied him.[5]

If the Jews left behind had known the townspeople the Nazis had taken into custody were shot, they might have begun to resist or even revolt, so the Nazis said they had sent them to labor camps.[6] They used a similar ruse to deceive those headed to a gas chamber at Auschwitz, telling them upon their arrival that they were going to be assigned to a work detail after getting a shower and a meal. The signs outside the chambers where they were gassed read BATH HOUSES,[7] and SS guards calmly advised those entering to carefully place their clothes on a hook in the undressing room and be sure to remember its number, because that was the way they would get their own clothing back after their shower.[8] The guards knew, however, that all their clothes would soon be brought to "Kanada," the name prisoners had given to huts at the camp where all the victims' belongings were sorted before being sent to Germany.

This elaborate charade didn't deceive some victims. In a statement written after his capture, Auschwitz Kommandant Rudolf Höss told how some women realized that they and their children were being herded to

Fig. 1. Hungarian Woman and Children Walking to a Gas Chamber at Auschwitz/Birkenau in May 1944: United States Holocaust Museum.

a gas chamber, not a bathhouse. They still managed somehow to find the strength to play with their children and talk to them lovingly while they all walked together to their death. He recalled how one woman, as she passed near him with her four children—all holding hands to help the smallest over the rough ground, pointed to her children and whispered, "How can you murder these beautiful, darling children? Don't you have any heart?"[9] (See Fig. 1.)

This book is about Heinrich Himmler and Rudolf Höss and people like them, supremacists who believe their group is better than all others and should be able to dominate and exploit everyone from an "inferior" group. Human history has been a continual story of supremacists slaughtering and enslaving people, of constant conquests and wars waged in the name of one ethnic group—or race, or religion—or another, from Alexander the Great to Genghis Khan, from the Crusades to European colonialism, from the Holocaust to the genocide in Rwanda.

It will tell how a people's natural pride in its own group can fester into prejudice against those from other groups and, in extreme cases, entitlement to take whatever it wants from the others: their labor, their land, even their lives. As we try to understand how people once justified practices now seen as profoundly wrong—like slavery, colonialism, and the exploitation of women—we will see how people can harm others, even in reprehensible ways, and still live with themselves by engaging in what social psychologists call *moral disengagement*.[10]

For example, if you're wondering how SS soldiers could continue to think of themselves as decent men after murdering women and children, part of the answer can be found in a speech Himmler gave to senior SS officers in the fall of 1943. He explained that the murders weren't wrong, because they were being committed for a worthy cause:

> One basic principle must be the absolute rule for the SS man: we must be honest, decent, loyal, and comradely to members of our own blood and to nobody else. [. . .] When somebody comes to me and says, "I cannot dig the anti-tank ditch with women and children, it is inhuman, for it would kill them," then I have to say, "You are a murderer of your own

blood because if the anti-tank ditch is not dug, German soldiers will die, and they are sons of German mothers. They are our own blood."[11]

Himmler squared the ethical circle with blood loyalty, the belief that people of Aryan[12] blood were so superior to everyone else that they were entitled to take whatever they wanted from others.

The first part of the book will contain case studies of three different supremacist ideologies—the first based on ethnonationalism, the next on race, and the last on gender. Each will tell how supremacists secured and maintained the dominance of their group and what their adversaries did to defeat them. All three studies will involve European countries whose citizens considered themselves to be among the world's most civilized people. And all three will be from the nineteenth and twentieth centuries to make sure any lessons are recent enough to be relevant today.

In the first chapter, Heinrich Himmler will make a cameo appearance. The main characters, though, will be Adolf Eichmann—one of his SS henchmen who tried to get all the Jewish people in Hungary to the death camp at Auschwitz before the advancing Soviet armies gained control of the country—and his Swedish nemesis, Raoul Wallenberg. In this chapter, we'll also meet Father Maximilian Kolbe, a Polish priest who took the place of another Auschwitz prisoner condemned to die in a starvation cell at the camp, and his moral opposite, Father András Kun, a Hungarian priest who urged a band of local fascists to "fire in the holy name of Christ" when massacring Jewish residents of Budapest. The chapter will end as the Soviet armies encircled Budapest and the Nazis set in motion a plan to slaughter all those still alive in the central Jewish ghetto.

The focus will shift in the second chapter to the race-based supremacism of King Leopold II of Belgium.[13] This section will tell how he convinced other colonial powers to let him take a large slice of the "African cake" they were dividing among themselves by promising to bring civilization, commerce, and Christianity to people living in the Congo region. Instead, he brought what Arthur Conan Doyle called a more efficient form of slavery by forcing the Congolese to provide labor for him in their own homeland.[14] While working as a clerk in the shipping company that brought goods to and from the Congo, E. D. Morel discovered that the king was robbing the Congolese. Following the model British abolitionists had used a century before, Morel launched a global public awareness campaign to wrest the Congo from Leopold, by then the wealthiest monarch in Europe.[15] With the help of a British consul who Joseph Conrad said used to emerge from months in the jungle as "serene" as if he had just been out "for a stroll in the park," Morel managed to get the British government to pressure Leopold into giving up the Congo. Then he worked to stop the Belgian government from allowing the king to keep his vast private estate there—booty Leopold hoped to hand down to a new generation of royal thieves.

The third chapter is about a worldwide supremacist ideology that cuts across all national, ethnic, racial, and religious lines: male supremacism. Our story begins in 1867, when the prominent English philosopher John Stuart Mill urged his colleagues in the British House of Commons to pass a bill enfranchising women on the same terms as men. Although that effort failed, during the next forty years, advocates of women's suffrage steadily gained support for their cause in the House of Commons, only to be repeatedly frustrated by opposition from political leaders concerned that the enfranchisement of women would hurt their own party's electoral prospects.

The situation reached a boiling point when the government "torpedoed" a compromise enfranchisement bill making its way through the House of Commons. After militants protested by planting bombs, setting buildings afire, and slashing paintings in museums, government support for women's suffrage plummeted. Then a group of suffrage societies led by Millicent Garrett Fawcett—who had watched Mill's speech from the Ladies' Gallery more than forty years earlier—took another tack. They put together a great pilgrimage in which thousands of supporters, many from the most remote parts of England and Wales, slowly made their way to London in the summer of 1913, with banners proclaiming they were seeking the vote in a nonviolent and law-abiding way. The pilgrims joined with others, fifty thousand strong, for a mammoth rally in Hyde Park. Just when it seemed the pilgrimage had turned the tide in the women's favor again, war intervened, splitting the suffrage movement between those who opposed the war and others who supported it. Fawcett soldiered on as she had for decades, convincing many of her colleagues to show themselves worthy of full citizenship by engaging in wartime relief work. The work they did during the war changed the minds of many British politicians, and an enfranchisement bill made its way through the House of Commons for the first time, only to face formidable opposition in the House of Lords.

The fourth chapter will consider whether different supremacist ideologies have common features that we can use to better understand how these ideologies work and how they can be overcome. It will also address several questions raised by the case studies, including:

- How could so many people living in Germany, one of the world's most civilized countries, help the Nazis carry out their genocidal plans?
- How did King Leopold's Catholic supporters in Belgium reconcile the murder and pillage committed by his soldiers with their Christian values? and
- How did a country that had abolished slavery decades before continue to limit English women to narrow lives in which they could perform only menial work, couldn't vote or attend a university, and, if they married, could be dominated by their husbands?

Although this chapter will include many examples from the three case studies, it's intended to be self-sufficient. You can bypass the case studies and go directly to this chapter if you'd prefer to do that. The case studies, though, describe in great detail the ways supremacists avoided shame and guilt for the harm they inflicted on others.

Any study of supremacism would be incomplete if it failed to address a type of supremacism that encompasses all others—the belief that we're superior to other animals and are entitled to take whatever we need or want from them. The next three chapters will apply what has been learned from the case studies of ethnic-, racial-, and gender-based supremacism to human supremacism to see whether it, too, involves causing unjustified harm to innocent members of a weaker group.

James Rachels, the author of a classic text on moral philosophy,[16] framed the issue this way:

> We kill animals for food; we use them as experimental subjects in laboratories; we exploit them as sources of raw materials such as leather and wool; we keep them as work animals—the list goes on and on. These practices are to our advantage, and we intend to continue them. Thus, when we think about what the animals are like, we are motivated to conceive of them in ways that are compatible with treating them in these ways. If animals are conceived as intelligent, sensitive beings, these ways of treating them might seem monstrous.[17]

The sixth and seventh chapters will consider whether animals raised for food are intelligent and sensitive beings or just robot-like creatures genetically programmed to act the way they do. These chapters will also evaluate whether the reasons people give to justify using animals for food are good ones, or if human exceptionalism is camouflage for another form of supremacism.

The final chapter will go from description to prescription, discussing practical actions each of us can take to prevent supremacist beliefs from taking root in the first place or at least combat them before they become virulent, an issue that has become critically important with the recent resurgence of nationalism and other group-based ideologies. Fortunately, in recent years, social scientists have learned a great deal about how supremacist ideologies work, how they spring from some people's desire for social dominance and are sustained by myths that legitimize oppression, how they can metastasize into a *supremacist syndrome* of dominance-related beliefs, and, most important, how they can be defeated. These findings, like the information included in other parts of the book, will be documented with extensive notes for those who want to dig more deeply.

Let's begin.

I

The Holocaust in Hungary

"After Being Rescued, My Mother Hugged and Kissed
Me and Said One Word: 'Wallenberg'"

Fig. 2. Walter Rosenberg (Rudolf Vrba)

1. MISSION IMPOSSIBLE: TO ESCAPE FROM AUSCHWITZ AND TELL THE WORLD ABOUT IT

[E]very escape attempt [from Auschwitz] posed a Herculean challenge.—Henryk Świebocki[1]

The young woman's face pressed close to her companion's as she whispered in his ear, "We'll meet again, darling. We'll meet again and it'll be wonderful. But . . . if we don't . . . it has been wonderful!"

The couple clung together, their lips pressed close, fingers biting into each other's back, until someone roared at the young man, "Get rid of that girl or go up on the lorry with her!"

The woman's grip relaxed. "Go, darling," she said softly. "*Go now!*"

Then she turned and ran for the truck that was going to take her to her death. For the parting took place at Auschwitz, and the young woman, Alice Munk, was being taken to a gas chamber, together with thirty-eight hundred other Jewish residents of the Czech "family camp" who were to be killed that day. When they became aware of their fate, the Czechs joined together and sang the Czech national anthem, "*Kde Domov Můj*" ("Where My Home Is"), and the Jewish song "*Hatikvah*" ("The Hope").[2,3]

The young man, a nineteen-year-old Slovak named Walter Rosenberg, had wanted to escape from Auschwitz since the first day he arrived there in June of 1942, almost two years earlier. The murder of the Czechs made him even more determined to try. Although a prisoner, he performed clerical work at Auschwitz II, the Birkenau extermination camp, and knew that when the Czechs had arrived six months earlier, the Nazis had classified them for *Sonderbehandlung* or "special handling" (one of the many Nazi euphemisms for murder) after they had been held for a six-month "quarantine" period. He also knew that another group of Czechs had arrived at Auschwitz the previous December, and the Nazis had given them the same classification; they were scheduled to be killed in about fifteen weeks. Although the Nazis had murdered hundreds of thousands of people in the gas chambers at Birkenau, they succeeded in keeping that a secret.[4] If only people knew the truth about Auschwitz, Rosenberg hoped, they would find a way to stop the killing.

As one Holocaust historian put it, "At Birkenau, illusion was the rule."[5] Camp officials disguised the platform where prisoners arrived as an ordinary railroad station, with signs in many languages pointing the way to departing trains,[6] although none of those arriving were going to be departing on a train. An orchestra of young girls in white blouses and navy-blue skirts greeted arrivals with light, happy tunes while camp doctors looked over the newcomers and decided who were going to be murdered right away.[7]

Camp officials reserved their deceptions for those who were destined for the gas chambers. They wanted prisoners, though, to understand what would happen to them if they ever attempted to—or even planned to—escape. They made this clear to Rosenberg a week after he arrived when, just before the evening roll call, two mobile gallows were brought in front of the kitchen at the camp.

As all the inmates looked on under the watchful gaze of Kommandant Rudolf Höss, a short SS officer bellowed:

> "Two Polish prisoners have been caught preparing to escape. This was made quite clear by the fact that under their tunics they were found to be wearing civilian shirts.
>
> "This is something which the camp administration will not tolerate. Any man found planning an escape will be punished by death on the gallows as these two prisoners are about to be punished now.
>
> "Let this be a warning to you all. The rules of the camp must be obeyed."

A prisoner standing next to Rosenberg muttered, "He's bluffing. He's just trying to scare us. I bet they only hang them by their wrists for half an hour or so."

The SS officer wasn't bluffing.

First, one prisoner was hanged, then the other. With the short-drop gallows used at Auschwitz, the victims only dropped a few inches after the platform on which they had been standing flew open, and they slowly strangled while their lungs fought a losing battle for air.[8]

By the time these prisoners were hanged, the short-drop gallows had become a standard feature of German concentration camps, part of a gruesome system first put in place by Theodor Eicke, a Kommandant at the Dachau camp obsessed with preventing escapes.[9] When a Slovakian friend of Rosenberg's tried to escape with four other men, SS troops caught all five and killed them before they had made it past the area around the camp the Nazis had populated with ethnic Germans likely to report seeing an escapee.[10] Then camp officials orchestrated a display Eicke had originally devised, placing five chairs in the middle of the camp where all the inmates would see them, strapping the men's bodies to the chairs, and attaching a large sign that read WE'RE BACK![11]

Eicke designed a fiendish humiliation for any escapee who was brought back alive. Before being killed, the victim was forced to parade throughout the camp beating a large drum, with a sign on his back that said HOORAY! HOORAY! I'M BACK AGAIN![12]

Camp officials put together a similar event when another friend of Rosenberg's, a French Army captain, was killed during an escape attempt. SS men dragged his body through the mud and placed it on display back at the camp. Once he saw this, Rosenberg went back to his barracks, filled a bowl with water, and gently wiped the blood and mud from his friend's face. When prisoners who worked in the mortuary came to pick up the man's body two days later, Rosenberg quietly told them, "This is Charles Unglick. He has been in the camp a very long time." They understood what he meant, carried Unglick's body to a washroom, cleaned it, and reverently wrapped it in two blankets before taking it to the mortuary.[13]

* * *

It often looked like Rosenberg wasn't going to live long enough to try to escape. Once, after he had contracted typhus, his number was on a list of those who were to be killed as part of camp authorities' attempts to quell an epidemic that had broken out. He barely managed to get his number off the list and then to survive the disease itself.[14] He was also flogged almost to death when he refused to tell officials the identity of a prisoner foreman (called a *kapo*) who was having an affair with another prisoner. When Rosenberg's wounds became infected, the grateful *kapo* made sure he was sent to the camp hospital and received the drugs and surgery he needed to recover.[15]

To further discourage escapes, camp officials exacted severe reprisals against those who had worked or lived with anyone who escaped. Usually, ten prisoners, sometimes more, would be sentenced to death. The way their death sentences were carried out made hanging on the short-drop gallows seem merciful. They were locked in a cell and kept there until they starved to death, which usually took several days. Despite this terrifying prospect, after a man standing beside him broke down when he was sentenced to a starvation cell, Father Maximilian Kolbe, a Catholic priest from Warsaw, stepped forward and volunteered to take his place. The SS officer in charge agreed and had Father Kolbe thrown into a cell with nine other men. Two weeks later, Nazi doctors killed him and the three other men who were still alive.[16,17]

All of these measures and the camp's elaborate security system were usually enough to drive any thought of escape from a prisoner's mind, but not from Rosenberg's.

By chance, he became friendly with Dmitri Volkov, a Soviet captain who had escaped from a German prisoner-of-war camp near Berlin, only to be recaptured by the Germans after he had made it all the way back to the Ukraine. Rosenberg gave Volkov his bread and margarine ration and, in return, Volkov let Rosenberg practice speaking Russian with him. The two men often discussed Dostoyevsky and Tolstoy and other, lesser-known Russian writers. At first, Volkov thought Rosenberg might be a German agent. He decided, though, that no German could appreciate Russian literature the way Rosenberg did and began to trust him.

Sensing that Rosenberg was thinking of trying to escape, Volkov told him all he had learned on his thousand-mile journey through enemy-occupied territory back to his homeland, which Rosenberg called a "manual of what every escaper should know." Some of the lessons were to travel only at night and to take a watch to time one's travels, a knife for self-defense, and a razor to kill oneself in case one was about to be recaptured.

Volkov also told Rosenberg he could elude the bloodhounds sent to catch him by taking with him Russian tobacco that had been soaked in gasoline and dried. The scent, he explained, would drive the dogs away. "Only Russian tobacco, remember," Volkov said. "I'm not being patriotic. I just know Machorka. It's the only stuff that works!"

Then the Soviet captain told Rosenberg, "We'd better not meet again because we have been seen talking together too much already and I intend to get out too, remember. Good-bye. . . . Good luck. Maybe we'll meet some other time, some other place."[18]

* * *

Rosenberg began putting together an escape plan with Alfréd Wetzler (see Fig. 3 on the next page), a twenty-five-year-old from his hometown in Slovakia who had been at Auschwitz even longer than he had. Like Rosenberg, Wetzler did clerical work at Birkenau and had a thorough knowledge of how it operated. The two men studied the camp's layout, searching for gaps in its defenses. Their jobs as clerks and couriers took them to areas outside the high-voltage fence that surrounded the inner camp. They noticed that when prisoners went to work in the morning, guards in the set of towers around the inner camp stood down and other guards began to man a second chain of watchtowers along an outer fence that surrounded the work areas.

Fig. 3. Alfréd Wetzler

They also noted that guards in the outer chain of towers were withdrawn at twilight each day, but only after camp officials made sure that all prisoners had returned from work areas to the inner camp. If one was missing at the evening roll call, sirens would trigger a systematic search of the entire area by hundreds of motorized SS troops with dogs, while guards continued to man the outer chain of towers until the prisoner was caught. After three days and nights, though, camp officials would assume an escapee had somehow managed to get beyond the fence on the outer perimeter, and the guards were withdrawn from the outer towers, leaving it to local police and SS patrols to apprehend the escapee.[19]

Rosenberg and Wetzler realized that any prisoner who could remain hidden for three days in a work area outside the inner camp stood a reasonable chance of getting through the outer fence at night, after the guards had left the towers on the perimeter. They just couldn't figure out how to remain hidden there for so long.[20] They learned how when another Slovakian prisoner, Sandor Eisenbach, told Wetzler that he and three other men were planning to escape and needed their help.

"You know the planks they've stacked for the new camp they're building?" Wetzler told Rosenberg. "Well, they've bribed some *kapos* to pile them so there's a cavity left in the middle. A hole big enough to hold the four of them."

Rosenberg and Wetzler immediately understood the plan. The four men were going to hide in a stack of lumber at a construction site just outside the inner fence and make their escape through the outer fence once the three-day manhunt ended.[21] They agreed to keep the four men abreast of what was happening while they were hiding.

A few days later, sirens went off and SS troops began sweeping through the camp. They often ran right past the pile of lumber but never thought to remove the planks on top of the men's hiding place.

On the first day, when all the searchers were quite a distance away, Rosenberg casually wandered over to the lumber pile and, without looking at it, said softly, "Can you hear me?"

"Yes."

Pretending to study some documents he was carrying, Rosenberg told those in hiding, "Everything's fine. They're over by the crematoria now. They've been past here a dozen times, but they never even looked at the wood."

"OK. Thanks."

Rosenberg and Wetzler kept the men briefed for three days. When Rosenberg whispered to them on the morning of the fourth day, he didn't receive any answer back. The men had gotten away![22]

A week later, though, smug SS troops brought all four of them back to the camp, an SS patrol having caught them near the town of Porąbka, about a third of the way to the Slovakian border. After Eisenbach assured them that no one had told camp officials how they had managed to escape, Rosenberg and Wetzler decided that they would be the next to try. They recruited two Polish prisoners to cover the top of the pile with planks as soon as they slid into their hiding place.[23]

Coordinating the travels of the four men so they would all meet at the stack of lumber proved almost impossible. The first four times they tried, one snag or another prevented someone from getting there on time. Each day, Rosenberg had promised an SS guard at the gate to the work area that he would bring him back a pair of socks. Every day, he had returned empty-handed. Finally, on the fifth day, the SS man growled, "If you don't bring me back those socks this time, you needn't bother coming back at all!" Rosenberg promised he wouldn't forget him, but hoped he wouldn't be coming back.[24]

As Rosenberg walked toward their meeting point, two SS guards stopped him and began to harass him. They started searching him and took some cigarettes he had in an overcoat pocket and threw them in the mud. If they had finished searching him, they would have found a watch he had taken from a sorting hut, as Volkov suggested. Camp officials thought just having a watch was proof that a prisoner was planning to escape. It was starting to look like Rosenberg would be hanged in front of the whole camp like the two Polish prisoners caught with civilian clothes under their striped tunics.

Then, in a stroke of luck, the SS men got tired of the whole thing. One of them walloped Rosenberg in the face with a baton and the two went on their way. When he arrived at the pile, Wetzler was already there and the two Poles were on top of the lumber, looking like they were working. No one spoke. The Poles moved some planks aside and gave Wetzler and Rosenberg an almost imperceptible nod.

* * *

The two men passed the point of no return at 3:30 p.m. on April 7, 1944, when they jumped on top of the pile and slid into their hiding place. The Poles put the planks back over their heads and left. Then Rosenberg and Wetzler both slathered on gasoline-soaked Russian tobacco as Volkov recommended and waited, their nerves taut.[25] (See Map 1.)

At first, everything went as planned. At evening roll call, the Nazis discovered the two men were missing and sirens shrieked, triggering a frantic search by SS troops and bloodhounds. Throughout the night and into the next day, shouts came closer and closer to the pile of planks and then faded away.

Just as the search seemed to be losing its fury, Wetzler and Rosenberg heard two Germans talking nearby.

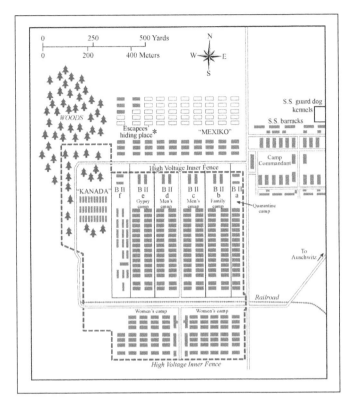

Map 1. Layout of Auschwitz/Birkenau Showing Rosenberg
and Wetzler's Hiding Place

One said, "They can't have gotten away. They must be in the camp still."

The other replied, "Otto . . . how about that pile of wood? Do you think they might be hiding under there somehow? Maybe they built themselves a little alcove or something."

"The dogs have been over it a dozen times," Otto said. "They'd have smelled them . . . unless, of course, they've some way of killing the scent."

Wetzler and Rosenberg crouched motionless in their cramped quarters and heard Otto say slowly, "It's a long shot . . . but it's worth trying. C'mon."

The Germans climbed onto the pile and began heaving one plank after another aside until just a few layers of lumber remained between them and their prey.

Suddenly, there was an uproar on the other side of the camp and Otto shouted, "They've got them! C'mon . . . hurry!" and the two men jumped off the pile and dashed off to see what the noise was all about, never to return.[26]

At twilight on the third day, Wetzler and Rosenberg heard the guards in the outer chain of watchtowers shouting their sing-song, "cordon down" call and tramping their feet as they marched back to the inner camp. When night had fallen, the two stood up and began pushing on the planks over their heads. They wouldn't budge! For a moment, it looked as if they had designed their own starvation cell! In desperation, they tried again. It took all the strength they had to push the planks up and to the side.

"Thanks be to God, those bloody Germans nearly found us!" Wetzler whispered. "If they hadn't moved those other planks, we'd be trapped!"[27] They climbed out into the cold night air and took the time to replace the planks on top of the pile so that other prisoners could use their hiding place. Then they crawled slowly to the grove that had given Birkenau ("birch trees") its name. There, they ran into something they hadn't expected: a ribbon of white sand about twenty-five feet wide that surrounded the camp. The trail of their footsteps would be a telltale sign for SS patrols, showing the route they had taken out of the camp.

They had no choice, though. They pushed on into the night, knowing they had to get as far away from the camp as they could before the guards returned to the towers on the outer chain in the morning.[28]

At daybreak, heeding Volkov's warning not to travel while it was light, they found a clump of large bushes, plunged into the interior, and covered themselves with leafy branches. When the sun climbed higher, they realized they were in a public park frequented by off-duty SS men strolling with their families and friends, but it was too late to leave.

Then they noticed two young children making a beeline for the bushes. The children saw them and called, "Pappa. . . . Pappa . . . come here . . . there are men in the bushes . . . funny men."

Wetzler and Rosenberg had their knives out and were ready to lunge when the man came over to investigate, looked at them, quickly gathered his wife and children, and left, apparently offended by the idea of two men lying together in the bushes at a public park.[29]

When it was dark, they headed out again, having only a vague idea of how to get to Slovakia, which Rosenberg had gotten by studying a map in a children's atlas he had come across in a sorting hut at Birkenau.[30] They tried to stay away from towns, but as the next day broke, they found they had wandered into the village of Pisarzowice, about ten miles south of the camp.

Realizing it would be nearly impossible to get out of the village without being seen, they decided they had to ask for help, to knock on a door even though the person answering the knock might be German. Luck was still with them: a Polish woman answered and invited them in.

She told them their only chance of avoiding German patrols was to wait until nightfall and travel through the open country to the mountains under the cover of darkness. If her sons were there, she said, they would have shown them the way, but one was dead and the other in a concentration camp. When night fell, they thanked her and headed toward the mountains.[31]

After traveling for two nights, they had made it another twenty miles and were almost halfway to the Slovakian border. At daybreak, they had laid down to rest on a hillside south of Porąbka—the town where Sandor Eisenbach and his companions had been captured—when rifle fire sang out from a German patrol on a hill across from them. They scrambled up the hill and made it to a small wood with the Germans in hot pursuit, their dogs howling. They plunged into a fast-moving stream to throw off the dogs, then zigzagged through the tall firs, running as fast as they could until they no longer heard the dogs.[32] (See Map 2.)]

Three days later, they stumbled upon an elderly Polish woman tending her goats on a hillside above the village of Milówka, about ten miles from the border. She could tell they were fugitives, but gave them food and let them rest in her goat hut. Later, she brought a friend who took them to the border.

Map 2. Route Traveled by Rosenberg and Wetzler during
Their Escape from Auschwitz

On the morning of April 21, eleven days after they had set off from
the camp, Rosenberg and Wetzler crossed into Slovakia. To complete
their mission, though, the two fugitives had to find someone who would
tell the world about the mass murders the Nazis were committing at
Auschwitz. Despite Volkov's warning to never trust anyone, they decided
they had to take a chance. Walking through the forest, they came across
a farmer plowing a field with a horse. They told him that they needed to
contact Jewish leaders in Čadca, the largest town near the border. The
farmer understood what was going on and said with a grin, "Don't worry,
gentlemen. I'm not going to give you away. You have my word for that . . .
my Slovak word! And once we get to Čadca, I can put you in touch with a
Jewish doctor I know, Doctor Pollack."[33] True to his word, the farmer took
Rosenberg and Wetzler to see the doctor, who quietly arranged for them to
meet with representatives of the Jewish Council in Žilina, the nearest city.

* * *

When the two men told members of the Jewish Council that most of the people deported to Auschwitz were killed in a gas chamber shortly after they arrived, skeptical council members produced a massive ledger with a list of Slovakians who had been deported and asked them if they could name any of the people who were on the transport to Auschwitz with them. Rosenberg gave them the names of thirty people who had been in his transport and saw the looks on the council members' faces turn to horror when they realized that he and Wetzler were telling the truth and that most of their countrymen had been murdered, not "resettled" as the Nazis had claimed.

To alert the rest of the world about what they learned, council members asked Rosenberg and Wetzler to tell them everything the two knew about Auschwitz. The next day, the council prepared a sixty-page account in German and Slovak[34] relating what the two men had informed them about the operation of the camp, how the Nazis decided whether a deportee was to be imprisoned or taken directly to a gas chamber, and the techniques used to gas and incinerate victims.[35] The report also warned that four months earlier, about three thousand prisoners had arrived at Auschwitz from the Czech concentration camp at Theresienstadt and been marked for "special handling" (i.e., murder) after a six-month quarantine period that was to end on June 20, 1944, only eight weeks away.[36]

The council sent copies of the report to the Jewish Agency in Istanbul, a Zionist agency in Switzerland, the Papal Nuncio in Slovakia, and Rudolf Kasztner, a leader of the Budapest Aid and Rescue Committee.[37] Kasztner asked that the report be translated into Hungarian too, so a translation was prepared and sent to him in Budapest.[38]

Rosenberg worried that the Hungarian Jews were going to be deported to Auschwitz soon. When he asked council members whether there was any news from Hungary, expecting to hear that Jews were resisting any attempts at deportation, they assured him that "Dr. Kasztner is looking after everything. He knows how to handle the situation. We can rely on him to take the right action at the right time. He's a man of vast experience."[39]

In the middle of May, Rosenberg saw a woman crying. When he asked her what the matter was, she sobbed, "They're deporting the Hungarians. Thousands of them. They're passing through Žilina in cattle trucks!"[40] Tormented by the knowledge of what was going to befall the people in the cattle trucks, Rosenberg couldn't help thinking all he and Wetzler had been through was in vain:[41] the miraculous escape, the days of blind travel at night through enemy territory, and the kindness of strangers who had risked their lives to help them.[42]

2. The Master of Mass Murder Arrives in Hungary

Adolf Eichmann bragged that "Müller [the Gestapo chief] said they had sent the master himself down there [to Hungary], in order to be quite sure that the Jews would not rebel as in the Warsaw Ghetto."—**David Cesarani**[1]

In June of 1943, Adolf Hitler gave Admiral Miklós Horthy, the regent of Hungary, a yacht on Horthy's seventy-fifth birthday. Horthy sent Hitler an effusive letter of thanks for "this colossal maritime token of affection" that, he wrote, "nearly took [his] breath away."[2] In truth, it was the idiocy of the gift that left the regent short of breath, considering that Hungary was landlocked. "What the hell can I do with a yacht," he scoffed privately, "cross over [from Buda] to Pest? . . . If he were a gentleman, he would send me a riding horse or a team of horses."[3] No, far from a fellow officer and gentleman deserving respect, Horthy thought the Führer was a "half-witted house-painter."[4]

The two men and their countrymen nursed many of the same grievances from the peace treaties the Allies had imposed on their countries after World War I. When he came to power, Hitler assured Horthy that the Nazis would help his kingdom recover the territory the Allies had taken away and distributed to its neighbors. After the war broke out, Hungary joined the Axis Powers and, in the spring of 1942, sent the 200,000 men of the Second Hungarian Army to fight alongside the Germans in Operation Barbarossa, the invasion of the Soviet Union.

The campaign had gone swimmingly at first. German Panzer Groups roared through Byelorussia and Ukraine all the way to the gates of Moscow.

By early 1943, though, the tide had turned. The Soviets had destroyed the Second Hungarian Army and vanquished the Germans' Sixth Army at Stalingrad. In the wake of these losses, Hungary's prime minister, Miklós Kállay, began to explore ways to exit the Axis Alliance.[5] In April of 1943, after Kállay refused the Germans' demands to move Hungary's Jewish residents to concentration camps and requested the return of Hungarian troops from the front, Hitler summoned Horthy to Schloss Klessheim, a Baroque-era castle on the outskirts of Salzburg, to discuss their differences.

Hitler complained bitterly to Horthy that the Hungarians weren't doing their part, in either the war against the Allies or the one against the Jews. In his catalog of complaints, the Führer accused Kállay of adopting a defeatist attitude by trying to reduce Hungary's role in the fighting on the Eastern Front and of adding insult to injury by also protecting Hungarian Jews.[6] Horthy came to the prime minister's defense, pointing out that Hungary had been the first European country to pass *numerus clausus* laws restricting the admission of Jews to universities, and later had passed laws limiting their ability to practice a profession, operate a business, or engage in a broad range of commercial activities. Hungary had done everything to the Jews that could be done within the limits of decency, he said, but could hardly murder them.[7]

Actually, murder was just what Hitler had in mind. Jewish people, he lectured Horthy, were "pure parasites." They must be eradicated like the tuberculosis bacteria that attacked a healthy body. Animals like deer must be killed when they became pests, he said, so why should more mercy be shown to the "beasts who would bring us bolshevism"?[8]

The regent continued to defend Prime Minister Kállay and refused to accede to the Führer's demands that Hungary begin deporting Jews. At the time, anti-Semitic sentiment was so strong in the Hungarian civil service, officer corps, and Parliament that Horthy was the only person standing between hundreds of thousands of Jewish people living in Hungary and their destruction.[9]

Ten days after the meeting at the Klessheim Castle, Joachim von Ribbentrop, the Nazi foreign minister, advised Hungary's ambassador to

Berlin that the Nazis were going to "resettle to the East" all Jewish people living in Germany and expected their allies to do the same. If Hungary failed to do that, he warned, sooner or later the Germans would probably do it themselves.[10]

By the time of Ribbentrop's tête-à-tête with the Hungarian ambassador, "resettle to the East" had become a Nazi euphemism for deportation to a death camp in Poland.[11] As late as May of 1940, though, Reichsführer Himmler had rejected any plan to murder Jews. In a memorandum to Hitler, he recommended shipping them to a colony in Africa or another distant location as a way to "purify" Europe of Jews, writing that coerced emigration "[was] still the mildest and best, if one [rejected] the Bolshevik method of physical extermination of a people out of inner conviction as un-German and impossible." Hitler approved forced emigration as the German policy and ordered that Himmler's six-page memorandum be distributed to political officials throughout the territories under German control.[12]

A year and a half later, the Nazis no longer saw the mass murder of Jews as impossible or un-German. In the late summer of 1941, Reinhard Heydrich, the head of the Nazi intelligence agency and secret police, told the man who headed his Office of Jewish Affairs, Lieutenant Colonel Adolf Eichmann, that the Führer had ordered the physical annihilation of the Jews.[13] Up to this time, the Nazis had tried to rid the Reich and territories they controlled of Jewish residents by using terror and draconian laws to coerce them to emigrate, taking much of any wealth they had by imposing steep "flight" and "export" taxes on those who emigrated. Now their murderous impulses joined the larcenous ones. As the Israeli attorney general who prosecuted Eichmann after the war put it, "[t]he previous order: 'Drive them out and rob them!' was replaced by: 'Kill them all and loot their property!'"[14]

Carrying out the Führer's order would require Nazi bureaucrats to untangle knotty problems involving intermarriage, Jewish workers in the armaments industry, and Jews who were citizens of another country—issues over which many agencies had some jurisdiction.[15] To coordinate the actions of government officials and ensure that the SS gained control over the new extermination policy, Heydrich asked Eichmann to invite the heads of all Nazi agencies with an interest in Jewish matters to a meeting. The invitation said that the goal of the meeting was to achieve "the same viewpoint by all central agencies concerned with the remaining work in connection with this final solution." It left the term "final solution" (*endlösung*) undefined.[16]

Those who attended the meeting quickly learned what it meant. Heydrich began by saying that they all knew previous attempts to "cleanse the German living space of Jews" through coerced emigration had failed and, until recently, there didn't seem to be any other solution. With the territory gained through the conquest of Poland, however, a better option presented itself: deporting Jews throughout Europe to death camps then under construction in occupied Poland.

Some officials raised concerns, not about a policy to murder millions of innocent men, women, and children, but about its implementation.[17] Half of the meeting was spent discussing the extent to which non-Jewish spouses in mixed marriages or the children of mixed marriages would be "evacuated,"[18] or the order in which the "evacuations" would take place. Finally, while butlers were pouring brandy for them, the guests debated the merits of different methods of mass murder, comparing the advantages and disadvantages of shooting, gassing in a mobile van, and gassing at a fixed site.

After the meeting ended, Heydrich, Eichmann, and Heinrich Müller (Eichmann's immediate superior) celebrated their success by sitting together around a cozy fireplace. Not one to relax completely, Heydrich used the quiet moments to clarify something about the record of the meeting. He told Eichmann to sanitize any references to violence. So, in the minutes sent to those who attended, discussion about the various methods of mass murder became an examination of "various possible kinds of solution" and people to be murdered were to be "dealt with appropriately."[19]

The Wannsee Conference and the setting up of death camps in Poland were closely guarded secrets. The minutes Eichmann prepared were marked "top secret," and copies were numbered. Only one of the thirty copies survived the war.[20]

* * *

Ribbentrop's warning to the Hungarian ambassador that Germany might take matters into its own hands if the Hungarians failed to "resettle" its Jewish residents wasn't an idle threat. On March 19, 1944, the Nazis occupied Hungary while Horthy was out of the country, Hitler having tricked him into meeting again at the Klessheim Castle. A regiment of German paratroopers spearheaded the operation, followed by eleven divisions that invaded the country from Austria, Slovakia, Serbia, and Romania.[21]

Although the Nazis were incensed by the Hungarians' delay in bringing about a speedy "solution to the Jewish question," the deteriorating military situation weighed more heavily in their decision to occupy Hungary.[22] Things were going poorly for their armies on both fronts. By the spring of 1944, the Western Allies had successfully invaded Sicily and were working their way up the Italian mainland toward Rome. In the east, the Red Army was continuing its relentless advance westward and was poised to enter Romania.[23] Many civilians had a stake in these ongoing military campaigns. Among them were more than 700,000 Hungarian Jews[24] whose fate depended on the outcome.

As soon as Horthy arrived back in Budapest, he called a Crown Council meeting. Prime Minister Kállay resigned but urged the regent to stay on. Horthy agonized about what to do, but ultimately decided to continue as regent, explaining to Kállay:

> I cannot let a usurper sit in this place. I have sworn to the country not to forsake it. I am still an admiral. The captain cannot leave a sinking ship; he must remain on the bridge to the last. Whom will it serve if Imrédy sits here? Who will defend the army? Who will save a million Magyar lads from being dragged away to the Russian shambles? Who will defend the honorable men and women in the country who have

trusted me blindly? Who will defend the Jews or our refugees if I leave my post?[25]

As Horthy expected, the Nazis asked him to appoint Béla Imrédy, an ardent Nazi sympathizer, as prime minister.[26] Horthy despised Imrédy[27] and rejected the idea outright. After three days of negotiation, he agreed to appoint Döme Sztójay, his long-time ambassador to Berlin, to replace Kállay. Although the new government wasn't ardently pro-Nazi, Sztójay's appointments of László Endre and László Baky (two notorious anti-Semites) as secretaries in the Ministry of the Interior effectively sealed the fate of Jewish people living in the country.[28]

Dispirited by the Nazis' occupation of the country, Horthy told the ministers of the new government that he was going to defer all matters concerning "the Jewish question" to them,[29] a Pontius Pilate–like step he took to avoid responsibility for what they were preparing to do to their country's Jewish citizens.[30]

* * *

The Nazis moved with lightning speed to launch their Final Solution in Hungary. Shortly before the invasion, the Gestapo chief ordered Adolf Eichmann and his chief lieutenants to put together a blueprint for Hungary. The group included Eichmann's closest collaborators, men who had years of experience implementing extermination programs in Poland, France, Belgium, Holland, and Czechoslovakia.[31] As soon as Eichmann and his men arrived in Budapest, officials in the new Hungarian government placed the instruments of state—the gendarmerie, civil service, and police—at their disposal.[32]

Eichmann was a radical anti-Semite, even more extreme than Hitler or Himmler, both of whom were willing to accept a ransom for Jews if the price was right. Not Eichmann. He thought any such deals were a sign of weakness.[33] He didn't just mindlessly carry out the Final Solution; he developed ways to make it more lethally efficient, including the use of a cyanide-based pesticide in gas chambers[34] that enabled Auschwitz to surpass all other Nazi death camps in its murderous capacity.

As soon as he arrived in Hungary, Eichmann introduced himself to members of the Central Jewish Council, saying, "So you don't know who I am? I am a bloodhound!"[35] In a businesslike presentation, he assured them that he was only there to expand industrial capacity for the Reich's war effort and that if Jews showed a proper attitude, they would enjoy the same treatment and pay as all other workers. He said that although Jewish residents would have to begin wearing a yellow star on their clothing, he would protect them from any violence and would severely punish anyone who tried to enrich himself by taking Jewish property. He also said that although the Germans would look to Jews to provide whatever they might need, they would give each owner a receipt for everything they took, down to the smallest item, and would either return the goods when they left or compensate the owner.[36]

In practice, the Germans just took whatever they wanted from Jewish people. They ordered the Central Council to supply offices and apartments for leading SS and Wehrmacht officers, complete with paintings, rugs, and musical instruments.[37] The Sztójay government didn't try to protect the country's Jewish citizens from the confiscations. Instead, it took a stake in them, entering into an agreement with the Nazis that once the occupation was over, it would get all the wealth taken from Hungarian Jews.[38]

As their counterparts in Germany had done, Hungarian bureaucrats developed what Randolph Braham, the foremost expert on the Holocaust in Hungary, called a "camouflage language" to conceal their anti-Jewish measures.[39] They referred to homes taken from Jewish residents as "abandoned apartments"; called furniture, clothing, and household items they hadn't been able to take with them when forced from their homes "property left behind"; and identified the owners of the property as "Jews who moved," "Jews who left," or simply "absent Jews."[40]

It had taken the Nazis several years to identify German and Polish Jews, then isolate and segregate them in ghettos. Racing to annihilate Hungarian Jews before the Red Army or Western Allies could liberate

Fig. 4. Hungarian Women and Children Awaiting Selection at Auschwitz/Birkenau in May 1944: United States Holocaust Museum.

them, the Nazis and their Hungarian henchmen mounted a ghettoization blitzkrieg in Hungary. It took them only ten weeks, from the middle of April to the end of June, to force hundreds of thousands of Jewish residents into 215 ghettos and collection camps throughout the country.[41]

In early May, Eichmann put together a deportation program, the next step in the annihilation process. If everything went according to his plan, it would only take a few months for all Hungarian Jews to be taken to Auschwitz. The deportations began on schedule in mid-May. Gendarmes crammed eighty people or more into each cattle car on a deportation train and supplied it with a single bucket of water and a waste bucket. Hundreds of the deportees committed suicide, and many others suffocated in the summer heat.[42]

The deportations began in the northern and eastern provinces, areas closest to the advancing Red Army. By mid-June, the Nazis and their Hungarian accomplices had shipped 250,000 Jews from the provinces to Birkenau[43] and had arranged to move the 200,000 Jewish residents of Budapest to yellow-star houses. Deportations from Budapest were scheduled to begin at the end of June. If the trains rolled from the capital at the same rate at which they had left the provinces—taking about 8,000 men, women, and children to Birkenau every day[44]—it would only take a month or so to liquidate all the Jews living in Budapest too. On June 30, Eichmann updated his superiors on his progress, saying that "the complete liquidation of the Hungarian Jews [was] an accomplished fact; technical details [would] only take a few more days in Budapest."[45]

No Allied army would be able to reach Budapest in time to rescue the Jews living there. Although the Red Army had entered northern Romania by then, it was still more than six hundred kilometers from the capital and the Allied Armies in Italy were no closer.[46]

* * *

At the same time that Eichmann was formulating his plan, Jewish leaders in Hungary received the Auschwitz reports compiled by Walter Rosenberg (known after his escape by his *nom de guerre* Rudolf Vrba) and Alfréd Wetzler. They decided not to disseminate the information in the reports at first, afraid it would create panic in their community.

Many people in the rest of the world learned about the reports the following month, after the head of the Budapest Palestine Office, Miklós Krausz, sent an abbreviated version to a diplomat stationed in Switzerland. He, in turn, provided copies to British and American intelligence organizations and news agencies in the United States, Great Britain, Sweden, the Vatican, and Switzerland.[47]

Almost overnight, newspapers in Allied countries began publishing accounts that included horrific details about Auschwitz gleaned from Vrba and Wetzler's reports. On June 18, the BBC broadcast a story about Auschwitz, and on June 20, the *New York Times* published the first of three stories about the camp, which included details about the use of gas chambers there.[48] Through a system of lies and elaborate deceptions, the Nazis had managed to carry out murders on a massive scale for three years.[49] Now, with the publication of the Auschwitz reports, their secret was out; the "unknown destination to the east" had a name, and the camp, formerly thought to be just one of the many labor camps in the area, was becoming known as the largest killing center in Europe.[50]

When people in the West learned about the ongoing Holocaust in Hungary, they pressed religious and political leaders into action. Pope Pius XII addressed a plea to Horthy on June 25. The next day, President Franklin D. Roosevelt followed suit, demanding an immediate end to the deportations and a cessation of all anti-Jewish measures.[51] Roosevelt backed up his demands with a threat of grave reprisals if the Hungarians failed to comply, warning that "[he relied] not only on humanity, but upon the force of weapons."[52] King Gustav of Sweden issued a personal plea to the regent four days later.[53]

In mid-June, Jewish leaders in Budapest began distributing copies of the Auschwitz reports to influential church and governmental leaders.[54] A member of the Central Council provided a copy to the regent's son, Miklós Horthy, Jr., which he and his wife showed to the regent during the second half of June.[55] Horthy was appalled by what he learned. In a conversation with a visitor, he described the measures taken against Jews as "beyond mere inhumanity," then wept uncontrollably.[56] Finally, at a Crown Council meeting on June 26, after Sztójay and some of his ministers had defended what the Germans were doing, Horthy brought the discussion to a close, saying, "I shall not tolerate this any further! I shall not permit the deportations to bring further shame on the Hungarians. . . . The deportation of the Jews of Budapest must cease! The government must take the necessary steps!"[57] He also ordered that Baky and Endre be removed from their positions, referring to them as "two sadist scoundrels, who [could not] be kept under control."[58]

Despite the regent's order, the deportations continued at a furious pace. During the next week, Hungarian gendarmes deported 28,000 more Jews from western and southwestern Hungary.[59] Sztójay also ignored Horthy's demand that he remove Baky and Endre from office.

Baky's response was more direct: he put together a complicated plan to arrest Horthy and take power himself. According to the plan, hired assassins would kill the secretary to the Council of Ministers and grab a key the man had to Horthy's private living quarters in the Royal Castle. Then the assassins would deliver the key to an air force officer so he could take the regent into custody.[60] On June 28, though, the plan fell apart when one of the assassins was killed in a firefight and the others fled without the key.[61]

The failure of the first plan didn't deter Baky; he met with Endre and Eichmann and put together another one. According to the new plan, thousands of provincial gendarmes would come to Budapest on the pretext of going to a flag award ceremony scheduled for July 2. After the ceremony, they would stay in Budapest "on furlough" and, on July 10, would begin putting the Jews of Budapest on trains to Auschwitz.[62]

Alarmed by rumors of the impending coup attempt, Horthy called off the flag award ceremony and asked the commander of his personal bodyguard, Major General Lázár, to assume military command in Budapest.[63] By chance, Lázár ran into Colonel Ferenc Kozorús, the commander of the Hungarian First Armored Division. When he heard about Baky's plan, Kozorús asked Lázár to "tell the Regent that if [he] received the command, [he] would get rid of the gendarme units with force!"[64]

Horthy gave the command, and on July 5, Kozorús brought his armored regiment to Budapest, occupied strategic locations in the city, and took control of all roads leading into it. Early the next morning, he sent an officers' patrol to Baky with an order that all gendarme units leave Budapest within twenty-four hours or he would force them to go. After a tense twenty-four-hour standoff, Baky relented and ordered the gendarmes to leave the city.[65]

Acting in concert with Baky and Endre, the minister of the interior, Andor Jaross, continued to circumvent Horthy's orders. During the first week in July, 30,000 more Jews were deported from the suburbs of Budapest.[66] On July 9, though, the regent was finally able to enforce his order, and the trains to Birkenau stopped rolling, at least for the time being.

By then, though, more than 400,000 Hungarian Jews had been deported to Birkenau. A staggering number had been killed there. To use a comparison Randolph Braham once made to show the magnitude of the killing,[67] on D-Day, the Axis forces killed 4,572 Allied soldiers during the first day of fighting.[68] At least 7,000 Hungarian Jews were probably killed at Auschwitz on D-Day, more than 8,000 having arrived there that day.[69] After the first day of fighting, the Allied death toll plummeted at Normandy. At Auschwitz, though, the murders continued unabated. In a genocidal frenzy, the Nazis killed more than 320,000 Hungarian Jews at the camp in eight weeks. Every day, day after day, week after week, they murdered more people there than they killed at Normandy on D-Day.

3. REPRIEVE

Adolf Eichmann exploded when he heard that Admiral Horthy had stopped the deportations from Hungary. A Gestapo colleague recalled that he said the Regent was an old *depp*—an Austrian word for nitwit—and barked, "Horthy's got no say in this. *We* decide what happens in Hungary."—**Guido Knopp**[1]

On July 9, when the last trains from the suburbs of Budapest and their forlorn human cargoes passed through Hegyeshalom in northern Hungary on their way to Auschwitz, a train from Berlin passed by, going in the opposite direction. It carried a thirty-one-year-old man headed to join the Swedish diplomatic mission in Budapest. Wearing a trench coat and carrying his belongings in two rucksacks,[2] he didn't look much like a diplomat. And anyone who encountered him probably wouldn't have guessed that he was from one of Sweden's wealthiest and most influential families—that he was a Wallenberg.

According to his younger half-sister, as a boy, Raoul Wallenberg (see Fig. 5 on the next page) had admired two intrepid and altruistic Scandinavians: Fridtjof Nansen and Elsa Brändström.[3] Nansen was a Norwegian polar explorer who had helped hundreds of thousands of people fleeing from violence find homes in another country as the League of Nations' high commissioner for refugees. Brändström, a Swedish nurse, had spent years caring for German and Austrian prisoners of war, first in Russian POW camps in Siberia, and later at a rehabilitation hospital in Germany.

After a brief stint as a banker, Wallenberg tried his hand at several business ventures, ultimately going to work in 1941 for the Central

Fig. 5. Raoul Wallenberg

European Trading Company, a Swedish firm that carried on an extensive import-export trade with countries in central Europe. Because the company's manager, Koloman Lauer, was Jewish and couldn't travel freely in central Europe, Wallenberg handled matters that required foreign travel, including trips to Hungary.

After the Germans occupied Hungary in the spring of 1944, Lauer asked officials in the Swedish Foreign Ministry to do what they could to protect seven of his relatives living there.[4] Other Swedes were also concerned about Hungarian Jews' increasing peril and began putting together plans to help them.[5,6] A newly created American executive agency, the War Refugee Board, had begun setting up its own rescue programs after the Secretary of the Treasury, Henry Morgenthau, Jr., sent President Roosevelt a devastating critique accusing State Department officials of not just failing to take any action to protect Jewish people from the Nazis, but also obstructing rescue attempts others made.

On May 23, eight days after deportation trains began arriving at Birkenau from Hungary, Secretary of State Cordell Hull informed the American minister in Sweden that "a systematic mass extermination of Jews" had started in Hungary and instructed him to ask the Swedish Foreign Ministry to strengthen its diplomatic mission there.[7] Iver Olsen, who represented the War Refugee Board in Stockholm, immediately saw an opportunity and began looking for a suitable candidate to carry out an agency-funded program in Hungary. By chance, Olsen's office happened to be in the same building as the Central European Trading Company, and when Olsen asked Lauer if he knew of a "reliable, energetic, and intelligent" person to conduct a rescue program in Hungary, Lauer recommended Wallenberg.[8]

The American minister in Stockholm was favorably impressed when he met Wallenberg and urged War Refugee Board officials to send him to Budapest with funding for a rescue program.[9] When Foreign Ministry officials asked the Swedish minister in Budapest about this, he said Wallenberg would be most welcome to join them after his deputy, Per Anger, told him he knew Wallenberg personally and thought he would be an excellent addition to the legation.[10] Anxious to accommodate the Americans, the Swedish Foreign Ministry agreed to appoint Wallenberg as an attaché to their Budapest legation and provide him with a diplomatic passport.

The Americans' offer fit in nicely with Wallenberg's own plans. He was already planning to make a trip to Budapest to help Lauer's relatives emigrate to Sweden and to buy foodstuffs for distribution to Jewish relief organizations, much as he had done earlier in the war when he helped the Red Cross obtain food in several central European countries. It might be a modest effort, though. Wallenberg's agreement with the Foreign Office provided that he could end his employment in as little as two months if he chose to.[11]

* * *

Although the trains to Birkenau had stopped running on the day Wallenberg arrived in Hungary, the man who ran them, Adolf Eichmann, the Master, was still in Budapest and determined to finish his "masterpiece" of mass murder by annihilating the Jewish residents of Budapest. He was enraged when he learned that Horthy had stopped the deportations.

Many in the Hungarian government didn't share the regent's opposition to the deportations. At a Council of Ministers' meeting three days after the deportations were stopped, Prime Minister Sztójay said they should be conducted more "humanely" in the future. He suggested that each deportee be provided with a seat on a deportation train, instead of being crammed into a wagon usually used for livestock.[12]

Eichmann refused to wait for the Hungarians to reach an agreement with the Germans about resuming the deportations. On July 14, he had SS troops round up 1,500 Jewish prisoners held in two internment camps near Budapest and bring them to a deportation train. As soon as leaders of the Central Jewish Council learned about this, they notified the regent, and, upon his order, soldiers intercepted the train after it had made it about forty miles from Budapest and brought it back.[13]

Having learned a lesson, five days later, Eichmann summoned members of the Jewish Council to his office and held them incommunicado. While he detained them, he had three SS platoons storm an internment camp and take 1,220 prisoners to a train a few miles away.[14] It sped across the Hungarian frontier in twelve hours.[15]

The Hungarians complained to the German government about Eichmann's defiance of their government's order.[16] To show them the Germans would decide what happened in Hungary, Eichmann had a Gestapo unit overpower the Hungarian staff at another internment camp five days later and deport another 1,500 internees to Auschwitz.[17]

While Eichmann continued to work on his "masterpiece," Wallenberg began his own work. A couple of days after he arrived, he met with Per Anger, who mentioned that the legation had issued a limited number of temporary passports to Swedish citizens who had lost their original passports or other protective papers.[18] Wallenberg looked at the documents and, after pausing, said: "I think I've got an idea for a new and maybe more effective document."[19] His idea was to draw up a new document called a protective passport (*Schutzpass* in German), which certified that the Swedish Foreign Ministry had approved the person's travel to Sweden.[20]

Soon after his arrival, Wallenberg also met with the Swiss vice-consul, Carl Lutz, who had already gained a reputation for zealously protecting Hungarian Jews. Earlier, Lutz had persuaded the Hungarian government to recognize the validity of protective letters issued by the Swiss legation called *Schutzbriefs*.[21] He then increased the protective value of these Swiss papers by setting up safe houses where *Schutzbrief* holders could live under Swiss diplomatic protection.

Wallenberg suggested that the delegation greatly increase the number of protective documents it issued, which prompted many hours of intense discussion.[22] Some of the diplomats were concerned that issuing large numbers of *Schutzpassen* to people with tenuous connections to Sweden would diminish the value of the protective documents they had already issued.[23] Others argued that Wallenberg's proposal went far beyond protecting and advancing the interests of their own country's citizens—their mission as diplomats.[24]

Fortunately for Wallenberg, the head of the legation, Carl Ivan Danielsson, was very sympathetic to the plight of Hungarian Jews.[25] A month before Wallenberg joined the legation, Danielsson had himself proposed that Sweden and other neutral countries try to save women, children, and elderly people facing deportation.[26]

In the end, Wallenberg prevailed. As one member of the delegation explained, "he won partly because he was so persistent, but finally because he had this very strong argument—it [would] save lives."[27] Anger recalled that Danielsson, an experienced diplomat, "slowly or step by step, became convinced that this was the only way to do it, to save people. . . . [I]t was remarkable to see how Wallenberg came every day to him with heaps of protective papers . . . and he signed them . . . without any comments. . . . Danielsson understood this situation, so when he was asked once [about] a paper which was false and asked if that was his signature, he said, 'Of course, I've signed that . . . of course.'"[28,29]

* * *

Shortly after he arrived in Budapest, Wallenberg learned how critical his mission was. On July 18, in his first dispatch to the Foreign Office, Wallenberg reported that, except for able-bodied men and young women, all the Hungarians who had been deported to Auschwitz were put to death when they arrived; he attached part of Vrba and Wetzler's report that described how the camp operated. He also learned that his mission wouldn't be entirely successful. With the dispatch, he enclosed a note to his mother, asking her to invite Koloman Lauer to dinner and break the news to him that members of his wife's family had already been deported to Auschwitz and probably had all been killed. "I haven't the heart to tell him," he wrote.[30,31]

In the meantime, negotiations about resuming the deportations remained at an impasse, but Eichmann's relentless pressure on Hungarian officials was having an impact. The interior minister capitulated, telling the Nazis' minister in Hungary, Edmund Veesenmayer, he would be willing to deport Jews from Budapest in a roundabout way despite the regent's prohibition. Horthy, for his part, explored the idea of replacing Prime Minister Sztójay with a loyal general, Géza Lakatos, and news about it leaked out.[32] Hitler was furious when word reached him. On July 17, Veesenmayer delivered a message to Horthy from the Führer. If he failed to carry out the planned deportations, Veesenmayer warned, Hitler would respond without scruples. After a grueling two-hour-long meeting, Horthy met with General Lakatos and told him that resignation seemed to be the only course left to him.[33]

The regent slowly regained his poise, even while two Panzer units Hitler had sent to back up his threat were parading around Budapest.[34] Having intervened to protect the Jewish residents of Budapest, he considered it a matter of personal honor that the deportations not be resumed.[35]

Eichmann felt differently. If he could complete the annihilation of Hungarian Jews, he hoped the Führer would summon him and thank him personally for all he had done.[36] To finish the job, he planned to round up all the Jewish residents of Budapest in a one-day blitz, take them to an internment camp at a brickworks north of the city, and deport them by the thousands beginning on August 5.[37]

On August 2, Interior Minister Jaross proposed that the Hungarians allow the Germans to deport all the Jewish residents of Budapest except for the twenty thousand or so who had converted to Christianity. It was all too much for Horthy. He dismissed Jaross and two other officials, including Béla Imrédy, the staunch anti-Semite he despised.[38]

Sztójay remained the prime minister, though, and assured Veesenmayer shortly after the reorganization that the deportations would resume within a week or two. The new interior minister gave a similar assurance to Eichmann on August 19.[39] Just as it had been a year earlier, the regent was the only person standing between the Jewish residents of Hungary and their annihilation.

In another move in the cat-and-mouse game he was playing, on August 17, Eichmann had three members of the Central Jewish Council imprisoned while SS units surrounded the city and held a massive German military parade. Unbowed, Horthy immediately ordered that the council members be released.[40]

While the regent sparred with the Germans, Wallenberg and his staff in the "Jewish Section" accelerated their efforts.[41] By early August, forty people were processing scores of *Schutzpassen* there every day. By mid-August, according to Anger's count, the delegation had issued some two thousand *Schutzpassen*.[42]

To increase the protective power of the *Schutzpassen*, Wallenberg went to visit Lieutenant Colonel László Ferenczy, the liaison between Eichmann's staff and the Hungarian gendarmes, to see whether the Hungarians would permit the Swedish legation to keep *Schutzpass* holders in protected houses, like the safe houses they allowed the Swiss to maintain.[43] Wallenberg didn't speak Hungarian, so he took Elizabeth Kasser, a Hungarian Red Cross volunteer, with him to translate. Ferenczy kept them waiting for quite a while and then made a long speech about how they should be ashamed of themselves for helping Jews and what awful people Jews were.[44] In the end, though, he agreed to allow the

Swedish legation to set up three safe houses for people under its protection, delighting Wallenberg. As Kasser recalled: "When we were out of sight of that building, we put our arms around each other and did a sort of Indian dance in the street."[45]

* * *

Meanwhile, the Germans finally reached an agreement with Hungarian government officials about resuming the deportations. Beginning on August 25, all the Jewish residents of Budapest would be deported, except for foreign citizens and about three thousand to whom the Hungarians had granted special exemptions.[46] When leaders of the Jewish Council learned about this, they pleaded with representatives of neutral countries and the Vatican to intercede.[47]

They did. Wallenberg and a group of neutral diplomats drafted an unusually frank note signed by Vatican Nuncio Angelo Rotta, Danielsson, and diplomats from Portugal, Spain, and Switzerland that read:

> The undersigned representatives of the neutral powers accredited to Budapest have learned with painful surprise that the deportation of all the Jews of Hungary is to be started soon. We also know, and from an absolutely reliable source, what removal means in most cases, even if it is masked as labor service abroad.
>
> The representatives of the neutral powers, motivated by feelings of human solidarity and Christian love, feel duty bound to lodge a strong protest against this unjustly motivated and inhumanely implemented process, as it is absolutely impermissible that people should be persecuted and sent to their death simply for their racial origin.[48]

The next day, the regent firmly told the Germans that, despite their threats, he wouldn't permit any more deportations.[49]

Then fate intervened. On August 23, Romania suddenly surrendered to the Allies and turned its troops against the Germans.[50] Alarmed by the defection, in the middle of the night, Himmler sent a telegram to the

SS chief in Hungary forbidding any further deportations.[51] The Germans didn't want to jeopardize Hungary's continued participation in the Axis Alliance, even if it meant they had to suspend their genocidal war against Jewish people for the time being.[52]

Eichmann was shocked by Himmler's order and immediately left Hungary.[53]

Taking advantage of his new leverage, five days later, Horthy dismissed Sztójay and appointed General Lakatos as prime minister. Lakatos purged the government of several officers who had designed and implemented the Sztójay government's anti-Semitic policies, including László Endre and László Baky, the two "sadist scoundrels" Horthy had wanted to dismiss for months.[54]

Eichmann's departure and the Lakatos government's more benevolent policies toward Jews prompted Wallenberg to begin phasing out the work of his "Jewish Section." On September 12, he reported to the Foreign Office that the reception office would be closed five days later and the rest of the staff let go as work diminished. Safe houses, though, would continue to be maintained to protect *Schutzpass* holders from any pogroms that might take place once the Germans withdrew from the city. On September 29, he let his mother know that he hoped to return home as soon as he had closed down the rescue section and wrote to Lauer reassuring him that he would be returning to Sweden before the Red Army, then eighty kilometers away, captured the city.[55]

Two weeks later, Wallenberg sent Iver Olsen what he expected to be a closing summary telling him about the work he had done with funds from the War Refugee Board and thanking Olsen for initiating and supporting the Swedish rescue programs.[56]

It looked like the Hungarian Jews' months-long nightmare was nearing its end. Instead, almost overnight, it became even more terrifying.

4. THE BLOODHOUND RETURNS

One morning, a group of these Hungarian fascists came into the [safe] house and said all able-bodied women must go with them. We knew what this meant. My mother kissed me and I cried and she cried. We knew we were parting for ever and she left me there, an orphan for all intents and purposes.

Then, two or three hours later, to my amazement, my mother returned with the other women. It seemed like a mirage, a miracle. My mother was there—she was alive and she was hugging me and kissing me, and she said one word: "Wallenberg."—Tommy Lapid[1]

The day after the Romanians defected to the Allies, Miklós Horthy reminded Edmund Veesenmayer that he had frequently warned Hitler they weren't reliable.[2] The German minister must have thought the regent was a shameless old rogue. Thanks to the many agents the Germans had, including some high-ranking officials in the Hungarian government, they knew that Horthy was himself looking for a way to extricate Hungary from the Axis Alliance.[3] To prepare for any defection, the Germans had entered into an agreement with a Hungarian fascist party, the Arrow Cross, regarding the composition of a new government under its leader, Ferenc Szálasi, and the transfer of power at the appropriate time.[4] In mid-September, Hitler also sent Major Otto Skorzeny, the commando leader who had rescued Benito Mussolini from his captors, to lead commando operations in Hungary should a coup become necessary.[5]

The appropriate time came in mid-October. Horthy had promised Hitler he would inform the Germans if Hungary ever decided to leave the Axis Alliance. He summoned Veesenmayer at noon on the fifteenth and told him that the Hungarians had reached an armistice agreement with the Soviets and were going to cease all hostilities.[6] An hour later, a Hungarian State Radio announcer read Horthy's proclamation about the armistice, igniting a celebration in the Jewish community. Some people tore off their yellow stars and left yellow-star houses, euphoric.[7]

The celebration was short-lived. The armistice never took effect. By late afternoon, the State Radio broadcast messages from Szálasi and Horthy's chief of staff, rescinding the armistice and ordering Hungarian soldiers to continue fighting alongside the Germans. The Nazis had seized control of the radio station and were preparing to attack the three-hundred-man security force in the Royal Castle.

Early the next morning, the regent and a loyal general were sitting on the steps of the Royal Castle, loading their pistols, when a German military car carrying Prime Minister Géza Lakatos and Veesenmayer pulled up to the castle's main gate. The German minister stressed the urgency of the situation to the regent, telling him, "It is my unpleasant task to take charge of your security, since in twelve minutes the attack will begin." Seeing no alternative, Horthy relented, telling the commander of the palace guard, "I don't want any shedding of blood. There will be no resistance. Cease all resistance!"[8]

The Germans took Horthy to another castle nearby. At noon, Szálasi met with him, expecting Horthy would ask him to form a new government. Instead, Horthy summarily dismissed him, telling him he was the last person in Hungary he would appoint as prime minister. When Szálasi came to see him again that evening, the regent told him the same thing.

The negotiations reached an impasse, and the Germans turned the screws. Skorzeny's commando unit had wounded and captured Horthy's son in a shoot-out the day before. The Nazis told the regent that if he didn't appoint Szálasi as prime minister and abdicate, they were prepared to use "the most brutal methods" and his son's life would be in danger. Finally, Horthy relented after receiving Veesenmayer's word of honor that his son would be allowed to join him the next day, when the two of them would be taken to Germany.[9]

* * *

As soon as the Arrow Cross took power, a reign of terror began. The night after the coup, fascist gangs dragged people from yellow-star houses and labor companies and shot them in the street or on quays by the Danube. In a small village west of Budapest, they slaughtered an entire 160-man Jewish labor company.[10]

The neutral legations went into overdrive defending people under their protection.[11] Raoul Wallenberg dashed around the city rescuing members of his staff who either had fallen into the hands of Arrow Cross militia units or were too frightened to leave their hiding places.[12] When police herded six thousand Jewish people into a large synagogue, he and Lutz immediately went there and secured the release of hundreds under Swiss or Swedish protection. The rest were released after neutral diplomats and prominent Hungarians lodged protests with Arrow Cross officials.[13]

The Jews' peril increased when Adolf Eichmann returned to Hungary two days after the Arrow Cross took power. He beamed with pleasure, telling members of the Jewish Council that the deportations would be resumed, this time on foot.[14] He planned to finish his work in installments. First, fifty thousand Jews would be herded on foot from Budapest to the Austrian border while the rest were held captive in ghetto-like camps around the city. Then, additional groups of fifty thousand would be expelled until Hungary was *Judenrein*.[15,16]

Concerned that the chaotic robbery and murder of Jewish people by Arrow Cross gangs were disrupting national stability, the Szálasi government tried to bring things under control. Three days after the coup, Gábor Vajna, the new government's anti-Semitic minister of the interior, issued the following thinly veiled warning to both anarchy-bent thugs and Jewish residents:

I have taken steps officially to ensure that the officers and executors of public administration, state security, and public order, knowing the present requirements, will do everything to preserve public order, calm, and state security. [. . .] Let me emphatically warn the Jews and those serving their interests that all the organs of state power are vigilantly watching their conduct. [. . .] I do not recognize Jews as belonging to the Roman Catholic, Lutheran, or Israelite denominations but only as persons of the Jewish race. I recognize no letter of safe-conduct of any kind, nor any foreign passport which a Jew of Hungarian nationality may have received from whatever source or person.[17]

Overnight, all the protective papers neutral nations had issued lost their protective power, and their safe houses were no longer safe.

Wallenberg went right to work. Danielsson had assigned him to deal with the Szálasi regime and its minister of foreign affairs, Baron Gábor Kemény.[18] He already knew the Keménys, having met Baroness Kemény soon after arriving in Budapest[19] and the Baron a few weeks later.[20]

As the Baroness recalled, it was typical of Wallenberg that he "nagged until he got something. . . . He visited [her] husband every day until he got what he wanted."[21] The visits and the nagging worked. The Szálasi government retracted its initial decision and broadcast a decree on Hungarian State Radio saying it would respect the protective papers issued by neutral governments, as Wallenberg had insisted.[22]

* * *

On November 10, Hungarian gendarmes began herding Jewish people on foot from an internment camp north of Budapest to Hegyeshalom on the Austrian border, 150 kilometers away. The marchers were supposed to be fed and housed along the way under guidelines issued by Interior Minister Vajna. The Hungarians ended up providing little food or shelter to the marchers, however, and the route became what Randolph Braham called a virtual highway of death.[23]

After interviewing some of the marchers and their guards, two members of the Swiss legation described the condition of people who managed to make it to the end of the march at the border:

> At Hegyeshalom we found the deportees in the worst imaginable condition. The extreme labor of the foot march, the almost total lack of food, made worse by the torturing steady fear that they were being taken to the extermination chambers in Germany, have brought these pitiful deportees to such a state that all human appearances and all human dignity have completely left them. [. . .] The denial of the most elementary human rights, the fact that they were usually totally at the mercy of the brutally behaving escorts, who in practice could do whatever they wanted with them—from spitting in their face to slapping and beating and shooting—left the mark of these horrors on the unfortunate victims.[24]

Wallenberg, Per Anger, Carl Lutz, and others traveled along the march route, distributing food, medicine, and warm clothing to the marchers. Wallenberg also carried his "book of life," a ledger with a list of Jews to whom the Swedes had issued protective papers.[25]

One of the marchers, Zvi Eyres, described how Wallenberg rescued him, his mother, an aunt, and a cousin:

> As we approached Hegyeshalom at the end of the march, we saw two men standing by the side of the road. One of them, wearing a long leather coat and a fur hat, told us he was from the Swedish legation and asked if we had Swedish passports. If we hadn't, he said, perhaps they had been taken away from us or torn up by the Arrow Cross men. We were on our last legs, but alert enough to take the hint and we said, yes, that was exactly what had happened, though in fact none of us had ever had a Swedish *Schutzpass*. He put our names down on a list and we walked on. At the station later we again saw Wallenberg [. . .] brandishing his list, obviously demanding that everybody on it should be allowed to go. Voices were raised and they were shouting at each other in German. It was too far away for me to hear exactly what was

being said, but clearly there was a tremendous argument going on. In the end, to our amazement, Wallenberg won his point and between 280 and 300 of us were allowed to go back to Budapest.[26]

Although some critics said the marches to Hegyeshalom were barbaric, Eichmann thought they were being carried out "in the most elegant way." He said he only saw two dead bodies along the entire route and both of them had been of elderly marchers. In any event, he said, "You can't make an omelet without breaking eggs."[27] When the marches began, he celebrated with his old friend László Baky, who was back in the government as a commissioner in the Szálasi regime.

A group of Eichmann's senior colleagues in the SS happened to pass by the marchers while headed to Budapest along the Vienna Road. One of them, General Hans Jüttner, was so offended by the condition of the marchers that he telephoned Heinrich Himmler and complained that the foot marches violated SS canons of decency. Himmler suspended them the next day.[28]

As usual, Eichmann persisted. He began deporting Jews to Austria in freight cars from Józsefváros Station, a freight depot southeast of the city center. Wallenberg persuaded the Hungarians to let him visit the station to make sure no one under Swedish protection was deported.[29]

Tamás Verés, a twenty-one-year-old photographer who went with Wallenberg to the station, recalled what happened when they arrived there:

> Wallenberg had his black ledger out. "All my people get in line here!" he called. "All you need to do is show me your *Schutzpass*."
>
> He approached the line of "passengers." "You, yes, I have your name here. Where is your paper?" The startled man emptied his pockets, looking for a paper he never had. He pulled out a letter. "Fine. Next!"[30]

* * *

Fig. 6. Hungarians Wallenberg Rescued at Józsefváros
Station Returning Back Home in November 1944:
United States Holocaust Museum

Most of the legation's rescue work was far less dramatic than Wallenberg's interventions on the death marches to Hegyeshalom or at the Józsefváros Station. After learning the Arrow Cross had forbidden the local ambulance service from providing care to Jewish residents, the legation "bought" two ambulances from the service for the price of one Swedish crown and put them on the road.[31] The Department of Provisions in Wallenberg's section served 1,500 of the city's most poverty-stricken residents breakfast, lunch, and dinner in a communal soup kitchen with food Wallenberg had stockpiled in Pest and Buda. By mid-December, the Swedes had opened hospitals with 150 beds and inoculated all those under their protection against typhus, paratyphus, and cholera. And by that time, seven thousand people were living in Swedish safe houses.[32]

Not everyone appreciated the work Wallenberg and his associates were doing. Eichmann, for one, didn't. In mid-December, he lost his temper in front of a Red Cross employee and said he intended to have "that Jew dog Wallenberg" shot. When the Swedish Foreign Ministry complained to the Germans about it, Veesenmayer defended Eichmann, saying that Wallenberg had acted illegally by handing out protective passports to foot marchers who were being taken to the Austrian border as part of a legal labor force.[33]

Soon, Eichmann became more concerned about his own safety than harming Wallenberg. On December 22, the Red Army began a massive offensive to capture areas to the north and west of Budapest and complete its encirclement of the capital. Eichmann barely escaped to Austria on Christmas Eve, two days before the Red Army gained control of the last roads leading out of the city.[34]

Like Eichmann, top officials in the Szálasi government fled the capital. With Eichmann and his Hungarian henchmen gone and liberation by the Red Army appearing imminent, it looked again as though the Hungarian Jews' long nightmare was nearing its end. Instead, as before, it became even more terrifying.

5. The Inferno

"Wallenberg's role took on heroic proportions during the siege."—Randolph L. Braham[1]

The reign of terror veered almost completely out of control on the day after Christmas, when the Soviet Army began a siege of Budapest.[2] During the siege, anti-Semites committed crimes against Jewish citizens that were without parallel anywhere in Nazi-dominated Europe.[3] Gangs of armed Arrow Cross youths roamed Budapest's streets, robbing and murdering defenseless pedestrians. To save bullets, they took people to a bank of the Danube, tied them together in groups of three, and shot the middle person in the back of the head so that his or her weight would pull the other two victims into the river.[4]

No one was safe from the mayhem. On December 28, a mixed band of Arrow Cross militia and SS troops attacked a Jewish hospital in Pest, terrorizing and robbing hospital patients and staff. Before leaving, they took twenty-eight young males to another building and murdered them two days later.[5]

The chaos increased when all utility services to the city were lost.[6] Wallenberg managed to get hold of miner's lamps for the surgeons and a hundred kilos of liquid paraffin to make candles so that surgeries could still be performed in the Swedish hospitals.[7]

On New Year's Day, Ernö Vajna, an official in the Ministry of Foreign Affairs, ordered all Jews living in the neutral governments' safe houses to move to the central ghetto in Pest, which the Hungarians had established in late November. Although Vajna claimed the move was "for military reasons," its real purpose was so that those living in the safe houses could also be murdered when the planned massacre of those in the ghetto took place.[8]

In late December, Wallenberg persuaded Pál Szalai, an Arrow Cross leader, to visit the ghetto with him. As Szalai recalled later, "When the gates to the ghetto opened, I felt as though I had entered the Middle Ages."[9] From then on, Szalai did what he could to protect the city's Jewish residents.

In early January, after an Arrow Cross militia unit stormed Wallenberg's office in Pest and headed to the Danube with people who had sought shelter there from ongoing air raids, a switchboard operator in the office got a message to Wallenberg. He quickly made his way to the scene with Szalai and several Arrow Cross police officers, who disarmed the Arrow Cross youths and released their captives.[10]

Arrow Cross violence escalated during the second week of January, when the Red Army began a house-to-house fight to take control of the city. On the eleventh, a gang invaded a Jewish hospital in Buda, threw patients out of their beds, trampled them, and killed anyone who couldn't walk. The aggressors ordered people who could walk to dig a large pit,[11] then killed them after Father András Kun—a rabidly anti-Semitic Minorite priest who traveled around the city with a revolver and cross dangling from the belt of his monk's cassock[12]—ordered shooters to fire in the "holy name of Christ."[13] Three days later, Arrow Cross militia units massacred 150 patients, doctors, and nurses at another Jewish hospital in Buda.[14]

Anti-Semitic violence raged across the Danube in Pest too. After Arrow Cross gangs and SS soldiers murdered forty-three Jews living in the ghetto, Szalai sent a hundred Hungarian police to protect the people held there.[15]

A hundred local police, though, would have been no match for the battalion of five hundred SS troops the Germans planned to have massacre everyone in the ghetto.[16] It looked as though this would be their last chance to achieve their Final Solution in Hungary, Soviet troops having reached the Great Boulevard near the ghetto.[17] On January 16, shortly before the attack was scheduled to begin, one of Szalai's officers learned about it and ran into his office to tell him. Szalai immediately went to see Ernö Vajna, who told him that he already knew about the Germans' plans and wouldn't do anything to stop them. Then Szalai rushed to see Major General Gerhard Schmidhuber,[18] the commander of all German combat groups on the Pest side of the river.[19]

Szalai told what happened next in postwar testimony:

> I asked him whether he was aware of the operation planned for the ghetto, and I also informed him that members of his unit were among those mobilized in the Royal Hotel. I warned him that according to Wallenberg's communication, if he did not prevent this crime he would be held responsible and would be called to account not as a soldier but as a murderer. Thereupon he summoned [Arrow Cross] Party member Vilmos Lucska, a barber's assistant, who would have commanded the entire operation in his position as [the] leader of District VII. He also summoned a German captain by the name of Mummi who was headquartered in the Royal Hotel and would have led the Germans. He further summoned Dr. Ernö Vajna and Police Commissioner Kubissy, whom he ordered to prevent this crime.[20]

To ensure that his orders were followed, Schmidhuber sent Wehrmacht soldiers to protect people held in the ghetto.[21]

On the same day, an Arrow Cross gang stormed the Swedish embassy, robbed several dozen people of food and jewelry, and lined them up in a courtyard in front of a machine gun. Janas Kandor was among the hostages, along with her husband, eleven-year-old son, and seven-year-old daughter. As she awaited her fate, she saw Wallenberg lead a group of people into the courtyard. "He seemed to me like an angel of mercy," Kandor recalled. "He was shouting this was an extraterritorial building. Little by little the shouting ceased, the Arrow Cross picked themselves up and left without taking what they gathered, the food, the rings. We could not believe our own eyes. He was victorious again, with his belief and his willpower. Then he left quietly."[22]

A few hours later, Wallenberg prepared to make a journey to Debrecen, 230 kilometers east of Budapest, which was the military headquarters of the Second Ukrainian Front and the provincial Hungarian government set up by the Soviets. As mentioned earlier, Wallenberg had planned to return home to Sweden before the Russians occupied Budapest. Then, with the help of an economist and medical and social service professionals, he put together a comprehensive plan to help Hungarians recover from the wreckage of the war. Realizing that any recovery program couldn't proceed without the support—or at least the consent—of the Soviets and the new Hungarian government, Wallenberg secured permission from the Soviet military commander in Budapest to go to Debrecen and ask for permission to implement the programs.[23]

When Wallenberg began putting the plan together, its original goal was to help Jewish people recover all they had lost during the war. By the time it was finished, its mission had grown to include all Hungarians hurt by the war.[24] The programs ranged from reuniting separated family members to providing food, housing, and medical care.[25]

Before leaving for Debrecen, Wallenberg went to see some colleagues who were still in Budapest. Two Uzbek soldiers and a Soviet colonel accompanied him. "These are assigned to me," he whispered to one of his colleagues. "I am not sure if I am a guest or a captive."[26]

The day before, the Soviet army had gained control of the area surrounding the safe houses in Pest. The 25,000 people living there[27] owed a great deal—perhaps even their lives—to the Swedes, Swiss, and other neutral nations whose representatives had protected them.

Then the Soviets captured the area around the ghetto and found 69,000 people still alive there. After another month of bitter fighting, another 25,000 Jewish men, women, and children emerged from their hiding places in convents, churches, and the homes of righteous Gentiles. In all, 119,000 Jews of Budapest had managed to survive the mayhem and Arrow Cross pogroms.[28]

For months, the Jews of Budapest had looked forward to being liberated by the Red Army. Liberation turned out to be a mirage. Once the Soviets took control of Hungary, they refused to let go. They held Raoul Wallenberg captive too, and never let him go.

EPILOGUE

Alfréd Wetzler was a true hero. His escape from Auschwitz, and the report he helped compile, telling for the first time the truth about the camp as a place of mass murder, led directly to saving the lives of 120,000 Jews: the Jews of Budapest who were about to be deported to their deaths. No other single act in the Second World War saved so many Jews from the fate that Hitler and the SS had determined for them.

—Martin Gilbert[1]

During the war, many Europeans fled from the Nazis. As the end of the war drew near and it became clear that the Nazis were going to lose, the tables turned. Then many Nazis and their henchmen fled themselves.

By the time the Red Army encircled Budapest in late December, as mentioned earlier, Ferenc Szálasi and his ministers had fled from the capital. Shortly before the Germans surrendered, American troops captured Szálasi in Austria and brought him back to Hungary, where he was hanged after a Hungarian court convicted him of war crimes.

Many of his ministers met the same fate. László Baky and László Endre were also captured and taken back to Budapest. They were sentenced to death by a Hungarian tribunal for the murder of Jews and crimes against the Hungarian state. The two men Miklós Horthy thought were sadistic scoundrels were hanged side by side in March of 1946.

As for Horthy, American troops found him in a Bavarian castle where the Nazis had held him. The Allies were torn about whether to try him as a war criminal. Ironically, considering that he was a fierce anti-communist, Joseph Stalin's intervention on his behalf tipped the balance in his favor and he wasn't put on trial, either by the Allies or the new Hungarian government.[2] He wasn't allowed to return to his homeland, though, and spent his last years in Portugal.

The man he appointed as prime minister after the Nazi occupation, Döme Sztójay, wasn't as fortunate. As the Red Army advanced, he, too, fled Hungary only to be captured by American troops and brought back. In 1946, a Hungarian People's Tribunal found him guilty of war crimes, and a firing squad shot him in the courtyard of the Academy of Music in Budapest.

The People's Tribunal acquitted a few defendants. Pál Szalai was among them, after leaders of the Jewish community testified about the protection he had provided to Jews living in safe houses and the Central Ghetto during the siege.[3] In 2009, the Israelis bestowed on Szalai the Righteous Among the Nations award, a recognition given to non-Jews who risked their lives to save Jewish people during the Holocaust.

Like many other Nazis, Rudolf Höss shed his uniform as the war was ending and assumed a false identity. A year later, though, British troops captured him. After he gave a detailed account of the Nazis' extermination camps at a war crimes trial in Nuremberg, the Allies handed him over to the new Polish government. A Polish court convicted him of murder, and he was hanged on the short-drop gallows at Auschwitz that had shocked Walter Rosenberg when he saw two Polish prisoners being hanged shortly after he arrived at the camp.

After their escape, Rosenberg and Alfréd Wetzler fought the Nazis with a Slovakian partisan unit until the end of the war. Both testified as witnesses for the prosecution at trials of Auschwitz officials and Adolf Eichmann's top aides. Rosenberg secured his doctorate in chemistry from a Czechoslovakian university, defected to Israel, and ultimately moved to Canada, where he died in 2006. Wetzler stayed in Czechoslovakia, married another Holocaust survivor, and worked as an editor, journalist, and author, dying there in 1988.

Of all the Nazis who fled, Eichmann was among those who fled the farthest. In 1960, though, he was captured in Argentina by Israeli operatives and taken to Israel, where an Israeli court tried him for war crimes, crimes against humanity, crimes against the Jewish people, and membership in criminal organizations. After a fifty-six-day trial that received worldwide attention, he was found guilty of all charges. In 1962, the Israelis hanged him, cremated his body, and scattered his ashes in the Mediterranean Sea.

Raoul Wallenberg's impression that he might be a captive when Soviet troops were escorting him to their military headquarters in Debrecen turned out to be correct. Initially, the Soviets denied ever having taken him into custody. In time, though, they admitted to imprisoning him but claimed that he had died in a Soviet prison of natural causes in 1947.

Over the years, Wallenberg was posthumously made an honorary citizen of Canada, Hungary, Australia, and Israel. The Israelis also honored him by planting a tree in his name on the Avenue of the Righteous Among the Nations in Jerusalem. In 1981, US Congressman Tom Lantos, who had lived in one of Wallenberg's safe houses and worked for him as a messenger, successfully sponsored a bill that made Wallenberg an honorary citizen of the United States.

II

King Leopold's Congo

"You Are Only Beasts Yourselves"

Fig. 7. King Leopold II

Fig. 8. E. D. Morel

1. A SLICE OF MAGNIFICENT AFRICAN CAKE

> I do not want to miss a good chance of getting us a slice of this magnificent African cake.—November 17, 1877, letter from King Leopold II to Ambassador Henry Solvyns[1]

The young clerk's suspicions rose during a routine meeting in Brussels between the directors of a Liverpool-based shipping company he worked for, Elder Dempster and Company, and one of its best clients, the Congo Free State. The meeting went well enough, until the Free State government's secretary of state leaned forward from his desk and complained that Elder Dempster had disclosed information about the last steamer bound for the Congo and a local newspaper had published a list of the ship's cargo. The list looked innocent enough, except it showed that the shipment included large supplies of ammunition and firearms.

Rising from his chair, the man denounced the shipping company's indiscretion in a trembling, high-pitched voice, his face becoming flushed with rage as he sawed the air with long, bony hands and repeated over and over that this information was a *secret professionnel*." The clerk left the meeting wondering why so much war materiel was needed in the Congo and why shipments there needed to be kept secret.[2]

The Congo Free State (L'État Indépendant du Congo) had become the personal possession of one man, King Leopold II of Belgium, by way of an organization he founded to develop trade in the Congo Basin—the Association Internationale du Congo (AIC). Leopold laid the groundwork for the AIC in 1876 by inviting forty well-known explorers, geographers, and philanthropists to a geographic conference on Central Africa at his palace in Brussels. On the first evening of the conference, the guests ascended a new baroque staircase of white marble to the throne room, lit by seven thousand candles,[3] where Leopold welcomed them, saying:

> The subject which brings us together today is one of those which must be a supreme preoccupation to all friends of humanity. To open to civilization the only part of our globe where it has not yet penetrated, to pierce the gloom which hangs over entire races constitutes, if I may dare to put it in this way, a Crusade worthy of this century of progress.[4]

Before adjourning, those in attendance set up a humanitarian organization, the Association Internationale Africaine (AIA), to establish medical and scientific stations in Central Africa, and elected Leopold as its president.

Not satisfied with bringing civilization to the Congo Basin, Leopold said he wanted to bring David Livingstone's other two European blessings— commerce and Christianity—there too, so he set up the AIC, a company of which he became the only stockholder. He hired the explorer who had found Livingstone in Central Africa, Henry Morton Stanley, to establish trading posts and stations along the Congo. Stanley gave tribal chiefs rolls of wire or bolts of cloth to get them to put an "X" on papers that said they granted the AIC the right to govern their tribal lands.

These "agreements" formed the legal basis of Leopold's claim that the AIC had the right to govern the Congo Basin as an independent state. Through a series of diplomatic maneuvers as complex as a game of three-dimensional chess, Leopold astutely played one great power against another and convinced delegates at the Berlin West Africa Conference to recognize the AIC as a sovereign state, as long as it complied with provisions of the Berlin Act of 1885, including requirements that it allow completely free trade there and grant no monopolies.[5]

It was a remarkable achievement. With few advantages, except his modest wealth and the work of a few men he employed, Leopold had acquired a colony the size of Western Europe.[6]

2. A Secret Society of Murderers

> It must be bad enough to stumble upon a murder. I had
> stumbled upon a secret society of murderers with a King for a
> croniman. And fifteen years previously this self same King had
> been acclaimed by Europe as a great philanthropist, invested
> with momentous trust, hailed as a champion of Christendom
> against the Arab slaver!—E. D. Morel[1]

Leopold's full name was Léopold Louis Philippe Marie Victor. The birth name of the shipping clerk who attended the meeting in Brussels was a mouthful too: Georges Edmond Pierre Achille Morel de Ville. He anglicized it to Edmund Morel after immigrating to England from France in 1891. His station in life wasn't as aristocratic as his birth name suggested. His father had been a minor official in the French Ministry of Finance before dying when Edmund was only four.

When he was eighteen, Morel started working as a 70-pound-a-year clerk at the Elder Dempster office in Liverpool. His ability and fluency in French led his boss, the tycoon Alfred Jones, to rely on him more and more when it came to the company's lucrative contract handling all the goods shipped in or out of the Congo Free State. By the time of the meeting in Brussels, Jones had made him the head of Elder Dempster's Congo department, although he was only in his mid-twenties.

Before the meeting with the Congo government official, Morel had heard rumors that Leopold's operations in the Congo weren't as benign as the king made them out to be. On the other hand, he also knew that many people had issued statements praising the Free State's treatment of natives. In the end, he decided that the men he worked with would surely have told him if they knew Leopold's soldiers were committing atrocities in the Congo, so he took the king's side at first. In an 1897 article in the *Pall Mall Gazette*, he vigorously defended Leopold against charges that he said came from "uncontrollable sources, dished up in the most sensational style" and went on to tell his readers the facts as he saw them, "not as disappointed adventurers, needy place-hunters and misinformed philanthropists would have [them] believe."[2]

After meeting two men from a Dutch firm that had done business in the Congo for many years, Morel began to worry that Leopold had "hoodwinked" him and almost everyone else.[3] The Dutchmen told him a story about the Congo government's treatment of the natives that was, he said, "so replete with details: so appalling, so bestial, so damnable" that he tossed and turned sleeplessly that night, "conjuring in mental vision burning villages and distracted human forms, men and women quivering beneath the lash, chained and bleeding, with tortured and mutilated bodies."[4] He decided the best way to calm his mind was to use what he had learned in more than a decade of work for Elder Dempster. Rather than attempting to weigh the credibility of the conflicting reports, he would look only at the objective facts.

In countries that had no currency, like the Free State, trade with Europeans usually involved paying natives for their products with goods manufactured in Europe. Morel's review of the manifests of ships bound for the Congo, however, showed that the cargo headed to the Congo included very little merchandise of any value to the Congolese. After deducting non-trade-related items like coal, steel, cement, and weapons (which couldn't legally be sold to natives), Morel calculated that from 1899 to 1903, trade-related merchandise worth a little over 25 million francs had been sent to the Congo as possible payment for rubber and ivory worth more than 230 million francs.[5] The ships that returned to the Congo weren't empty though; they were full of weapons instead of goods sent back in trade.

He made another discovery too. Comparing records from the Antwerp market to those published by the Free State, he found that the amount of Congo rubber sold in Belgium far exceeded that shown in the government's records, and that the Free State's officials had cooked its books to disguise the enormous quantities of rubber Leopold was extracting from the country. It looked to Morel as though Leopold was robbing the natives at gunpoint.[6]

He shared what he had discovered with his boss, hoping it would prompt Jones to lead a campaign to reform the Free State—he recognized that a man of great wealth and influence like Jones stood a much better chance of success than he did. Jones promised to raise Morel's concerns with Leopold on his next visit to Antwerp. When he returned, Jones told Morel the king had assured him that he would make reforms, but that it would take time.[7]

Disregarding the impact it would have on his continued employment at Elder Dempster, Morel pressed on with the zeal of the newly converted, publishing a series of articles on the millions of francs the king was taking from the Congo each year. In time, Morel realized he would have to leave Elder Dempster if he wanted to continue pressing for reforms in the Congo, so he did and began working as a freelance journalist. At the time, the movement to reform the Congo had no momentum, either in England or in Belgium.[8]

The articles Morel wrote prompted Congo reformers in the British House of Commons to ask for his help in drafting a formal request that the British government work with other Berlin Act signatories to halt Leopold's ongoing violations of the act. Morel agreed, drafted the resolution so that it would appeal to both humanitarian and economic concerns, and provided talking points to the speakers.[9]

A few days before a debate on the resolution was to take place,[10] Alfred Jones asked Morel to meet him in London and talk things over. Hoping that Jones would suggest a set of reforms that were acceptable to Leopold, Morel agreed to meet with his old boss and a group of other men. When they made no progress at the meeting, Jones suggested that Morel continue to meet alone with a Belgian member of the group, who, Morel recalled, displayed a touching concern for my welfare. [. . .] "Did I expect to be successful against the King, who was very, very powerful? What would come to me from all this? What did I stand to gain? . . . I was a young man. I had a family—yes? I was running serious risks." And then, a delicately, very delicately veiled suggestion that my permanent interests would be better served, if . . . "A bribe?" Oh! Dear no, nothing so vulgar, so demeaning. But there were always means of arranging these things. Everything could be arranged with honour to all sides. It was a most entertaining interview, and lasted until a very late hour. "So nothing will shake your determination?" "I fear not." We parted with mutual smiles.[11]

The debate on the Congo resolution went forward in the House of Commons. Herbert Samuel, the Liberal member who sponsored it, focused on the humanitarian issues, denying that he was one of the "short-sighted philanthropists" who thought the natives should be treated as if equal to a white man. Instead, he argued:

> The rights of liberty and of just treatment should be common to all humanity, and especially should those rights be received from a State which was avowedly founded for the purpose of elevating the negro population, and introducing among them the benefits of civilization.

"If the administration of the Congo State was civilization," he asked, "what was barbarism?"[12]

Several other members condemned Leopold's violation of the free-trade guarantees of the Berlin Act. Lord Cranborne, the under-secretary for foreign affairs, initially spoke against the resolution, saying that the government couldn't support what amounted to an indictment of Belgium, a friendly nation. Then, seeing the strong support the resolution had throughout the Commons,[13] he asked only that the language in the original resolution regarding the Free State's constant violations of the Berlin Act be stricken. Samuel agreed, and on May 20, 1903, the House of Commons unanimously adopted a resolution requesting the British government to confer with other signatories of the Berlin Act and adopt measures to abate the evils that prevailed in the Free State.[14]

3. "POOR PEOPLE; POOR, POOR PEOPLE"

[C]rouching over the fire in the otherwise unlighted room, as the shades of a December evening gathered; unfolding in a musical, soft, almost even voice, in language of particular dignity and pathos, the story of a vile conspiracy against civilization, the difficulties he had to overcome, the traps laid for him, the consternation his unexpected presence upriver had occasioned to the agents of the King. Not once were the tones raised, but ever and anon by emphasis of expression, by a slower enunciation, a glimpse of the deeps to which his soul was stirred revealed itself. For hours he talked on, with now and again a pause, as the poignancy of recollection gripped him, when he would break off the narrative and murmur beneath his breath, "Poor people; poor, poor people."—E. D. Morel's description of what British consul Roger Casement told him regarding his investigatory journey upriver in the Congo Free State[1]

The British government's secretary of state for foreign affairs, Lord Lansdowne, wasn't anxious to get into a diplomatic spat with the Belgian king over the resolution passed by the House of Commons. In a play for time, he decided to put off approaching the other nations that had signed the Berlin Act; instead, he directed the British consul in the Free State, Roger Casement, to investigate the allegations that had prompted the resolution and file a report about what he found.[2]

Until then, the fate of millions of Africans in the Congo had largely depended on a contest between Leopold and Morel, two men who had never set foot there. That was about to change when Casement, a European who had spent his entire adult life in Africa, became involved.

He went to the Congo in 1884 at the age of nineteen and began working for Leopold's AIC, building a railroad around the impassable cataracts of the Lower Congo. Six years later, while working for the Congo Railway Company, he met Joseph Conrad, who later said of him:

> There is a touch of the Conquistador in him, too; for I have seen him start off into an unspeakable wilderness, swinging a crookhandled stick for all weapons, with two bulldogs, Paddy (white) and Biddy (brindle) at his heels and a Loanda boy carrying a bundle for all company. A few months afterwards it so happened that I saw him come out again, a little leaner, a little browner, with his stick, dogs, and Loanda boy, and quietly serene as though he had been for a stroll in the park.[3]

The next year, Casement joined the British Colonial Service and, ten years later, was appointed as British consul in the Congo Free State. Before taking up his post, he went to Brussels and had lunch with King Leopold, who asked the newly appointed consul to advise him privately if there was anything he could do to improve things in the Free State.[4]

On June 4, 1903, two weeks after the passage of the House resolution, telegrams from the Foreign Affairs Office caught up with Casement, requesting that he complete an investigation.[5] He left the next day.

When he reached Leopoldville, he could have spent a few weeks touring areas within easy reach of the comfortable brick house where he was staying and submitted his report. Instead, he hired a small steam launch from the Baptist Missionary Union[6] and began what was to be a thousand-mile journey up the Congo River and some of its tributaries.

The first place he reached in the rubber region was Chumbiri, a line of villages he had visited sixteen years earlier. Natives there told him that a government raiding party headed by a white officer[7] had killed eleven men, three women, and a child and confiscated forty-eight goats and two hundred twenty-five fowl to punish villagers for their failure to provide enough food for the government's station at Leopoldville and for

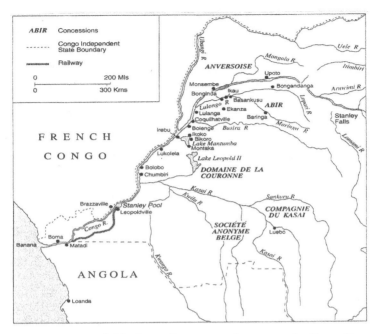

Map 3. Route Traveled by Roger Casement on Journey up the Congo River

passengers on government steamers. The raiders also took ten villagers as hostages but, when the natives' friends came up with a ransom of sixteen goats, released them all, except for a child who had died while in captivity. When he learned what the government soldiers had done, the *inspecteur d'état* in Leopoldville was furious and paid the relatives of the victims a total of 950 francs—about the value of three goats for each person killed.[8] Hoping he would find the violence in the Chumbiri villages an unfortunate exception, Casement headed farther upriver into the Crown Domaine—some of the richest rubber country in the entire Congo, an area ten times the size of Belgium that the king had reserved entirely for his own use. After learning that people had abandoned their homes in a village near Lake Leopold II (now Lake Mai-Ndombe), Casement decided to find them and ask why they had left. He walked ten miles to the place where they had gone, crossing several streams and swamps on the way. When he found them, one of the men explained why they had fled to a village belonging to another tribe:

It used to take us ten days to get the twenty baskets of rubber—we were always in the forest and then when we were late we were killed. We had to go further and further into the forest to find rubber vines, to go without food, and our women had to give up cultivating the fields and gardens. Then we starved. Wild beasts—the leopards—killed some of us when we were working away in the forest, and others got lost or died from exposure and starvation, and we begged the white man to leave us alone, saying we could get no more rubber, but the white man and their soldiers said "Go! You are only beasts yourselves, you are *nyama* [meat]."[9]

Four years earlier, in his novel about a trip on the Congo River, Joseph Conrad had called what the white men were doing there "just robbery with violence."[10] A chief living in a village on Lake Tumba told Casement that nothing had changed. Local officials hadn't made any payment to him after taking a canoe he used to deliver the weekly requisition of fish. When Casement suggested that he pursue the matter with the station master, the chief pulled up his loincloth, pointed to scars from being flogged with a razor-sharp hippopotamus-skin whip called a *chicotte*, and said, "If I complained I should only get more of these."[11]

Everywhere he went, Casement investigated the claims of men working for Leopold that the Congolese were "adequately remunerated" for the work they did.[12] He found the payment they received was a sham. For instance, using figures from a government bulletin, he determined that villagers living around Lake Tumba provided the government with gum copal worth about 9,000 francs a year, but were paid only 250 francs.[13]

Although tormented by a persistent fever, Casement journeyed even farther upriver into the Equateur District, an area ruled by the private army of the Abir Congo Company, which had a monopoly on trade and taxation in the region. At the American mission there, a missionary showed Casement an entry in his diary from four years earlier. It read:

M. Roy (the Chief State Prosecutor) called on us to get out of the rain, thinking this was the S.A.B. (Trading Company); and in conversation

with M. Guindini (State Telegraph Poseur on the line), in the presence
of myself and Van Beers, said [. . .] "The S.A.B. on the Bussira, with 150
guns, gets only 10 tons (rubber) a month; we, the State, at Momboyo,
with 130 guns, get 13 tons per month." "So you count by guns?" I asked
him. "*Partout* (everywhere)," M. Roy said. "Each time the corporal goes
out to get rubber, cartridges are given to him. He must bring back all
not used; and for every one used, he must bring back a right hand."
M. Roy told me that sometimes they shot a cartridge at an animal in
hunting; then they had to cut off a hand from a living man. As to the
extent to which this is carried on, he told me that in six months they,
the State, on the Momboyo River, had used 6,000 cartridges, which
means that 6,000 people are killed or mutilated.[14]

In early September, after traveling two hundred kilometers up
a tributary of the Congo River to reach another station of the Abir
Company, Casement decided that he had seen and heard enough. He
headed downriver to his post at Boma and took the first ship to London.[15]

His ship landed in Liverpool on the evening of November 30. The
next day, he took a train to London and told officials at the Foreign
Office what he had found. They asked him to submit a report as soon
as possible. Eleven days later, he submitted a fifty-six-page typewritten
report to Lord Lansdowne. It described what he had found in great detail,
but was precise and understated. Lansdowne congratulated him, saying
it was "proof of the most painfully convincing kind."[16]

* * *

Leopold had expected trouble. While at Boma awaiting his return
to England, Casement had summarized his findings in a letter to the
governor-general of the Free State:

> The system is bad, hopelessly and entirely bad. [. . .] Instead of raising
> the indigenous peoples who are subjugated and suffer from it, it

can only lead, if it is maintained, to their final extinction and to the universal condemnation of the civilized world.[17]

Leopold warned officials at Elder Dempster that the Free State might not renew its contract if the British government took any action against the Free State.[18] Alarmed by the prospect, Alfred Jones—a man Casement thought was "a bold and original liar"[19] and "a poisonous serpent"[20]— called on Foreign Office officials, asking them to soften the report[21] or at least provide Leopold with an advance copy.[22]

Some in the Foreign Office thought it would be best not to publish the report but to give it instead to an international commission to conduct an investigation and carry out any needed reforms. The British minister to Brussels, Sir Constantine Phipps, opposed publication too. He didn't believe that the Belgians, a cultivated European people, could have acted with such cruelty and explained to Lord Lansdowne that the concessions employed private armies only to protect the rubber harvesters while they worked.[23] With rumors circulating that the report contained some sensational revelations, and realizing that members of Parliament were expecting it to be published, Lansdowne decided that the Foreign Office had to publish it.[24]

Shortly before submitting his report, Casement met with E. D. Morel at a house in London owned by a mutual friend. Until then, Leopold's relentless public relations campaign had even affected Morel, causing doubts that assailed him, he said, "like a thief in the night." Morel further said:

> In the wakeful hours when sleep refused its solace and I turned the whole thing over and over in my mind the evil seemed almost too monstrous to be systematic and deliberate. It appeared almost incredible that a European Parliament should associate itself with such a colossal crime; that men should be found in almost every land to deny its existence; that nearly five hundred missionaries labouring on the spot should keep silence—so far as the world knew to the contrary—on the subject. Might it not be a hideous nightmare: a delusion of the brain?[25]

When Casement told him that his indictments of Leopold were "in every particular sound" and read passages from the report that were almost identical to those he had written himself,[26] Morel's doubts vanished.

Casement told Morel the only way they could free the Congolese people from Leopold's clutches was to found a new organization dedicated exclusively to reform in the Congo.[27] Morel agreed. He thought Casement would be the perfect man to lead the new organization. Casement thought just the reverse. He wasn't willing to leave the Foreign Office and told Morel that he must lead the organization himself.

Morel was appalled by the prospect of starting a new group and leading it himself. The two men talked into the early morning hours. When they parted, Morel shrank from making any commitment.

Casement persisted. He visited Morel and his wife, Mary, at their home in a small Welsh village near Liverpool. Mary agreed entirely with Casement; she thought that they should form a new organization devoted to Congo reform and that her husband should lead it.[28] Her support and encouragement tipped the scales for Morel.[29] He agreed to meet Casement in Ireland and begin putting the new organization together.

So began a deep friendship between the two men. In time, the tenacious, indefatigable, barrel-chested Morel became Bulldog in Casement's correspondence to him, and the lithe, high-strung Casement became Tiger in Morel's. And Leopold became the King of Beasts to them both.

* * *

In March of 1904, a month after the Foreign Office published Casement's report, Morel, Casement, and another Irish advocate of reform in the Congo officially formed the Congo Reform Association. It had assets of just 378 pounds (9,450 francs).[30] By then, its adversary had amassed the largest fortune of any European monarch and was a member of the Coburg dynasty, related by blood or marriage to many European royal families, including to Edward VII, the current regent of the country the association hoped would take the lead in Congo reform.[31] And, as Morel knew well, Leopold had handily overcome all his previous critics, some of whom were wealthy and powerful.

The same month, Leopold sent a thirty-seven-page response to the Foreign Office, challenging the reliability of Casement's findings. The depopulation of Congolese living in the region had been caused by an epidemic of sleeping sickness, he said, not the depredations of government soldiers and the private armies maintained by concessionaires. He defended forced labor as necessary to generate a work ethic in the natives and claimed that the accounts of pillage and plunder were made by "untruthful Congolese and biased Protestant missionaries."[32] While arguing that Casement's proofs were an "insufficient basis for a deliberate judgment," Leopold conceded that "the particulars in question [required] . . . [being] carefully and impartially tested."[33]

He asked to be provided with a complete copy of Casement's report, including the identities of witnesses—whose names the Foreign Office had redacted from the published report—so authorities in the Free State could arrange for appropriate inquiries to be made. Lansdowne responded that if Leopold appointed an independent commission with sufficient resources to investigate the allegations thoroughly, the Foreign Office would provide it with an unredacted copy of Casement's report.[34]

4. Leopold's Commissioners Journey to the Heart of Darkness

> It should be always borne in mind that in spite of the progress
> achieved, the natives of the Congo are still in a large measure
> savages. Twenty centuries were necessary to create from Gaul,
> of the time of Caesar, the France and Belgium of today and
> if our ancestors were, in the eyes of the conquering Romans,
> barbarians, one can, we think, say that they were civilised
> people in comparison with the inhabitants of the immense
> territory of the Free State at the moment of its constitution.[1]
> —*The Congo: A Report of the Commission of Enquiry Appointed by
> the Congo Free State Government; A Translation*

In July of 1904, Leopold set up the commission Lord Lansdowne had
suggested, giving it no other instructions except "to devote all its efforts to
the complete and entire discovery of the truth." He gave the commissioners
the power to subpoena witnesses and the resources they would need for a
complete investigation, including the assistance of interpreters, translators,
physicians, and experts.[2]

In early October, the three commissioners he appointed—judges from
Belgium, Italy, and Switzerland—arrived in the Congo and immediately
went to work. They traveled to two dozen native villages, tracing the
route Casement had taken to Lakes Leopold II and Tumba and the region
controlled by the Abir Company. Ultimately, they went all the way to
Stanleyville, two hundred miles farther upriver than Casement had
gone. In February of 1905, they made their way back downriver, went to
Belgium, and put together their report.[3]

Morel worried that it would be a whitewash. He had good reason to worry. A commission Leopold had appointed to investigate reports of atrocities eight years earlier hadn't led to any reforms.[4] As with the earlier commission, Leopold had handpicked the three members of the present one; they included a Belgian presiding officer who was unlikely to criticize the conduct of his countrymen, and an Italian who had been employed by the Free State.

In November of 1905, seven months after the commissioners submitted their report to him, Leopold finally released it. Much like Casement's account, the 167-page report began with an introductory section extolling the contributions Belgians had made in the Congo by suppressing the slave trade and building railroads, schools, hospitals, and courts.[5]

Then the commissioners addressed claims that the Free State engaged in state-sponsored terrorism. The Belgian judge who served as the president of the commission admitted to a British official that the evidence the commission collected agreed in all essential details with Casement's findings.[6] Unlike Casement, however, the commissioners found justifications for the violence Leopold's soldiers used against the natives. Among the questions the commission addressed, and its conclusions, were:

Was coercion used to force the natives to work? Yes. The negro's dislike for all kinds of work, his extreme aversion to rubber gathering, and his indifference to the payment proffered made compulsion necessary.[7]

Did the coercion include the taking of hostages? Yes, women and children were taken as hostages and, in some cases, held for several months. Some officials defended the practice, explaining that the hostages weren't poorly treated and the conditions of their captivity were usually less oppressive than the animal-like life they led in their own village.[8]

Did the violence include murder and pillage? Yes. Soldiers had punished villagers for failing to come up with the rubber or provisions requisitioned by the government or a private concession and the results were "frequently murderous."[9] Soldiers often acted like they were at war with villagers.[10] They killed men, women, and children, sometimes while they were fleeing.[11] But, in delicate operations to take hostages or intimidate natives, the commissioners found, supervisors were not always able to hold in check the savage instinct of their black soldiers.[12]

In a final chapter titled "Justice,'" the judges concluded that while Europeans had committed some wrongs, fairness required considering the difficulties that surrounded them in the Congo:

> They left Europe filled with respect for human life and they soon see in the barbarous circle into which they are transplanted, that this has no value. They were taught from infancy to love one's neighbor and they note amongst the savages around them an absolute ignorance of the sentiment called charity—the negro, in fact, cannot realize that a thing can be done except from fear or hope of personal gain; they are witnesses in the villages of the miserable plight of the weak and the infirm upon whom the chiefs and head men always let fall the heaviest burdens; they see the women degraded to the condition of beasts of burden, labouring without interruption and performing every task.[13]

As judges, the commissioners were likely familiar with a "yes, but . . ." form of pleading, known in European courts as "confession and avoidance." In this defense, a person—often faced with irrefutable evidence of wrongdoing—can attempt to justify what he or she has done by claiming that the ordinary rules of conduct shouldn't be applied in their case because of the circumstances that prevailed at the time. The commissioners decided that this was true in the Congo, that European ideas of justice and ethics didn't apply to the treatment of the Congolese because they were an inferior race of lazy, uncivilized, animal-like savages who hadn't yet gained a sense of morality or fairness.

The publication of the commission's report put Leopold on the spot but he carried on with tenacity, appointing a fourteen-member Committee of Reforms to "study the conclusions of the Report of the Commission of Enquiry, to formulate the suggestions which they necessitate and to investigate the practical means for realizing the same."[14]

* * *

Before the new committee began working, the publication of books by two Belgians added to Leopold's difficulties. The first, written by Félicien Cattier—a law professor who had once supplied Leopold with opinions supporting the legal system in the Free State—included a detailed account of the great wealth Leopold was extracting from the Congo. Cattier told how Leopold had spent much of this money in Belgium instead of on building a working state in the Congo. Among the financial details he reported were:

- In addition to the 31.8 million francs Leopold had borrowed from the Belgian government ostensibly to develop the Congo, over the years, he had gotten 130 million francs in loans from banks and bondholders in the name of the Free State to cover the deficits it supposedly incurred. A close review of the Free State's financial records, however, showed that its actual deficits totaled only 27 million francs.[15]
- During the previous decade, Leopold had made at least 70 million francs in profits from the sale of rubber harvested by natives in the vast tract he had set aside for himself known as the Crown Domaine.[16]
- He had quietly spent more than 18 million francs to buy more than a hundred properties in Brussels and Ostend in the name of a charitable foundation[17] and spent another 35 million francs on grandiose construction projects at his palace at Laeken, the Royal Museum at Tervuren, and the Arc de Triomphe–like Arcade du Cinquantenaire in Brussels.[18]

In all, Cattier said, Leopold had extracted more than 200 million francs (1 billion dollars in today's value) from the Congo, in the form of either profits or funds he had borrowed to develop the Congo but hadn't spent there.

Cattier also evaluated the extent to which Leopold had established a government in the Free State that provided essential services to its citizens. He concluded:

> The clearest and most incontrovertible truth arising from this report is that the state of Congo is no colonized state, barely a state at all, but a financial enterprise. [. . .] The colony is not administered in the best interests of the natives, nor even in the economic interests of Belgium: to provide the sovereign with the greatest possible financial gain, that was the motivation.[19]

In the final chapter, Cattier concluded that the necessary reforms would never take place in the Free State unless Belgium annexed it from Leopold.

The second book, written by Arthur Vermeersch—a priest and professor of moral theology at a Jesuit university in Belgium—discussed Cattier's findings but approached the matter from a different point of view. While Cattier had based his critique on legal principles and progressive colonial policies, Vermeersch rooted his in Christian ethics.

He reminded readers that under the Berlin Act, Leopold had promised to preserve the native tribes and improve their moral and material well-being. Citing liberally from Cattier's revelations and the findings of the Commission of Enquiry, Vermeersch said that Leopold had abused and plundered people he agreed to protect, violating not just his own promises but also Christian moral principles.[20]

In a sarcastic comment, Vermeersch said that by appropriating vast tracts of land in the Congo for himself and granting monopolies to concessions in exchange for a large share of their profits, Leopold had effectively fulfilled the promise he made at the Berlin Conference to make the Congo Basin a free-trade zone. As he explained, commerce was entirely free in the Free State, but because the state owned everything, there was nothing for anyone to buy or sell.[21]

Critics of the Free State were invigorated. In February of 1906, Émile Vandervelde, the leader of the Belgian Labour Party, called for a debate about annexing the Free State from Leopold. Unlike his earlier attempts, this time the idea drew broad support from both Liberal and Catholic party members of the Belgian Chamber of Representatives.[22]

During the debate, Free State defenders argued that Parliament shouldn't take any action until Leopold's newly appointed Committee of Reforms issued its report. Vandervelde replied that he expected few meaningful reforms from the committee's work, considering that nine of the fourteen members of the committee either worked for the Free State or were concessionaires exploiting the natives. He said: "It is precisely as though one called in a slave trader to a conference to abolish the slave trade!"[23]

When Vandervelde argued that the Free State had made natives serfs by appropriating all uninhabited land and barring them from traveling from one village to another without a permit, a colleague interrupted, saying that Free State officials were treating the Congolese more like cattle than serfs.[24]

Georges Lorand, the leader of the Liberal Party, rose to support Vandervelde, quoting extensively from the Commission of Enquiry's findings about the violence government soldiers had used against the natives. Prime Minister Paul de Smet de Naeyer, one of the Free State's most loyal defenders, responded:

M. DE SMET DE NAEYER: [. . .] [The commission's] report justifies coercion by the natural indolence of the native.

    M. MASSON: Is it by coercion that you intend to lead the natives to work?

    M. DE SMET DE NAEYER: In the earlier stages a certain amount of coercion cannot be avoided (interruption—uproar)

    M. JANSON: It is with such arguments that slavery is justified.[25]

In a debate three years earlier, the prime minister had claimed that because the natives' work was payment in lieu of taxes and that the government owned the land where the rubber vines grew, "they [the natives] [were] not entitled to anything. What [was] given to them [was] a veritable gratuity."[26] Lorand reminded the prime minister of what he had said, commenting:

> The natives are entitled to nothing, you said. For them, therefore there are no rights. I have said, and I maintain, that that is an atrocious sentence. [. . .] [T]he native has the rights of a man, he has the right to live, the right of personal security, the right of personal property, the right to the produce of his labour, the right of coming and going, and we know that, in the majority of cases, even that right is denied to the native. We have allowed the Congo and the pernicious influence which the Congo has exercised on a portion of our countrymen, to reach the stage of denying to our black brothers—those brothers whom you gentlemen desire to Christianise; men who, it is true, have not our culture, but who are, for all that, men like us—these elementary rights of humanity, which we must, on the contrary claim for every human being.
> M. BEERNAERT: It is abominable![27]

Vandervelde and Lorand also cited extensively from Cattier's book about the great wealth Leopold was extracting from the Congo, prompting the prime minister to call Cattier a pamphleteer who only saw matters to criticize in the Congo.[28] He questioned Cattier's accounting, saying that, according to his calculations, Leopold had only taken 18 million francs in profits from the Crown Domaine, not 70 million as Cattier had claimed.[29]After four days of debate, the time came to vote on three resolutions. The first, requiring the Free State to produce financial records and accounts that would allow the Belgian government to evaluate the consequences of any annexation, lost by a vote of 86 to 60. The second cited the grave abuses documented in the Commission of Enquiry's report and called on the government to stop sending officers to the Congo until "a new state of affairs was inaugurated compatible with the dignity of the Belgian army." It lost 88–26.

The third was moved by Auguste Beernaert, a Catholic who had been an original member of Leopold's AIA and had served as prime minister from 1884 to 1894. The resolution paid homage to Belgians who brought civilization to the Congo and expressed confidence in the work the Committee of Reforms was doing. Then it called on the Belgian government to examine the legal framework of annexation without delay. When Leopold instructed the prime minister to make sure that Beernaert's resolution would fail, de Smet de Naeyer had to tell Leopold that despite the majority his Catholic Party had in the Chamber of Representatives, the government would fall if it opposed the resolution.[30] In the end, the Belgian Chamber of Representatives unanimously approved Beernaert's resolution, setting the annexation process in motion.

5. Belgium Takes over the Congo: Will the New Boss Be the Same as the Old Boss?

> The standard of emancipation is now unfurled; let all the enemies of the persecuted blacks tremble. I will be as harsh as the truth and as uncompromising as justice.
>
> I am in earnest. I will not equivocate. I will not excuse. I will not retreat a single inch: And I will be heard."—**William Lloyd Garrison**[1]

After the debates concluded in the Belgian Parliament, E. D. Morel doubled down, perhaps feeling that the wind was at his back. He secured a shorthand transcript of the debates, translated it into English, and had it published in a 200-page book, all in less than three months. While doing that, he managed to keep up with work at the Congo Reform Association, often putting in sixteen-hour days. In the first six months of 1906, he mailed over 15,000 pamphlets and wrote 3,700 letters, in addition to handling the association's daily correspondence.[2]

Somehow, he also found time in 1906 to finish his third book, *Red Rubber*. This time, he adopted a different approach than in previous books and pamphlets. As he explained to a supporter, "For six years I have appealed to the head and now I am appealing to the heart, the head having been captured."[3,4] The book described many poignant scenes like the following, which was based on a letter Morel received from a missionary about a hostage house where women whose husbands had failed to meet their rubber tax quota were held until the quota was fulfilled:

Look inside that hostage house, staggering back as you enter from the odours which belch forth in poisonous fumes. As your eyes get accustomed to the half-light they will not rest on those skeleton-like forms—bones held together by black skin—but upon the *faces*. The faces turned upwards in mute appeal for pity: the hollow cheeks, the misery and terror in the eyes, the drawn parched lips emitting inarticulate sounds. A woman, her pendulous, pear-shaped breasts hanging like withered parchment against her sides, where every rib seems bursting from its covering, holds in her emaciated arms a small object more pink than black. You stoop and touch it—a new-born babe, twenty-four hours old, assuredly not more. It is dead, but the mother clasps it still. She herself is almost past speech, and soon will join her babe in the great Unknown.[5]

In language reminiscent of Garrison's, he closed the book by telling what he and other Congo reformers were seeking:

Nothing impracticable, nothing unrealisable is being demanded on behalf of the Congo natives. No grandmotherly legislation, no sentimental legislation, no sentimental claims are being urged in their interest. Only justice. They have been robbed of their property. We demand that their property shall be restored to them. They have been robbed of their liberty. We demand that their liberty shall be restored to them. They are bound in chains. We demand that those chains shall be rent asunder. For fifteen years they have been degraded, enslaved, exterminated. We demand that this shall stop, not fifteen years, or five years, or one year hence, but now.[6]

* * *

Although he was then seventy-one years old, Leopold continued his duel with Morel with his usual tenacity. While Morel worked in the study of a small house in a Welsh village, Leopold put together an elaborate battle plan at Cap Ferrat on the French Riviera while living on his 1,500-ton royal yacht or at his villa, the Leopolda.

The plan consisted of a series of defenses, like the moat/drawbridge/ garrison strategy used to defend medieval castles. First, he would resist annexation. If that failed, he would fight to ensure that no reforms were financial, that income from the Crown Domaine and the private concessions would continue to flow to him. Finally, he took the wealth he had accumulated in dozens of financial structures, consolidated it into a private foundation called the Fondation de la Couronne, and prepared to move it to Bavaria, the ancestral home of the Coburg dynasty.

Attempting to defuse Belgian support for annexation, he had the Free State issue twenty-four decrees on June 3, 1906. Among other reforms, he appointed inspectors to protect natives and took the power to collect taxes away from concessionaires.

Two documents Leopold issued with the reform decrees provoked a strong response from the Belgian Parliament. The first was a codicil to the will he had executed in 1889, bequeathing his holdings in the Congo to Belgium. The codicil added a new condition to the bequest: Belgium would only get the legacy if the revenue from the Crown Domaine and the concessions continued to go to Leopold's Fondation de la Couronne, not to the Free State or Belgium. The second document was a cover letter addressed to the secretaries-general of the Free State but intended for the Belgians. In it, Leopold said he retained the exclusive right to determine if and when Belgium would be able to annex the Congo:

> My rights to the Congo are not for sharing; they are the fruits of my labours and my expenditures. [. . .] The adversaries of the Congo are pressing for immediate annexation. These persons no doubt hope that a change of regime would sabotage the work now in progress and would enable them to reap some rich booty. I consider myself morally bound to inform the country when [. . .] I feel the moment is approaching and is becoming favourable for examining the question of annexation. I have nothing to say at present.[7]

Leopold's "royal manifesto"[8] was a game changer for many in the Parliament. The issue of annexation was no longer just about the Congo.

For them, it had become a constitutional issue: whose will was to be supreme, that of a constitutional monarch or that of the country's elected representatives?[9] They were determined not only to annex the Congo, but to do so on their own terms and without further delay.[10] In December of 1906, facing almost certain defeat if he continued to support Leopold, de Smet de Naeyer announced that his government now supported annexation, and Parliament appointed a seventeen-member commission to work out the details under the chairmanship of Frans Schollaert, the president of the Chamber of Representatives.[11]

The following April, de Smet de Naeyer lost a critical vote on an unrelated matter and resigned, to be succeeded by Jules de Trooz and another Catholic Party administration. In July, eight negotiators, consisting of equal representatives of the Belgian government and representatives of the Free State, began working on a Treaty of Cession. Congo reform advocates worried that the four Belgian representatives included two men who were very close to Leopold, one of whom having worked for many years in the Free State and the other having been his minister to China.[12]

The future of Leopold's 100,000-square-mile (250,000-square-kilometer) private estate, the Crown Domaine, was among the major issues in dispute. The estate contained much of the richest rubber-producing land in the Free State. As mentioned earlier, according to Cattier's estimates, Leopold had already reaped at least 70 million francs in profit from rubber that grew there.

After four months of work, the negotiators reached agreement and submitted a draft Treaty of Cession to Leopold and the Belgian Parliament for ratification. At first glance, Article I of the treaty didn't seem controversial. It read like the standard language used in commercial transactions at the time:

> His Majesty King Leopold II, Sovereign of the Independent State, hereby cedes to Belgium the sovereignty of the territories composing the Independent Congo State, together with all the rights and obligations

appertaining thereto. The Belgian State hereby accepts this cession, takes over and accepts the obligations of the Independent State [. . .] and undertakes to respect the existing interests in the Congo, together with the legally acquired rights of third parties, native and non-native.[13]

By agreeing to this, though, the Belgian negotiators had caved to Leopold's demand that he continue to receive the revenue from the Crown Domaine as if annexation had never taken place.

Morel was aghast when he learned about the terms of the proposed treaty. It seemed like nothing would change after annexation. All the evils found by Casement and the Commission of Enquiry would continue unabated in the Congo: the taking of hostages, the setting afire of villages, the flogging of innocents, the mutilations, the terror. Had all his work— all the long workdays and sleepless nights, and his continual struggle to support his family while working as the unpaid honorary secretary of the Congo Reform Association—been for naught? In the end, would all the hard-fought victories they had won in the British Parliament count for nothing? Was the damned old scoundrel, as Casement called him,[14] going to outwit everyone once again?

* * *

The death of Prime Minister de Trooz on New Year's Eve and the formation of a new government under Frans Schollaert gave British reformers more time to bring pressure on their government. They took advantage of it. On February 21, they held a massive rally at the Queen's Hall in London. According to the *Daily Chronicle*, the hall, which could hold 2,500 people, "was packed from floor to topmost ceiling, and the scene outside before the doors opened was one that [was] witnessed only on some great national occasion."[15] The lord mayor of London presided in his robes of office, supported by his sheriffs, forty members of Parliament, and religious and philanthropic leaders from throughout Great Britain. People at the rally adopted a resolution that "no scheme of annexation which [did] not restore to the native population its rights and liberties . . . [could] be acceptable to the people of Great Britain."[16]

Five days after the rally, the House of Commons took up the matter. Secretary Sir Edward Grey—whose great-granduncle, Earl Grey, had introduced the bill that abolished slavery in Great Britain some seventy-five years earlier—was outspoken in his criticism of the Free State. He said that the condition of natives in the Congo "[amounted] to slavery, which [could not] be regarded only from the point of view of treaty rights. It [was] a violation of the ordinary rules of civilized government." He went on to say conditions in the Congo were in such stark contrast to Leopold's philanthropic and humanitarian pledges that the Free State had forfeited every right to international recognition. As a result, the government would do all it could to see that reforms were made to fulfill the noble aspirations that had moved Britain to recognize the Free State in the first place.[17] Grey backed up his remarks by releasing a recent report from a consul to the Free State that said, consistent with Casement's report, that "[t]he system which gave rise to these abuses still [continued] unchanged, and so long as it [was] unaltered the condition of the natives must remain one of veiled slavery."[18]

The proposed Treaty of Cession wasn't well received in Belgium either. Prime Minister Schollaert had the unpleasant task of advising Leopold that it would be impossible to get Parliament to approve it unless he agreed to abandon his interests in the Crown Domaine. In their discussions, Schollaert was just as tenacious as Leopold. When Leopold flew into a rage, Schollaert calmly left the room and waited in an adjoining one until it subsided, then returned to continue their discussions. At one point, Leopold offered to explain to Schollaert how he could delay annexation. Schollaert replied, "Sire, I don't want to know."[19]

Finally, Leopold relented. Under the agreement they reached, Leopold retained only a 155-square-mile (400-square-kilometer) private estate in the Crown Domaine. Although Schollaert had wrested a vast tract of land from Leopold, it came at a high price. In exchange, Belgium would pay 45 million francs to complete several lavish building projects Leopold had begun in the country, and the Congo State, on the receiving end of a parting insult, would pay him 50 million francs for what he had done there. Like from lashes of the *chicotte*, the Congolese would suffer from this payment in a series of installments over fifteen years. The Belgian Parliament approved the agreement in the summer of 1908, and on November 15, 1908, the flag of the Free State—a single yellow star on an azure field—was lowered in the Congo for the last time.[20]

EPILOGUE

Any theory which involves the claim that racial or ethnic groups are inherently superior or inferior, thus implying that some would be entitled to dominate or eliminate others, presumed to be inferior, or which bases value judgments on racial differentiation, has no scientific foundation and is contrary to the moral and ethical principles of humanity. [. . .]

Racial prejudice, historically linked with inequalities in power, reinforced by economic and social differences between individuals and groups, and still seeking today to justify such inequalities, is totally without justification.—UNESCO's **Declaration on Race and Racial Prejudice**[1]

Leopold never saw the estate he retained in the Crown Domaine; he failed to survive a sudden illness in December of 1909, having never set foot in the Congo. In a final deceit, he claimed in his will: "This is my testament. I inherited from my parents fifteen millions (francs). These fifteen millions I have religiously preserved through many vicissitudes. I possess nothing else."[2]

His death left no one to keep his wealth hidden. Contrary to Joseph Conrad's comment in a 1903 letter to Casement that wealth never has a bad odor,[3] financial autopsies performed after Leopold's death gave off an unmistakable stench. They showed that Leopold had moved assets worth tens of millions of francs to a foundation he secretly set up in Bavaria, with instructions to divide the income between certain male members of the Coburg dynasty and grandiose public works projects he had undertaken in Belgium.[4] With typical cunning and sophistication, Leopold had devised a plan to take the booty from the Congo and establish a dynasty free of the constraints imposed by the Belgian Parliament.[5]

His plan died with him. After his death, the Belgian government and his daughters tore down the fabric of trusts he had created and fought over the shreds.[6] The Belgian government successfully seized 90 million francs from Leopold's foundation in Bavaria—to repay Congo-related loans he had borrowed—and the proceeds from the sale of bonds he had issued in the name of the Free State but never invested there.

After annexation, the Congo Reform Association pressed the British government to withhold recognition of the new government in the Congo until the latter had enacted land reforms and abolished forced labor.[7] In June of 1913, having made sure that the Belgians had made sweeping changes to liberalize trade policies and the treatment of the Congolese, Britain finally granted recognition to the Belgian Congo. A month later, the Congo Reform Association formally dissolved, having spent 12,425 pounds (about 1.5 million dollars in today's value) to wrest control of the Congo from Leopold.[8]

In the end, as Edward Grey said, Leopold's treatment of the Congolese had been a matter of right and wrong. Even the commissioners he appointed to investigate allegations of state-sponsored oppression in the Free State admitted that Leopold's soldiers had terrorized the Congolese to make them harvest rubber for him and provide food for his soldiers. The commissioners justified this, though, by saying that they thought the natives were savages and that coercion was needed to teach them the value of work and a sense of Christian charity. Lashing with a *chicotte* was a common way government soldiers tried to teach natives these lessons. A Belgian who worked in the Congo as a magistrate described the process:

> The station chief selects the victims. [. . .] Trembling, haggard, they lie face down on the ground. [. . .] [T]wo of their companions, sometimes four, seize them by the feet and hands, and remove their cotton drawers. [. . .] Each time the torturer lifts up the *chicotte*, a reddish stripe appears on the skin of the pitiful victims, who, however firmly held, gasp in frightful contortions. [. . .] At the first blows, the unhappy

victims let out horrible cries which soon become faint groans. [. . .] In a refinement of evil, some officers, and I've witnessed this, demand that when the sufferer gets up, panting, he must graciously give the military salute.[9]

Few Europeans who spent time in the Congo expressed shock at this violence. As Adam Hochschild asked in *King Leopold's Ghost*:

[What] made it possible for the functionaries in the Congo to so blithely watch the *chicotte* in action and [. . .] to deal out pain and death in other ways as well? To begin with, of course, was race. To Europeans, Africans were inferior beings: lazy, uncivilized, little better than animals. In fact, the most common way they were put to work was, like animals, as beasts of burden. In any system of terror, the functionaries must first of all see the victims as less than human, and Victorian ideas about race provided such a foundation.[10]

Morel had a different moral compass. He saw the Congolese people's capacity to suffer as the reason they deserved better treatment, saying:

The realisation of a great human tragedy will be vivid and historically enduring in the measure in which we are able to fashion for ourselves a mental vision, which shall also be an accurate one, of its victims. This is especially required when its victims belong to a non-white race, for the Anglo-Saxon type of mind, although inspired with a genuine desire to be just, and still susceptible of being moved to anger by cruelty, is not naturally and intuitively sympathetic towards coloured races. It is not quite easy for us to understand that despite differences of colour, climate, environment and evolution, the main channels along which travel the twin emotions of suffering and joy are much the same in all races.[11]

In the century since Morel wrote this, his insights have endured and Leopold's ideas about racial supremacy have been thoroughly discredited.

III

Votes for Women

Fig. 9. Millicent Garrett Fawcett

1. "Milly, after Elizabeth and I Open the Universities and Medical Professions to Women, You Must Get Us the Vote"

Ray Strachey, a friend of English suffragists Emily Davies and Elizabeth Garrett, wrote about an event that became part of British suffragists' lore:

Emily, the story runs, went to stay with the Garretts at Aldburgh, and at night the two friends sat talking together by Elizabeth's bedroom fire. Millicent Garrett, then quite a small girl, sat nearby on a stool, listening, but saying nothing. After going over all the great causes they saw about them, and in particular the women's cause, to which they were burning to devote their lives, Emily summed the matter up. "Well, Elizabeth," she said, "it's quite clear what has to be done. I must devote myself to securing higher education while you open the medical profession to women. After these things are done," she added, "we must see about getting the vote." And then she turned to the little girl who was sitting quietly on her stool and said, "You are younger than we are, Milly, so you must attend to that."[1]

In late May of 1867, a young woman led a man to the chamber of the British House of Commons. The man was Henry Fawcett, a Liberal member of Parliament who was a strong advocate of women's suffrage. He had been blind since being accidentally struck by a shot from his father's gun while hunting nine years earlier and was determined to carry on just as if he could still see, in part to assuage the guilt his father felt.[2]

Henry Fawcett's nineteen-year-old guide and bride as of a month earlier, Millicent Garrett Fawcett,[3] was keen to watch the proceedings herself. That day, for the first time, there was going to be a debate in Parliament about whether women would be allowed to vote.

A bill to extend the franchise to more working-class men drew the most attention on the day's legislative calendar. The year before, then-Chancellor of the Exchequer William Ewart Gladstone had introduced an ambitious franchise reform bill, only to have it narrowly defeated in the House of Commons after eight nights of intense debate, with many debates lasting well into the early morning hours. The wounds from this defeat caused the Liberal government to fall.

After the defeat of Gladstone's bill, "one man, one vote" advocates seeking universal male suffrage organized demonstrations that drew out hundreds of thousands of demonstrators in England's largest cities.[4] In London, after police blocked the entry of people headed to a rally in Hyde Park, crowds pulled down some of the iron railings around the park and flooded in. In the wake of these demonstrations, Gladstone's nemesis, Benjamin Disraeli, the chancellor of the exchequer in the new government, brought forward the Conservative government's own bill to enfranchise more men.

The philosopher and member of Parliament John Stuart Mill had a different kind of franchise reform in mind. An ardent supporter of equality for women, he filed a motion to amend the government's franchise reform bill by replacing the term "man" with "person," an amendment that would extend the government franchise to women.

Mill began the debate on his motion by saying that enfranchising women who were qualified to vote except for their gender shouldn't be controversial because it wouldn't favor one party or social class, issues that were often determinative for members of Parliament. He then appealed to his colleagues' sense of fairness. Their country's failure to give women the right to vote violated a constitutional maxim accepted by most Englishmen: that those who paid money into the state's treasury should be able to help decide how the funds were spent. The present arrangement was unfair, he said, because some women who paid taxes couldn't vote, while men who paid the same amount of taxes could.

Then he turned to the objections he anticipated opponents would raise, beginning with the claim that women didn't need the vote because their interests were already protected by the courts and by their male relatives, who could vote. Mill pointed out that women couldn't always rely on men for protection, that sometimes those closest to them posed the greatest threat, one from which judges often failed to protect them:

> I should like to have a Return laid before this House of the number of women who are annually beaten to death, kicked to death, or trampled to death by their male protectors; and in an opposite column, the amount of sentences in those cases in which the dastardly criminals did not get off altogether. I should also like to have, in a third column, the amount of property, the unlawful taking of which was, at the same sessions, [. . .] by the same judge, thought worthy of the same amount of punishment. We should then have an arithmetical estimate of the value set by a male legislature and male tribunals on the murder of a woman, often by torture through years, which, if there is any shame in us, would make us hang our heads.[5]

If women were enfranchised, Mill argued, they could contribute more to the community, and everyone would benefit. He told how Millicent's sister, Elizabeth Garrett, had been refused admission to medical schools in England because of her gender but still pursued medical studies and passed medical examinations given by the Society of Apothecaries, an organization that had neglected to prohibit women from taking the exams.[6,7]

As soon as Mill finished his remarks, opponents made arguments that anti-suffragists would make for decades. Edward Karslake, a Conservative from Colchester, began by pointing out that he hadn't received a single letter from a woman supporting women's enfranchisement, showing that most women had no interest in voting.[8] He thought this was because English women were content with the advantages granted them under English law and preferred things to remain as they were. To give women the vote, he said, wouldn't ennoble them as Mill had suggested; instead, they would lose their gentleness, affection, and domesticity.[9]

Then Henry Fawcett spoke in support of Mill's motion, saying that giving women the same opportunities as men wouldn't make them less feminine, pointing to what had happened at Cambridge University when girls recruited by Emily Davies were allowed to take junior and senior class examinations on a trial basis three years earlier. The proposal had been bitterly opposed by some at first, but became so successful that the university later adopted it by unanimous vote.[10]

During the debate, one of Mill's supporters asked William Gladstone whether the principle he had set forth three years earlier in a House debate on a bill to enfranchise more men—that absent a good reason for disqualification, every person deserved the vote[11]—would apply to Mill's motion. The Liberal leader exclaimed, "No, no!"[12]—the first recorded evidence of Gladstone's stance against women's suffrage, opposition that would become a major barrier to women's enfranchisement for the next twenty-five years.

Although Mill's motion was defeated, Millicent Fawcett was encouraged by the vote—196 votes against the motion and 73 in favor—because the campaign for women's suffrage had just begun, and many expected the motion would only garner a few stray votes.[13,14]

* * *

Consistent with a maxim, attributed to Gandhi, that people who work for fundamental social change are met with laughter in the early stages of their campaign,[15] five days after the debate in the House of Commons, Mill was the butt of an article in the satirical magazine *Punch*. The piece was said to be a transcript of a lecture by Professor Barnowl on the "enfranchisement of persons," in which the professor said it was strange that Mill, an eminently logical man, had failed to see why women were unfit to be voters. The reason, he explained, was:

[I]n many things women are cleverer than men. They have intuitions which transcend reason. But that same reason is the one thing needful for the free and independent voter. No reason, no vote. Now the fact is, that women, wonderful as many of their endowments are, women in general, are not endowed with reason.[16]

Other critics tied Mill's support for female enfranchisement to his lack of masculinity. Several political cartoons showed him as a woman in a dress and bonnet or referred to him as Ms. Mill.[17]

The ridicule failed to dissuade Mill. In 1869, he published *The Subjection of Women*, a withering critique of the ways English men dominated and oppressed women.[18] Their refusal to grant women the vote, he said, was another way men perpetuated their domination of women.

Much like the way E. D. Morel would later invoke the memory of British abolitionists in his campaign to rescue the Congolese from Leopold, Mill said English men should see the subjugation of women in Victorian England like they had seen slavery forty years earlier—as a barbaric practice of an earlier time. In many ways, he wrote, an English wife was no better off than a slave: she could own no property of her own, and if she left her husband, he could make her come back or seize any money she earned.[19,20] That kind of oppression was not new, Mill said. He traced the exploitation of women back to the twilight of human society, when men used their greater strength to hold women in bondage. Over time, though, the belief that stronger people deserve to exert their will over weaker ones—that might makes right—had been abandoned in advanced nations like England.[21]

Ethics had progressed, according to Mill, but English men had not. They still used violence and coercion to oppress women. He noted that what had become customary was commonly seen as natural. He then asked:

[W]as there ever any domination which did not appear natural to those who possessed it? There was a time when the division of mankind into two classes, a small one of masters and a numerous one of slaves, appeared, even to the most cultivated minds, to be the natural, and the only natural, condition of the human race.[22,23]

Three days after *The Subjection of Women* was published, the Irish journalist, feminist, and social reformer Frances Power Cobbe wrote to Mill, thanking him for having written the book. Anyone who had read an essay Cobbe had written for *Fraser's Magazine* six months earlier would likely not have been surprised by her enthusiasm for *Subjection*. In the essay, Cobbe lampooned the one-way provision of the English common law of coverture—whereby all the money or other personal property a woman owned became her husband's upon their marriage— by recounting an allegorical conversation between an interplanetary visitor to Earth and his native guide:

"Ah," we can hear him say to his guide as they pass into a village church. "What a pretty sight is this! What is happening to that sweet young woman in white who is giving her hand to the good-looking fellow beside her, all the company decked in holiday attire, and the joy-bells shaking the old tower overhead? She is receiving some great honour, is she not? The Prize of Virtue, perhaps?"

"Oh, yes," would reply the friend, "an honour certainly. She is being Married." After a little further explanation, the visitor would pursue his inquiry:

"Of course, having entered this honorable state of matrimony, she has some privilege above the women who are not chosen by anybody? I notice her husband has just said, 'With all my worldly goods I thee endow.' Does that mean that she will henceforth have the control of his money altogether, or only that he takes her into partnership?"

"*Pas précisément*, my dear sir. By our law it is *her* goods and earnings, present and future, which belong to him from this moment."

"You don't say so. But then his goods are hers also?"

"Oh dear, no! not at all. He is only bound to find her food; and truth to tell, not very strictly or efficaciously bound to do that." [. . .]

"One question still further—your criminals? Do they always forfeit their entire property on conviction?"

"Only for the most heinous crimes: felony and murder, for example."

"Pardon me: I must seem to you so stupid! Why is the property of the woman who commits Murder, and the property of the woman who commits Matrimony, dealt with alike by your law?"[24]

Like Mill, Cobbe thought that men's domination of women in Victorian England was a relic of the ancient law of the strongest. As she put it:

In past ages, the case was simple enough. No question of right or duty disturbed the conscience of Oriental or Spartan, of Roman or Norman, in dealing with his wife, his Helot, his slave, or his serf. "*Le droit du plus fort*" was unassailed in theory and undisturbed in practice.[25]

When other groups, such as children working in Dickensian factories, were endangered or tyrannized by those with power over them, Cobbe said, the law stepped in to protect them. Not so with women. Rather than give married women a measure of independence by letting them keep their own personal property and what they earned, English marriage law didn't allow that, making them even more vulnerable to abuse and exploitation. Cobbe compared the status of women in Victorian England to a metaphorical creature in the London Zoo:

Do we not seem to hear one of the intelligent keepers in the Zoological Gardens explaining to a party of visitors: "This, ladies and gentlemen, is an inoffensive bird, the *Mulier Anglicana*. The beak is feeble, and the claws unsuited for grubbing for worms. It seems to be only intelligent in building its nest, or taking care of its young, to whom it is particularly devoted, as well as to its mate. Otherwise it is a very simple sort of bird, picking up any crumbs which are thrown to it, and never touching carrion like the vulture or intoxicating fluids like the macaw. Therefore, you see, ladies and gentlemen, as it is so helpless, we put that strong chain around its leg, and fasten it to its nest, and make the bars of its cage exceptionally strong. As to its rudimentary wings we always break them early, for greater security; though I have heard Professor [T. H.] Huxley say that he is convinced it could never fly far with them, under any circumstances."[26]

Cobbe not only wrote essays and magazine articles condemning English laws that allowed men to exploit women, she also worked to change them. Six weeks after Mill's motion to amend the 1867 franchise reform bill was defeated, Cobbe helped found the London National Society for Women's Suffrage. Millicent Fawcett was one of the founding members of the society too, thus embarking, as a biographer put it, on the assignment that Emily Davies and Millicent's own sister Elizabeth had given her when she was a small child.[27]

2. THE THIN END OF THE WEDGE

In an 1868 essay, Frances Power Cobbe compared marriage under the English law of coverture to relations between tarantulas:

> As most persons are aware, when one of these delightful creatures is placed under a glass with a companion of his own species a little smaller than himself, he forthwith gobbles him up; making him thus, in a very literal manner, "bone of his bone" (supposing tarantulas to have any bones) "and flesh of his flesh." The operation being completed, the victorious spider visibly acquires double bulk, and therefore may be understood to "represent the family" in the most perfect manner conceivable.[1]

After spreading their message by distributing thousands of pamphlets and writing essays published in newspapers and English periodicals, supporters of women's suffrage had to overcome a formidable barrier. Other successful English reformers gained momentum and legislative credibility by holding well-attended public meetings and staging massive rallies. These events, though, could become rowdy affairs, like the 1866 rally mentioned earlier, in which supporters of universal male suffrage tore down some of the railings around Hyde Park. Many people considered it improper for women to attend such events, much less give speeches at them. Being well aware of this, suffrage groups began by holding small meetings in local clubs and drawing rooms. They realized, though, that to have any chance of success, they would have to start holding large public events and brave the disparagement that would follow.

In July of 1869, the London Society held its first public meeting in the gallery of the Architectural Society. Twenty-two-year-old Millicent

Fawcett was among the speakers, along with the wife of another member of Parliament. A few days later, a colleague of her husband's mentioned on the floor of the Commons that the wives of two MPs had disgraced themselves by speaking in public, but as a gentleman, he wouldn't bring further dishonor upon them by mentioning their names.[2]

A short time later, when Millicent Fawcett and her husband were dining with friends in Cambridge, she found that the MP who thought she had disgraced herself had been asked to escort her into dinner. She told him she regretted the unfortunate position in which he found himself and asked if he would like her to request that he be allowed to escort another woman. He declined her offer. As she recalled later:

> I found him to be quite an agreeable neighbour at the table, and so far as I knew he never again publicly held up any woman to contempt for advocating the enfranchisement of her sex. After all, what he had said was very mild compared to [writer] Horace Walpole's abuse of [feminist philosopher] Mary Wollstonecraft as "a hyena in petticoats."[3,4]

Fawcett frequently spoke at suffrage meetings and rallies, although she dreaded it. Her speeches often included a point-by-point rebuttal of all the arguments made by opponents of women's suffrage, delivered with the same courtesy and rational analysis as those of her friend and mentor, John Stuart Mill. As she pointed out, many of the anti-suffragists' arguments were at odds with one another. Some opponents claimed that women weren't interested in gaining the franchise, while others worried that if they got it, they would outvote men. And some argued women were so easily influenced that their nearest male relative would end up having two votes, while others said they were so obstinate that enfranchising them would lead to endless family discord.[5]

Cobbe had an explanation for these contradictory arguments: opposition to women's suffrage was rooted in custom and sentiment, not reason.[6]

Another suffrage supporter, Fred Pethick-Lawrence, had a different explanation. He thought many men's opposition to women's suffrage flowed from their love of domination, which sometimes led to their blunt rejoinder—"Votes for Women, indeed; we shall be asked next to give votes to our horses and dogs."[7]

Charles Dilke, an MP who spoke at the London Society's meeting at the Architectural Society, had suggested the year before that the most pragmatic strategy would be to secure the parliamentary franchise in installments as working men had done, beginning with getting the right to vote in local elections.[8] Several suffrage leaders agreed, seeing the municipal franchise as the "thin end of the wedge" that would, in time, help them get the vote in national elections.[9,10]

Their first opportunity arose in 1869, when Dilke and another advocate of women's suffrage, Jacob Bright, moved to amend a pending municipal franchise bill to grant the vote to single women and widows who, except for their gender, met the qualifications for voting. After the home secretary indicated that the government didn't object to the amendment, the House of Commons adopted it with virtually no debate. It was even quietly accepted by the House of Lords after a supporter made clear that the bill didn't concern "the wider and more doubtful question of extending to women the right to vote at government elections."[11]

The wedge was driven in a little deeper the next year with the passage of the Elementary Education Act, which established local school boards and gave women the right to vote in a school board election and even to stand for a seat on the board. It was beginning to feel like 1870 might be a banner year for English women, when the Commons voted 124–91 to have a committee review a bill, introduced by Jacob Bright, granting some women the parliamentary franchise. During the debate on Bright's bill, the home secretary indicated that the government hadn't had the time to thoroughly study it and hadn't decided whether to support it or not.[12]

Eight days later, Prime Minister Gladstone announced his government's decision during a debate on the bill. He prefaced his remarks by explaining that the government hadn't taken a position earlier so as not to invade the liberties of the independent members of the House. Then he proceeded to do just that, saying that when the vote was taken, he would "cheerfully" join those in opposition.[13] His invocation of Liberal Party loyalty was dramatic, precipitating a swing to 159 votes against the bill from the previous majority of 33 votes in favor to a hostile majority of 126 against.[14] When Bright's enfranchisement bill was soundly defeated, many suffragists began to realize how difficult their mission would be.[15]

* * *

That fall, Elizabeth Garrett found a group of men from the Marylebone Working Men's Association waiting for her when she returned home. The men were husbands and fathers of patients at a dispensary she had helped start in a poverty-stricken section of London. By that time, she was Elizabeth Garrett, M.D., having secured her medical degree from the Sorbonne after being denied admission to English medical schools.

The men had come to ask her to run for election to the newly established London School Board.[16] She was already working long hours but decided she couldn't refuse, writing to her childhood friend, Emily Davies:

> [I]t is no use asking for women to be taken into public work and yet to wish them to avoid publicity. We must be ready to go into the thing as men do if we go at all, and in time there will be no more awkwardness on our side than there now is on theirs. Still I am very sorry it is necessary, especially as I can't think of anything to say for four speeches! And after Huxley,[17] too, who speaks in epigrams![18]

In the election, Garrett faced off against several other candidates in a vast electoral district torn by many social, political, and religious rivalries.[19] She turned out, though, to be a gifted campaigner: buoyant, quick-witted, hardworking, and articulate. She divided her day into performing surgeries in the morning, attending factory meetings at lunchtime, and dispensing medications in the afternoon. Then she headed to committee meetings in the early evening, followed by a speech or two, after which she often dashed across the city to support another female candidate.[20]

People were also pressing Garrett's friend Emily Davies to run for the school board in another part of London.[21] At first, Davies was torn between the advice of her mother and Garrett—both of whom encouraged her to be a candidate—and that of her brother, who warned that an ignominious defeat would harm the women's movement.[22] Her days were already full too, with her duties at Britain's first women's college, which she'd helped found the year before. In the end, she decided to run, hoping, like Garrett, to further women's participation in public life. She found campaigning painful but gritted her teeth and persevered, hoping that the next speech would be easier than the last.[23]

Elizabeth Garrett, in contrast, found it all great fun, speaking from the stage in a cavernous hall as confidently as from an orange box or beer barrel.[24] At the end of the campaign, she roused a large crowd at a rally in Greenwich to support her friend's candidacy, as Davies described in a letter to a supporter:

> You would have liked Miss Garrett's speech—it was only too generous—and the meeting was enthusiastic. The Hall was fuller than it would hold (it holds 1,000) and the women came crowding into the committee room at the end to shake hands and promise their votes.[25]

By polling day, Garrett felt good about her chances. Still, she wasn't prepared for the final tally. She slipped out of the polling place at midnight to send her campaign manager—and soon-to-be husband, Skelton Anderson—a card giving him the news. She had gotten nearly 48,000 votes, three times more than T. H. Huxley, who finished second, and more than any other candidate in London.[26] Emily Davies was the top vote-getter in her district too, finishing 2,000 votes ahead of the next candidate.[27] While Davies and Garrett were among the first female school board members, they were far from the last. By the end of the decade, there were some seventy women on local school boards, many of them drawn from the ladies' educational societies that Davies had helped establish.[28]

* * *

Throughout the 1870s, the British government ping-ponged between Gladstone and Disraeli. Neither of them had a minister introduce a women's suffrage bill. Still, the suffragists kept at it, arranging to have MPs introduce private member's bills almost every year.

All these bills failed. Each government exercised a great deal of control over the parliamentary calendar, and, absent its support, a private member's bill had to follow a path that was steeply uphill. Another legislative route, less taxing at first, was to amend any government franchise reform bill to include women, as Mill had attempted in 1867. An opportunity to do this arose again in 1884 when, during Gladstone's second term as prime minister, the government introduced a bill to enfranchise more men living in rural areas, much like how the 1867 franchise reform law had given the vote to more men living in cities and towns.

In February, women's suffrage supporters in Parliament decided that a Liberal colleague, William Woodall, would move to amend the pending franchise reform bill. Whereas Gladstone claimed he had opposed Bright's earlier bill to enfranchise single women because it didn't enfranchise married women too, Woodall's amendment did just that. Whatever their marital status, all women would be granted the vote under his amendment if their gender was the only reason they were disqualified from voting. Nevertheless, Gladstone passionately opposed Woodall's amendment too, concluding his remarks in a floor debate thus: "I offer it the strongest opposition in my power, and I must disclaim and renounce all responsibility for the measure should my Hon. Friend succeed in inducing the Committee to adopt the Amendment."[29]

Conservatives voted 95–28 in support of the amendment, but Liberals voted 236–33 against it, and it was overwhelmingly defeated.[30] More than a hundred Liberal members who voted against the Woodall amendment had previously pledged to support women's suffrage.[31] Looking back years later, Fawcett thought their betrayal sowed the seeds of the militant movement to come.[32]

For the time being, though, suffrage supporters kept working quietly. The breadth of support they gained was evident in 1897 when House members voted 230–159 to move forward with a private member's enfranchisement bill, after suffrage societies displayed a monster petition—signed by 257,796 people—on tables in Westminster Hall outside the House chamber.[33] The government declined to support the bill, though, and opponents managed to obstruct and delay legislative proceedings until it died. For the next several years, anti-suffragists used a variety of tactics to derail suffrage bills, sometimes just engaging in filibusters on bills that preceded a suffrage bill on the legislative calendar until no time was left to take it up. Liberal and Conservative party leaders acquiesced to this while continuing to say they were committed to democracy and representative government.

For more than thirty years, suffragists held thousands of meetings and rallies throughout the country and collected the signatures of hundreds of thousands of their countrymen on petitions in support of their request: that women who were fully qualified to vote under the country's laws—except for their gender—be allowed to vote. Although they worked to change the laws, the suffragists continued to abide by them, eschewing violence even though they knew that millions of men had gotten the vote in their country through campaigns stained by violence and intimidation. Shortly after the turn of the century, though, some suffrage advocates began to take a different tack.

3. CONSTANCE LYTTON: MAKING A TRACK TO THE WATER'S EDGE

I saw a desert and I saw a woman coming out of it. And she came to the bank of a dark river; and the bank was steep and high. And on it an old man met her. [. . .] And he asked her what she wanted; and she said, "I am woman; and I am seeking for the Land of Freedom."

And he said, "It is before you." [. . .]

She said, "How am I to get there?"

He said, "There is one way, and one only. Down the banks of Labour, through the water of Suffering. There is no other."

She said, "Is there no bridge?"

He answered. "None."

She said, "Is the water deep?"

He said, "Deep."

She said, "Is the floor worn?"

He said, "It is. Your foot may slip at any time and you may be lost."

She said, "Have any crossed already?"

He said, "Some have *tried*."

She said, "Is there a track to show where the best fording is?"

He said, "It has to be made."

She shaded her eyes with her hand; and she said, "I will go."

—Olive Schreiner[1]

If she had never become a suffragette,[2] Lady Constance Lytton would probably never have gone to jail, much less been imprisoned four times. She was from one of England's first families. Queen Victoria had made her father, Robert Bulwer-Lytton, the Earl of Lytton for his service as viceroy of India and had appointed her mother as one of her ladies-in-waiting. One of her brothers was a Conservative member of the House of Lords, and her older sister was married to Prime Minister Arthur Balfour's brother.

When members of a militant suffrage group, the Women's Social and Political Union (WSPU), began using nonviolent civil disobedience to promote women's suffrage in 1905, Constance Lytton[3] was in her mid-thirties. She shared a quiet life with her mother on the family's estate in Hertfordshire and shrank from controversy and notoriety.

The WSPU's tactics, in contrast, were designed to ignite conflict and generate publicity.[4] WSPU suffragettes began baiting politicians when they spoke in public, just as radical male reformers had done in their country throughout the nineteenth century.[5] Their anger escalated in the spring of 1908 when H. H. Asquith—a Liberal MP who had imbibed his opposition to women's suffrage from William Gladstone—became prime minister. In many ways, according to historian Martin Pugh, Asquith's prejudice in the matter was even more deep-seated than Gladstone's. Nothing in his upbringing or experience as a member of a series of comfortable men's clubs had awakened any sympathy in him for women's subordinate status or opened his mind to their abilities.[6]

Shortly before Asquith became prime minister, Gladstone's son Herbert said in a House of Commons debate that Parliament shouldn't pass a women's suffrage bill until its advocates had demonstrated there was broad public support for their cause, as men had done by organizing massive rallies like those that had sparked the passage of franchise reform acts in 1832, 1867, and 1885, during his father's time. "Of course," he went on to say, "it is not to be expected that women could assemble in such masses."[7] Women's suffrage supporters picked up the gauntlet and began putting together a rally to make the younger Gladstone regret his comment.

In June, many MPs, clerics, constituents, and a host of well-dressed women were relaxing in the shade on the terrace of the House of Commons, sipping tea and dining on watercress sandwiches, when a boatload of suffragettes steamed down the Thames next to the terrace.

Flora Drummond, nicknamed "the General" for marching at the head of WSPU processions in epaulets and a peaked cap,[8] used a megaphone to invite MPs to the Women's Sunday rally that would take place three days later, seasoning her invitation with inducements like "there will be no arrests" and "you shall have plenty of police protection."[9]

Any MPs who had attended the Women's Sunday rally—held in Hyde Park like the famed 1866 men's Reform League rally, which had attracted some 67,000 people[10]—would have joined a throng. One of the organizers claimed that "the numbers who came to the park that day were greater than had ever been gathered together before on any one spot in the whole history of the world."[11]

A correspondent to the *Times*, a paper hostile to the women's cause, used superlatives in describing the rally too:

> Its organizers had counted on an audience of 250,000. That expectation was certainly fulfilled and probably it was doubled, and it would be difficult to contradict anyone who asserted that it was trebled. Like the distances and numbers of the stars, the facts were beyond the threshold of perception.[12]

An account in the *Daily Express* used the 1866 Reform League rally as a measuring stick: "Men who saw the great Gladstone meeting years ago said that compared with yesterday's multitude, it was as nothing."[13] Among the multitude were Millicent Fawcett, Elizabeth Garrett Anderson, and Emily Davies.[14]

Four months earlier, a women's franchise bill had won a 273–94 majority in the House of Commons, but the government had refused to give it time on the parliamentary schedule. The day before the rally took place, Prime Minister Asquith promised a delegation of sixty Liberal MPs who supported the bill that the government would grant it time on the calendar if there was evidence of widespread support in the country for giving women the vote. The massive turnout at the Women's Sunday rally in Hyde Park apparently wasn't sufficient. Pressed by suffragettes two days after the rally, he said he had nothing to add to what he said earlier.[15]

Six days later, Asquith refused to see a delegation of suffragettes. Two took a taxi to Downing Street and threw stones at the windows in his residence. One of them reportedly said, "It will be a bomb next time."[16]

* * *

In the summer of 1908, a friend invited Constance Lytton to spend a two-week holiday with her at Littlehampton, a seaside resort town. Lytton rarely left home but, at her mother's suggestion, accepted the invitation, "little realizing," as she put it later, "that this visit would lead to a most unexpected series of experiences."[17]

The friend, Mary Neal, shared Lytton's sympathy for the plight of British working women. A decade earlier, Neal and a colleague, Emmeline Pethick, had set up the Maison Espérance, a dressmaking cooperative in London that paid seamstresses double the customary wage, limited their workday to eight hours, and spread the work evenly throughout the year to avoid the privation that usually resulted from the seasonal nature of the dressmaking trade.[18] They also bought a large house in Littlehampton so working women could spend a holiday by the sea and named it the Green Lady Hostel;[19] this was the place Neal invited Lytton to visit.

Upon arriving at the Green Lady, Lytton met Emmeline Pethick (by then Emmeline Pethick-Lawrence, having married Fred Pethick-Lawrence in 1901) and Annie Kenney, two leaders of the WSPU. For the first couple of days, though, Lytton didn't realize the women were suffragettes, although she sensed at once they were strong women who radiated a force greater than themselves.[20] She learned she was among militants one evening when the women heard Annie Kenney's younger sister Jessie talk about her experiences at Holloway Prison in London while serving a month-long sentence for disturbing the peace as a member of the deputation Asquith had refused to see after the Women's Sunday rally.[21]

Even after several heart-to-heart talks with Kenney and Pethick-Lawrence, Lytton continued to believe that the WSPU's militant tactics were unreasonable and politically irresponsible.[22] She changed her mind, though, after seeing what happened to an animal.[23]

While walking around Littlehampton one morning, she came across a crowd surrounding a misshapen sheep. The animal had escaped while on the way to a slaughterhouse and, with increasing fear and distress, ran around in desperation. People in the crowd jeered at it. After two men caught the animal, one gave it a cuff in the face. Unable to take any more, Lytton ran up to the men and scolded them: "Don't you know your own business? You have this creature absolutely in your power. If you were holding it properly, it would be still. You are taking it to be killed, you are doing your job badly to hurt and insult it besides." The men seemed ashamed, and the crowd slunk away.[24]

Seeing what had befallen the sheep led to an epiphany for Lytton. As she said later:

> [O]n seeing this sheep it seemed to reveal to me for the first time the position of women throughout the world. I realised how often women are held in contempt as beings outside the pale of human dignity, excluded or confined, laughed at and insulted because of conditions in themselves for which they are not responsible, but which are due to fundamental injustices with regard to them, and to the mistakes of a civilisation in the shaping of which they have had no free share.[25]

Lytton began her suffrage work quietly, writing a thirty-two-page pamphlet distributed by both the WSPU and Fawcett's National Union of Women's Suffrage Societies (National Union). As Fawcett had done more than three decades earlier, she patiently rebutted the claims of suffrage opponents with wit and verve, although she pointed out that, over the years, many of the opponents' arguments had not only become threadbare, they had worn into holes.[26]

Lytton also brought warm clothing and bedding to suffragettes imprisoned at Holloway. After attending a breakfast reception for some of them who had been released, she began to feel guilty for not contributing more herself.[27] Finally, in February of 1909, she agreed to join a deputation.

By then, sending groups of suffragettes to Parliament, even after having been told they would be unwelcome there, had become a regular feature of WSPU campaigns. After holding a women's parliament in a nearby hall, a group would head out on foot toward the Houses of Parliament. Somewhere along the way, cordons of police on foot and horseback would block their way and order them to turn back. They would keep on going, and a scuffle would usually break out. People in the crowd around them— some friendly, some not—often joined in.[28]

This being Lytton's first experience as part of a WSPU deputation, a young woman was assigned to accompany her, who explained to Lytton that whatever happened, the only thing she must remember was not to turn back. To Lytton, this was more than just an instruction for the evening; it was the essence of the suffragette's creed.[29]

Squads of police met members of the deputation as soon as they stepped out into the street, even though the Houses of Parliament were about a kilometer away, and closed in from both sides. Lytton, of frail health to begin with, was soon out of breath and doubled over in the crush. To make things worse, a policeman grabbed her around the ribs, squeezed the remaining breath from her, and threw her up in the air. Fortunately, the crowd had pressed so tightly around her that she didn't hit the ground when she came down.

She wasn't as fortunate later when police officers twice threw her to the ground. Each time, a friendly German woman helped her up and kept the crowd away while Lytton leaned against a railing or the woman's shoulder and regained her strength. Finally, she stopped and said to the stranger, "I can't go on; I simply can't go on." The angelic stranger quietly replied, "Wait for a little, and you will be all right presently."[30]

Somehow, Lytton soldiered on and made it to the House of Commons. There, two police officers took her into custody and brought her to the nearest police station. She found Pethick-Lawrence and some other members of the deputation at the station too. Many had been thrown to the ground or kicked, and one had blood streaming from her nose. Lytton tasted the sweetness of solidarity there with those who shared her newfound passion, trading stories with them about the evening's adventures.[31,32]

After a supporter bailed the suffragettes out, Lytton made her way to her younger sister's flat in London to stay for the evening. Her other sister, Betty, was visiting too, and comforted Lytton as she tried to recover from the battering she had taken, lamenting, "Oh! Con, you are not fit to go to prison." In the morning, the sisters discussed how best to comfort their mother, Edith, whom Constance hadn't told about her decision to join the delegation of suffragettes.[33]

Instead of telling her mother about her plans before she left home, Lytton had written a letter to her when she arrived at King's Cross Railway Station in north London, explaining that she was joining a WSPU deputation and might be in Holloway Prison in London by the time the letter arrived. She knew her mother despised the militants' methods and grieved over her daughter's increasing involvement with them. In the letter, Constance tried to reassure her mother that prison conditions had improved and that she would easily be able to handle them.[34]

The next day, a judge sentenced her to a month at Holloway Prison after one of the police officers who arrested her testified that she had said, "I must see Mr. Asquith. I must get to Mr. Asquith." She could have avoided imprisonment by agreeing to "keep the peace" in the future but in good faith couldn't do that.[35]

After sentencing, police kept her in a cell at the station until a van came to take her to the prison. Both of her sisters and her younger brother came to bid their goodbyes at the station. Several friends told her, "Well done." The pleasure of seeing friends and family members was spoiled for her, though, when she noticed that no one had visited a quiet cellmate. Then, just as she was being taken out, Lytton's gloom lifted when three kind-looking women came to the cell window and her cellmate sprang up to greet her friends.[36]

Arriving at Holloway, Lytton was disappointed to find that prison officials forced her and the other suffragettes to wear prison uniforms like ordinary criminals. When the first suffragettes had become imprisoned

Fig. 10. Constance Lytton Wearing a WSPU Ribbon Commemorating Her First
Imprisonment at Holloway

in 1906, Home Secretary Herbert Gladstone had allowed them to wear
their own clothes and have other privileges.[37] By Lytton's time, though,
he had grown tired of the suffragettes' militancy and had begun treating
them like common criminals, not prisoners who were imprisoned for
political activities.[38]

Lytton was also disappointed to find that prison officials were aware
of her heart condition[39] and had assigned her to the prison hospital.
Patients in the hospital unit were waited on by other prisoners, and she
was adamant that she shouldn't receive any special privileges.[40]

Although prison officials knew of her aristocratic lineage—a half-page
photo of her having appeared in the Daily Mirror with a story about her
trial[41]—she didn't know whether the other prisoners were aware of it until
some overheard the prison chaplain addressing her as "Your Ladyship."
When it dawned on her that the chaplain was treating her more respectfully
than he did the other prisoners, it also occurred to her that the dress jacket
prison officials had given her was much newer than the ones they had
given to other prisoners and didn't have white arrows on it, signifying the
person was a prisoner. Exquisitely sensitive to issues of class and privilege,
she swapped her jacket with that of a prisoner from another suffrage group,
the Women's Freedom League—one that was well worn.[42]

Lytton had another taste of solidarity with her suffragette companions at the prison. They had arranged with a kind-hearted wardress to get together and tell stories on the evening before some Freedom League prisoners were scheduled to be released. When the time came, nine of them sat in a circle in the hospital ward. The fire-lit faces of the women beamed as each told a story or read a poem that had special meaning for her. Even the wardress joined in.

When it was Pethick-Lawrence's turn, she told an allegory written by a South African woman, Olive Schreiner. The story reminded Lytton warmly of her father, Robert, it having been a favorite of his.[43]

In the story, a woman crossing a desert sees an old man, Reason, and asks him for directions to the place she had been searching for, the Land of Freedom.

> He said, "There is one way, and one only. Down the banks of Labour, through the water of Suffering. There is no other." [. . .]
>
> She said, "Is there a track to show where the best fording is?"
>
> He said, "It has to be made." [. . .]
>
> And she said, "For what do I go to this far land which no one has ever reached? I am alone! I am utterly alone!"

But soon, she hears the sound of feet, "a thousand times ten thousand and thousands and thousands," and they beat toward her:

> He said, "They are the feet of those that shall follow you. [. . .] Have you seen the locusts, how they cross a stream? First one comes down to the water-edge, and it is swept away, and then another comes and then another, and then another, and at last with their bodies piled up a bridge is built and the rest pass over." [. . .]
>
> She said, "And of those that come first, some are swept away and are heard of no more; their bodies do not even build the bridge?"
>
> "And are swept away, and are heard of no more—and what of that?" he said.
>
> "And what of that"—she said.
>
> "They make a track to the water's edge."[44,45]

4. NO SURRENDER!

Before long I heard the sounds of force feeding in the cell next
to mine. It was almost more than I could bear[;] it was Elsie
Howey, I was sure. When the ghastly process was over and
all quiet, I tapped on the wall and called out at the top of
my voice, which wasn't much just then, "No surrender," and
there came the answer past any doubt in Elsie's voice, "No
surrender."—Constance Lytton[1]

In the months after Constance Lytton and her companions were
released from Holloway, the mutual ill will between the suffragettes
and the Asquith government grew even more intense. In late June of
1909, after the government declined to support a suffrage bill that
included some votes for women, another group of WSPU supporters
attempted to see Asquith. As before, members of the delegation were
arrested and sentenced to prison despite their claim at trial that they
had a constitutional right to petition the government for redress of their
grievances.[2]

They also made their case at St. Stephen's Hall in the Palace of
Westminster, where a WSPU member, Marion Wallace-Dunlop, stamped
a message on the wall which read: "Women's Deputation. Bill of Rights.
It is the Right of the subjects to petition the King, and all commitments
and prosecutions for such petitioning are illegal."[3] The last sentence was
a quotation from the 1689 English Bill of Rights.

A judge sentenced Wallace-Dunlop to prison for causing ten shillings'
worth of damage to St. Stephen's Hall.[4] When she arrived at Holloway to
serve her sentence, Wallace-Dunlop told the prison governor that unless
he gave her the privileges and relaxed regimentation accorded prisoners

of conscience, she would not eat. When he refused, she began a hunger strike. Staff left a special tray of delicacies in her cell to tempt her, but she remained steadfast.[5] Concerned about her increasing weakness, a prison doctor came to check her regularly. She always met him with a smile. "What are you going to have for dinner today?" he asked one evening. "My determination," she replied. After having fasted for ninety-one hours, she grew weak, and the prison governor set her free, even though she had more than three weeks left on her sentence.[6]

News of what Wallace-Dunlop had done spread quickly. Upon their arrival at Holloway, other suffragettes told the prison governor that they, too, would begin hunger strikes unless he treated them as political prisoners—the way Irish nationalists and socialists were treated. He allowed them to keep their own clothes but warned them that when a committee of magistrates visited the prison, he would charge them with mutiny. The women repeated their request in petitions to Herbert Gladstone, the home secretary, but received no response. When the magistrates arrived, they sentenced the women to solitary confinement for violating prison rules. True to their word, the suffragettes began fasting. After several days, they, too, were released.[7]

Hunger strikes gave the suffragettes a way to reduce the length of their imprisonment, if at great cost to themselves. This only lasted a couple of months though. In September of 1909, prison officials began responding to a hunger striker by overpowering and restraining the suffragette, forcing her mouth open with a wooden or steel gag, jamming a long tube down her throat, and pouring liquid nourishment into the tube. To regain the upper hand, Gladstone had decided that "for the present these women must be treated like prisoners with defective minds who [were] not amenable to the prison regulations."[8]

By then, Constance Lytton had recuperated from her stay at Holloway and was traveling around the country for the WSPU, speaking at meetings and rallies in England, Wales, and Scotland. In October, Emmeline Pankhurst, the charismatic leader of the WSPU, took Lytton to visit a nursing home in Birmingham where some of the first force-fed hunger strikers were recovering. As had happened when she first met suffragettes who had been imprisoned at Holloway, Lytton felt guilty about not having contributed more herself. By the time she left, she had made up her mind to join the hunger strikers in prison.[9]

A few days later, Lytton and another suffragette destined to become well known,[10] Emily Wilding Davison, waited by the side of a road in Newcastle where they thought a car carrying Chancellor of the Exchequer David Lloyd George would be passing by.[11] Lytton threw a rock at a wheel of an official-looking vehicle, careful not to hit the chauffeur or any passenger. Wrapped around the stone was a message to Lloyd George that read: "Rebellion against tyrants is obedience to God." Two police officers in plain clothes arrested her immediately.[12]

At her trial, the authorities made every effort not to convict her, but she insisted to the judge that she had intended to be disorderly. He found her guilty and sentenced her to a month in Newcastle Prison with several other suffragettes.[13]

When she arrived at the prison, Lytton and another prisoner— Jane Brailsford, the wife of a prominent journalist—were housed in a separate part of the prison and given privileges not granted to the other suffragettes. Prison officials put the others in punishment cells upon their announcing their intention to fast and had them force-fed. Lytton and Brailsford began hunger strikes to protest the treatment their colleagues were receiving and were released in a couple of days without having been fed against their will.[14]

Suffrage supporters charged the government with having a double standard. Brailsford's husband wrote to the *Times*, saying that if force-feeding was too horrible for some, it was too horrible for all.[15] George Bernard Shaw also wrote to the *Times*, congratulating Gladstone on his decision not to feed Lytton by force and suggesting that he treat the other suffragettes the same way. If he declined to do that, Shaw invited him to enjoy a banquet at which "[t]he rarest wines and delicacies shall be provided absolutely regardless of expense" but on the condition that "Mr. Herbert Gladstone shall partake through the nose."[16]

Gladstone responded to critics concerned about the health of force-fed suffragettes by assuring his colleagues in the Commons that a physician carefully checked every woman who was force-fed for evidence of heart disease. When asked about Lytton and Brailsford's early release from Newcastle Prison, he denied that the government treated suffragettes with political connections any differently from other citizens, saying, "[T]here is not the slightest ground for the insinuations which are being freely made that Lady Constance Lytton was released because she was a peer's sister. She was released solely on medical grounds."[17]

Lytton came up with a way to test the government's claim that it treated all suffragettes equally and was blind to issues of social class or political influence: she decided to get imprisoned while disguised as an ordinary seamstress. When she learned that Selina Martin, one of the suffragettes she had met at the nursing home in Birmingham, was imprisoned in Liverpool and likely being fed against her will, she arranged with WSPU organizers in Liverpool to lead a group to the jail and call upon the governor to release the suffragettes.

After attending WSPU events in Manchester, she put together her disguise. She had her hair cut short in early Victorian style and purchased an entire working-class outfit, topping it off with an unfashionable cloth hat she bought at an inexpensive dry goods shop.[18]

Fig. 11. Jane Warton (Constance Lytton)

When she approached the jail in Liverpool, Lytton was taken with the thought that prison staff might be force-feeding Selina Martin at that moment, writing later: "I felt so feeble, had so little faith in the utility of what I was about to do, yet I was athirst to do it."[19] When the women arrived on the prison grounds, Lytton threw some stones over a hedge into the governor's garden. Two policemen seized her and took her to the nearest station. Although she had planned to go to prison alone, two other women broke a window of the governor's house so they would be arrested and could accompany her.[20]

One of the women was released, but the judge sentenced Lytton (under her pseudonym, Jane Warton) to Walton Gaol for a fortnight and the other suffragette, Elsie Howey, for six weeks. Upon arriving at the jail, Howey politely advised a wardress that they would refuse all food unless treated as prisoners of conscience. She explained: "We are sorry if it will give trouble; we shall give as little as possible; but our fast is against the Government, and we shall fight them with our lives, not hurting anyone else."[21] After being placed in her cell, Lytton wrote a quotation from Thoreau's *Duty of Civil Disobedience* on the wall with a slate pencil: "Under a Government which imprisons any unjustly, the true place for a just man (or woman) is also a prison."[22]

After she refused food for a couple of days, prison officials had Lytton put in a punishment cell. Two days later, the senior medical officer and five wardresses came with feeding equipment. Wardresses grabbed Lytton's arms, legs, and head while the doctor forced her mouth open with a steel gag, rammed a plastic tube down her throat, and poured a mixture of milk, egg, and brandy into the tube. Lytton immediately threw it up all over her hair and clothes. As the doctor left, he slapped her on the cheek. Before long, she heard a clamor in the cell next to hers. She was sure it was Elsie Howey being force-fed. Once it was over and quiet returned, she tapped on the wall and said, as loudly as she could, "No surrender!" Soon, Elsie's reply came back: "No surrender!"[23]

Despite Gladstone's assurance that a doctor carefully examined each prisoner before she was force-fed, Lytton wasn't examined until she began to shiver uncontrollably while being force-fed for the third time. The doctor who was feeding her summoned another doctor; he put a stethoscope to her heart briefly and exclaimed to his colleague, "Oh ripping, splendid heart! You can go on with her!"[24]

After being overpowered and fed six times, Lytton was a broken woman. She longed for death and felt she could take no more. Remembering her pact with Elsie Howey, though, she made herself get up from her bed and walk around her cell until she recovered her resolve.[25]

In the meantime, rumors began to circulate that the prisoner in Walton Gaol wasn't a seamstress named Jane Warton but Lady Constance Lytton. Her sister Emily received a telegram from the *Daily News* meant for Lord Victor Lytton, asking whether the rumor was true. She called the prison at once and quickly put the pieces of the puzzle together. Prison officials arranged for Emily to pick her sister up the next day. When Emily met with the prison governor, he told her he had never seen such a bad case of force-feeding, and that Constance had been almost asphyxiated every time.[26]

Constance Lytton returned home to recover, having lost about twenty-five pounds in the ordeal.[27] Victor Lytton requested that the Home Office investigate her claims that she hadn't been examined before being fed by force, that the senior medical officer struck her, and that the examination finally made by another doctor had been cursory. A Home Office official replied that the doctor had felt her pulse before force-feeding her for the first time and hadn't slapped her but had just patted her cheek to comfort her. The official also claimed that the symptoms of heart defects like hers varied from time to time and were difficult to detect.[28]

In a letter to the *Times*, Victor pointed out that the same person, when known to be Lady Constance Lytton, had been judged to be too ill to be force-fed, but when thought to be Jane Warton, had been force-fed eight times, and that prison officials only stopped when they discovered she was actually Lady Lytton.[29]

* * *

While Constance Lytton was going through her ordeal at the Walton Gaol, Henry Brailsford, the husband of her companion in Newcastle Prison, was putting together a group of MPs from all political parties who supported women's suffrage. Ever since the Liberal landslide in the 1906 election—which brought in 200 new Liberal members and 29 Labour members, most of whom had never sat in Parliament before—a clear majority in the House of Commons supported some type of women's suffrage.[30] They disagreed, however, on what form it should take. Some preferred a moderate approach, enfranchising only single women and widows; others supported giving the vote to women, regardless of marital status, on equal terms with men; a third group wanted to radically expand the franchise to include all adults, regardless of gender.[31]

Encouraged by the prospect that an all-party group of MPs would be able to put together a women's franchise bill that could become law, on January 31, 1910, Emmeline Pankhurst announced that the WSPU was suspending all militant actions for the time being.[32] Within a few months, the group of legislators—which became known as the Conciliation Committee because it was working to reconcile the diverse viewpoints of its members—reached agreement on a moderate bill that would enfranchise about a million women.[33]

The bill won a comfortable 109-vote majority when it came up for its first vote in July of 1910. Bowing to pressure from his cabinet ministers—a majority of whom favored the enfranchisement of women—Asquith agreed to provide the bill with time on the legislative calendar as the committee requested.[34]

The following November, Edward Grey announced that the government wouldn't be able to provide time on the calendar for the Conciliation Bill when Parliament reconvened.[35] This ended the truce. Eight days later, Emmeline Pankhurst led 300 suffragettes on a march to the Palace of Westminster. Police were brought in from London's East End who were used to handling working-class men and women with violence. On what came to be known as Black Friday, they assaulted the marchers, kicking and punching them and grabbing their breasts.

Although the police arrested 115 women, government officials dropped all the charges the next day.[36]

* * *

By the time the Conciliation Bill came up for another vote in May of 1911, the committee had revised it in response to concerns some opponents raised. The second bill fared even better than the first, the majority having grown to 166 votes. It had become a true all-party bill, securing majority support from members of all four parties.[37] Despite the resounding majority, the government declined to afford the bill any more government time in 1911 but agreed to provide it with all the time it needed during the next session.[38]

A month after the vote, 10,000 women marched in a seven-mile-long procession to Albert Hall in support of the second Conciliation Bill. Constance Lytton walked at the front of the parade with 616 other women, all of whom were dressed in white and carried silver staves. Each had served time in prison for the cause; Lytton and 86 others had been hunger strikers. Both of Lytton's sisters and a brother joined the march. Her other brother, Lord Victor Lytton, spoke at Albert Hall after the rally.[39]

It was beginning to look as though the hundreds of meetings and rallies, the Black Friday assaults, and the hunger strikes hadn't been in vain. "With sure and certain steps the cause of women's suffrage is marching to victory," read a story in the *Daily Chronicle*.[40] Two days after the march, London's evening newspaper, the *Star,* predicted: "Nothing can prevent the triumph of the cause which behind it has such reserves of courage and conviction."[41]

In years past, women's suffrage supporters assumed that the passage of a franchise bill by the Commons would only be the preliminary skirmish to a more forbidding battle in the House of Lords, the stronghold of anti-suffrage sentiment.[42] In August of 1911, though, the Lords lost a dominance struggle with the lower chamber and bowed to the king's threat that if they didn't approve passage of a bill removing their ability to veto legislation passed by the Commons, he would appoint enough Liberal peers to ensure its passage.[43] From then on, the Lords would only be able to delay any suffrage bill for two years, not veto it altogether, bringing success even closer for suffrage supporters.

In early November, Asquith announced that the government would introduce its own bill to enfranchise the four million men who weren't eligible to vote under the existing franchise laws. WSPU leaders saw this as a ploy to undermine the Conciliation Bill. They weren't alone. The *Evening Standard and Globe* said: "We are no friends of female suffrage, but anything more contemptible than the attitude assumed by the government . . . is difficult to imagine."[44] The *Evening News* predicted that the government's bill was so incompatible with the second Conciliation Bill that it would blow the Conciliation Bill to smithereens.[45] Asquith's chancellor of the exchequer, David Lloyd George, admitted that was the goal, bragging at a Liberal meeting later in November: "We have torpedoed the Conciliation Bill."[46]

Relations between the suffragettes and Asquith, already strained, deteriorated even further. Two weeks after Asquith's announcement, the WSPU began its "broken windows" campaign.[47] Equipped with bags of stones and hammers, suffragettes smashed windows in government buildings, offices of the Liberal Federation, and West End shops.[48] The next month, matters spiraled even further out of control when Emily Wilding Davison set three mailboxes afire by dropping burning linen into them.[49] The Post Office worked to turn public opinion against the suffragettes by delivering the charred fragments of mail to the addressees in special envelopes, which explained the reason for the damage.[50]

Shortly before the second Conciliation Bill came up for another vote in March of 1912, the WSPU organized two more window-smashing campaigns in London.[51] A friend wrote a cheerful letter to Lord Cromer, an anti-suffrage leader, saying he was sure supporters of the Conciliation Bill had lost ten votes for every pane of glass the suffragettes broke.[52] When the bill came up for a vote in the Commons, the 166-vote majority it had gotten ten months earlier turned into a majority of 14 votes against it, a reversal Martin Pugh attributed to the backlash against the WPSU's "broken windows" campaign.[53] Majority support for the enfranchisement of women, gained little by little through decades of patient work, had been quickly lost. Then the militancy became even more extreme: suffragettes began planting bombs, setting buildings afire, and slashing paintings in museums.

5. THE GREAT PILGRIMAGE TO THE VOTE

Lord Curzon wound up the debate on the afternoon of the 10th of January, and as he rose to speak there was a hush of excitement. One of the policemen at the door, friendly as the police always were to the women, went along the passage to the committee-room, where a number of them were gathered, and put his head round the door. "Lord Curzon is up, ladies," he announced, "but 'e won't do you no 'arm." And so it was. For the President of the Anti-Suffrage League was forced to strike his colours."—Ray Strachey[1]

The WSPU's increasingly violent militancy added another level of complexity to the work of Millicent Fawcett and her suffragist[2] comrades. The contest was no longer just between them and those who opposed allowing women to vote. Now they were also caught in a crossfire between the militants and their foes. Even though the suffragists refused to engage in violence, opponents often used the same brush to tar them and the suffragettes, as one did in a debate about the second Conciliation Bill:

It is not only of the financial support furnished to the militant movement by constitutional suffragists that I complain, but it is also the moral support that is forthcoming from them on every possible occasion. They co-operated with them in processions; they appeared with them on platforms. The very Committee which is responsible for this Bill is up to the neck in complicity with these militants. The chairman of the committee, Lord Lytton, appears constantly with them on public platforms and deplores the outrages.[3]

The WSPU's campaigns put the suffragists in a bind. If they refused to be militant, suffragettes accused them of lacking enthusiasm for the cause; if they joined in the militancy, opponents denounced them as disruptive law-breakers.[4] Fawcett's approach was straightforward: she supported the militants when they were victims of violence and denounced them when they engaged in it themselves.[5] She thought the arson, bombing, and destruction of art were barbaric and set back the women's cause. As she explained in a letter to a friend:

> I can never feel that setting fire to houses and churches and letter boxes and destroying valuable pictures really helps to convince people that women ought to be enfranchised. That half-savage men did worse things half a century ago does not make it any better in my eyes. [. . .] I do so intensely believe in the sort of work that helps to evolve a finer kind of civilization, and so intensely disbelieve in the work that helps to push us back into barbarism and the reign of brute force.[6]

Although Fawcett was appalled by the suffragettes' violence, in the end, she accepted it as part and parcel of a social reformer's work. She tried to comfort other suffragists by reminding them of what a biographer had said of William Gladstone's continued support for Irish Home Rule after Irish nationalists had committed arson and assassinations: "No reformer is fit for his task who suffers himself to be frightened off by the excesses of an extreme wing."[7] Her belief that the crimes committed by Home Rulers had doomed the efforts of Home Rule advocates—including those of her nemesis, William Gladstone—was probably less comforting to her, as was the prospect that the suffragettes' destructive campaigns would end up dooming women's suffrage in the same way.[8]

* * *

When the House of Commons killed the second Conciliation Bill in March of 1912, Prime Minister Asquith continued to believe, as he had argued in the House of Commons some twenty years earlier, that most women had little interest in voting, that they were "watching with languid and imperturbable indifference the struggle for their own emancipation."[9]

The following spring, the chairwoman of a regional suffrage society suggested at a National Union committee meeting that they could show the breadth of support for their cause throughout the country by organizing a massive demonstration in London, like the celebrated Women's Sunday rally in Hyde Park five years earlier. This time, though, those going to the rally wouldn't just meet in London; they would walk there in a great pilgrimage, some from the farthest reaches of England more than three hundred miles away![10]

It was a bold idea. Of course, tens of thousands of well-mannered women might get to London without incident, generating much goodwill and recapturing the public support the suffragettes had squandered by their destructive sprees.[11] Many less favorable outcomes were possible too. Some of the pilgrims might fall victim to miscreants they encountered on their journey, and hooligans might disrupt the meetings and rallies they planned to hold along the way, having harassed suffragettes for years. It was also possible that the pilgrimage would end up proving what their opponents always claimed: that there was no wellspring of support for women's suffrage in the country. People living in the cities they passed through might ignore the pilgrims or, even worse, greet them with hostility, not realizing that while they were working to get women the vote, they were doing it nonviolently. And it might turn out that few of their supporters would have a commitment deep and strong enough to leave families and jobs and embark on an odyssey with such uncertain prospects.

Undeterred by the risks, the National Union decided to go ahead with a pilgrimage and invited each of its nineteen regional federations to send a delegation. Each federation was notified, however, that it would have to make arrangements for everything its pilgrims would need along the way.

Every federation quickly signed on. Organizers set the Hyde Park rally for July 26 and emphasized that the pilgrims should set themselves apart from militant suffragettes—who were continuing to plant bombs and set buildings afire—by making clear they were law-abiding. To drive the point

Fig. 12. Pilgrims from Carlisle Leaving Thame in July 1913

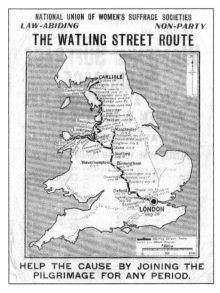

Map 4. Poster Showing Route Traveled by Pilgrims from Carlisle

home, two marshals were to march at the front of every procession with banners proclaiming that the marchers weren't militant. A group traveling along the Watling Street route from Carlisle even included three babies in baby carriages who had the words NON-MILITANT stitched into their hats.[12]

Millicent Fawcett joined the pilgrims at several places along the many routes they took to London. She especially enjoyed walking through Cambridge with friends she and Henry had made while living there and marchers from Newnham College, which she had helped found more than forty years earlier.[13]

Her visit to travelers along the Great North Road in Nottinghamshire was much less pleasant. Hooligans threw dead rats at the suffragists and spewed obscenities at them. While she was appalled at the nastiness with which some had greeted them, Fawcett was proud that her colleagues had shown their mettle by responding nonviolently.[14]

Another group of pilgrims had their mettle even more severely tested in Thame, a town near Oxford. Two days before they arrived, a local anti-suffrage group warned a crowd that the marchers were a danger to life and limb.[15] When opponents disrupted one of the pilgrims' meetings, police broke it up but were unable to stop ruffians from heading to a wooden caravan the pilgrims had taken with them on their journey from Carlisle. As one of the women recounted in *Diary of the Great Pilgrimage*, other police summoned by a local doctor arrived in the nick of time to prevent the mob from setting the caravan afire with three women inside. When the women emerged from their sanctuary, they found the police sifting through rubble. The ruffians had slashed a tent in which two of them slept and strewn its contents around. The corn they carried for Noah, a horse who pulled "the Ark" (the name they had given the caravan), was also scattered on the ground. Before heading to London the next day, the women held another meeting in the middle of town and explained what they were doing and why.[16]

The pilgrims traveled to London from cities, towns, and villages throughout England and Wales—from Newcastle on the North Sea and Land's End on the Celtic Sea to Dover on the Channel and Liverpool on the Irish Sea, and hundreds of places in between. Members of suffrage societies far from a major route walked on secondary ones until they joined their comrades. Small streams of travelers became great rivers by the time they arrived in London, tributaries of pilgrims having joined together along the way (see Figure 12 on p. 134).

Three days after leaving Thame, the suffragists traveling from Carlisle made it to London, thirty-seven days and more than three hundred miles after having left home (see map on p. 134). Noah appeared star-struck by the city, calmly taking in all its sights and sounds. Despite their tight schedule, Noah took his time, ignoring a groom who tried to speed him up by waving a white handkerchief in front of him.[17]

The rally in Hyde Park began at five o'clock on the dot. Seventy-eight speakers addressed a multitude—fifty thousand strong[18]—from nineteen platforms, one for each regional federation. They spoke of their desire to improve the lives of people they had met on their journey, the need for a "mother spirit" to enrich communities, and the redemptive prospect of enfranchisement. Sensibly, organizers allotted only an hour for speeches. At six o'clock, bugles sounded and each federation passed a resolution: "That this meeting demands a government measure for the enfranchisement of women."[19]

The next day, hundreds of pilgrims wearing the red, white, and green sashes of the National Union assembled in Trafalgar Square and walked together in procession to St. Paul's Cathedral. They sat in seats reserved for them under the cathedral's magnificent dome. Many thought it highly appropriate that the first psalm for the evening service told of believers who had sown their crops in tears and, after many trials, reaped in joy.[20]

Some government ministers were favorably impressed by the pilgrimage.[21] David Lloyd George called it "one of the best political moves in recent times," and Home Secretary Reginald McKenna, an anti-suffragist, said he admired the pilgrims' courage and thought they had helped their cause.[22] Prime Minister Asquith agreed to meet with a committee from the National Union, but his opinions about women and their qualifications to be voters hadn't changed much. When a member of the committee suggested that the government's new reform bill include a provision enfranchising women and the bill be retitled the Representation of the People Act, he asked why the title of the legislation should be changed. A suffrage supporter answered, "Well, women are people, aren't they?" "I suppose so," he replied, apparently unconvinced.[23]

Still, the suffragists seemed to be making progress. Then war overtook them and their countrymen.

* * *

On August 4, 1914, while many suffragists were meeting in Kingsway Hall to plan a peace rally, the government announced that Britain was joining the war breaking out in Europe. This added still another level of complexity to the suffragists' work. In a letter posted the day after the Kingsway Hall meeting, Lord Robert Cecil, a leader of the pro-suffragist Conservatives in Parliament, complained to Fawcett that under the circumstances, planning a peace rally was so unreasonable that it had shaken his belief in the fitness of women "to deal with the great Imperial questions."[24]

The war split suffragists into three camps. Some wanted the National Union to lead an anti-war campaign; others thought it should conduct a public education campaign about ways to prevent conflict between nations; and a third group wanted it to support Britain's participation in the war.[25]

Fawcett tried to bridge the split by urging her colleagues to focus on war relief work. Now that all hope of peace had vanished, she said, they should come to the aid of their countrymen, especially women and children threatened with destitution.[26] In a column published in the National Union's newspaper three days after the government's declaration of war, she wrote: "Now is the time for resolute effort and self-sacrifice on the part of every one of us to help our country. . . . Let us show ourselves worthy of citizenship, whether our claim to it be recognized or not."[27]

Whatever their position on the war, almost all the suffrage societies set up relief programs. Forty-five local suffrage societies became Red Cross centers; others opened maternity centers and baby clinics.[28]

Several suffrage societies trained women for wartime production work. The London Society opened a workshop to teach women acetylene welding. Workers there were delighted when the queen made a surprise visit in the summer of 1916 and took a cup of tea with them while seated on an overturned packing case.[29]

Suffragists with medical training also offered their services to the country, only to be rebuffed at first. When Dr. Elsie Inglis, a founder of the Scottish Federation of Women's Suffrage Societies, asked the head of the Royal Army Medical Corps in Scotland what she and other female doctors could do to help Britain, he replied, "Dear lady, go home and keep quiet."[30]

When Inglis approached Fawcett about the idea, though, the latter was enthusiastic, and they immediately began putting together Scottish Women's Hospitals units. The physicians and nurses, orderlies, drivers, and domestic staff who worked in the units were all women, mostly members of suffrage societies. The hospitals cared for soldiers at the front in Corsica, Salonika, France, and Serbia.[31] By the end of the war, they were providing care in more than 1,800 beds.[32]

Militants with medical training pitched in too. Dr. Louisa Garrett Anderson, Elizabeth Garrett Anderson's daughter, raised and headed a well-equipped hospital unit in France also staffed by women. After the war, the surgeon general of the Royal Army Medical Corps said the women were "worth their weight, not in gold, but in diamonds."[33]

While the war raged, the British press carried stories about the courage women were showing in their wartime work. After an explosion at a shell factory in northern England killed twenty-six women and injured many more, newspapers told how the women helped care for the wounded and then carried on with their work at the factory.[34] Another time, when a troopship was torpedoed, the cry went out to "save the women first!" The nurses on board stood back from the lifeboats, though, and insisted, "Fighting men first; they are the country's greatest need."[35]

All of this had an impact on the anti-suffragists in Parliament, even Prime Minister Asquith. In the fall of 1915, he spoke to his colleagues in the House of Commons about "the imperishable story" of Edith Cavell, a British nurse in Belgium who had been executed by the Germans for sheltering British soldiers trapped behind enemy lines: "She has taught the bravest man amongst us a supreme lesson of courage. Yes, Sir, and in this United Kingdom and throughout the Dominion of the Crown there are thousands of such women, but a year ago we did not know it."[36]

The following summer, Asquith mentioned the women's contributions again when introducing a government bill to update the national registry of eligible voters, saying that in light of what the women had given to the country, they deserved to be heard in discussions about postwar Britain.[37]

The same month, Walter Long, a longtime anti-suffragist, suggested that Parliament submit issues about updating the electoral registry and qualifications for voting to a non-party conference made up of members of both houses, presided over by the speaker of the House of Commons, James Lowther.[38]

* * *

Two months later, the House of Commons voted to set up the electoral reform committee Long had suggested. It included members of all parties: thirteen Conservatives/Unionists, twelve Liberals, four Nationalists, and three Labour members.[39] Lowther agreed to chair the conference without enthusiasm, telling Prime Minister Asquith he believed it was a fool's errand and that it would be almost impossible to achieve anything approaching unanimity on the most critical issues.[40]

Enfranchisement of women was among those issues. Conference members, like Parliament itself, were split between members who opposed any form of women's suffrage and others who favored one form or another—ranging from full adult suffrage to enfranchisement for only single, propertied women, and other points in between. Even if a majority of the conference ended up endorsing one arrangement, it was uncertain whether the government would agree to include it in a franchise reform bill. And this was the same Parliament that had killed every women's suffrage bill that had come before it, including the modest second Conciliation Bill.

Fawcett shared Lowther's pessimism, but for a different reason. As she saw it, one anti-suffragist (Long) had suggested that the conference be set up, another (Asquith) supported the idea, and a third (Lowther) presided over said conference.[41]

At their first meeting, Lowther advised conference members to start with minor issues and work their way toward bigger ones. They ignored his suggestion and immediately came to a complete deadlock.[42] After the meeting, one member, Sir Edward Grey,[43] advised a colleague that there was "not the slightest chance of [their] being able to make a unanimous recommendation on any subject."[44]

Conference members then put off any discussion of women's suffrage but had heated disagreements about other franchise-related issues. Three Conservative members resigned after being outvoted in divisions. They called for the conference to be dissolved, arguing that because Lloyd George had replaced Asquith as prime minister after the conference had begun its work, the government in whose name the conference had been appointed no longer existed.[45] Lloyd George resolved the issue by advising Lowther that he was anxious to receive a report from the conference.[46]

Lowther didn't replace one of the members who resigned but replaced the other two—diehard anti-suffragists—with two staunch friends of the women's cause.[47] Fawcett, who was closely monitoring the conference's work, thought this was "a blessed change."[48]

As members of the conference kept working, Lowther continued to put off any discussion about women's suffrage. He hoped that if committee members reached agreement on other issues, they might be more inclined to reach agreement on women's suffrage too.[49]

In January of 1917, the conference was nearing the end of its work, and the issue couldn't be put off any longer. In the first vote, members voted 15–6 to recommend some form of women's enfranchisement but then rejected a proposal for suffrage on the same terms as men by a vote of 12–10.[50] Finally, one of Fawcett's close associates,[51] Willoughby Dickinson, had his chance. As he recalled later:

> I was then allowed to put forward my proposition, which was that
> the vote should be accorded to all women who were either "occupiers"

themselves or wives of occupiers. The division showed nine "for" and eight "against." Thus, by one vote we secured for women's suffrage a place in the report that Mr. Speaker brought up to Parliament.[52]

In his report to Parliament, the speaker said that the conference had decided some form of women's suffrage should be conferred. If Parliament agreed, he said the most practical arrangement would be the one proposed by Dickinson: to enfranchise women of a specified age who were currently able to vote in a local election (i.e., single women and widows who met the same qualifications for men) and the wives of men able to vote in the election. He went on to say that conference members had discussed various ages at which women might be eligible to vote and that thirty and thirty-five years of age had received the most support.[53]

* * *

Once Lowther issued his report, Fawcett's first task was to get all factions of suffragists to support it.[54] That a higher age limit was applied for women than for men rankled her. She thought it was indefensible logically but was reminded of Disraeli's remark that "England [was] not governed by logic, but by Parliament."[55] She understood the reason behind the higher age limit though. At the time, women outnumbered men in the country and it was doubtful whether the House of Commons would agree to go from women having no vote at all to becoming the majority of voters in one fell swoop.[56]

Women who worked in shops and factories were the most concerned about the higher age limit for women voters. They believed they, more than anyone else, needed the protection of enfranchisement, which many of them wouldn't gain because they hadn't reached the minimum age. Over the years, though, most working women had learned to trust Fawcett and took her at her word when she assured them that the National Union would treat the proposed arrangement as only the first installment in a larger campaign. As a result, she was able to tell Prime Minister Lloyd George that if the government brought forward a bill that included the recommendations of the Speaker's Conference on women's suffrage, all suffragists would support it as long as it had a thirty-year-old threshold, not thirty-five.[57]

Fawcett's next task was convincing the prime minister to include the recommendations of the conference report in the government's franchise reform bill. In late March, she headed a delegation of female war workers to see him, including ambulance drivers, nurses, munitions workers, oxy-acetylene welders, textile workers, Scottish Women's Hospitals workers, and representatives of more than forty other trades and professions.[58] Members of the group made clear their support depended on women's enfranchisement's being included in the government's bill from the outset.[59] The prime minister overcame any hard feelings he might have had from having been heckled by suffragettes for years and having had some plant bombs in a home that was being built for him. He assured members of the delegation that he had instructed the government draftsman to include the conference's recommendations about women's suffrage in the bill but that, while the government would push for the bill's passage, it would leave members of both houses free to vote on the women's suffrage provisions as they pleased.[60]

Although she was approaching her seventieth birthday, Fawcett took it upon herself to call upon every government minister, many being already stretched thin with war-related responsibilities. She saw some ministers very early in the morning, others late at night—visiting them in Parliament, in a government office, or at their own homes, seeing each one whenever and wherever it was convenient for him.[61]

The first critical vote on the women's suffrage provisions in the Representation of the People Act came on June 19, 1917. While resounding majorities supported other recommendations of the Speaker's Conference in earlier votes, the women's suffrage provisions were very similar to a bill the same members had rejected four years earlier when it had been brought forward by Willoughby Dickinson.

During the debate, one opponent said that women were hysterical and sentimental, "likely to be affected by gusts and waves of sentiment."[62]

Another argued that they were unfit to be enfranchised because they were illogical and hardheaded, that "when a woman [had] made up her mind, you [could not] move her, and arguments [were] of no avail."[63] And, as Asquith had argued for decades before he began supporting women's suffrage, some opponents claimed that most women didn't want the vote at all.[64]

After more than six hours of debate, the House voted 385–55 to support enfranchising women with the thirty-year-old age threshold. When Fawcett saw the vote from the Ladies' Gallery, some fifty years after having seen from there the vote on John Stuart Mill's motion, she was encouraged but realized at once that it had only set up a battle with far more formidable opponents in the House of Lords.[65]

* * *

The head of the anti-suffragists in the Lords was its leader, Lord Curzon, the president of the National League for Opposing Woman Suffrage.[66] When the debate began in January of 1918, no one knew how it would come out.[67] One suffrage supporter, Lord Haldane, thought the outcome would depend on the votes of "fifty dark horses."[68]

Lord Loreburn opened the debate for the opponents, arguing that the higher age limit for women was a slippery slope. He said that in a short time, it would be repealed, making women a majority of the electorate and giving them the power over imperial policy, questions of peace and war, and in the end, the destiny of the nation itself.[69] He wondered whether women had it in them to exercise dominion over the hundreds of millions of people living in India and the other Crown colonies. Ceding such power to women who had no experience in wielding it, he said, would be "a very dangerous leap in the dark."[70]

After several hours of debate, with soaring oratory on both sides, mixed with insincere flattery and polite insults for those with opposing views, Lord Curzon closed the debate. He, too, argued that if the current bill passed, women would inevitably gain the vote on equal terms with men and become the majority of voters. While some opponents of women's suffrage worried that women wouldn't be strong enough to help make imperial decisions, he feared the contrary. He thought women would be too strong and try to dominate men, to control their work and wages, subject them to conscription and send them to war, and even tell them how much they could drink. And he worried whether men would respond with chivalry as in days past, or would defend their interests with physical force.[71]

In extended remarks, Curzon argued that giving the vote to women would be ruinous to the country and destroy the stability and order that Englishmen had enjoyed for centuries. Then he paused. Just when it seemed he was about to make a final impassioned plea to remove the women's suffrage clauses from the bill and send it back to the Commons, he made a stunning about-face, asking, "[A]re you prepared to embark on a conflict with a majority of 350 in the House of Commons, of whom nearly 150 belong to the Party to which most of your Lordships belong?"[72] He said he wasn't prepared to do that himself and would abstain when the vote was called.[73]

As Fawcett recalled, the effect of Lord Curzon's announcement was dramatic. The anti-suffragists were white with rage, the suffragists flushed with thoughts of victory. When she asked a supportive lord standing nearby how large their majority would be, he replied, "Quite thirty."[74] Their margin of victory was more than twice as large, with 134 voting in favor and 71 against.

Constance Lytton's brother, Victor Lytton, was among those who voted in favor.

Less than a month later, King George V gave his royal assent, and the Representation of the People Act became the law of the land, granting the government vote to more than eight million women.[75] For Fawcett, it was the greatest moment in her life. As she put it: "We had won fairly and squarely after a fight lasting just fifty years. Henceforth, women would be free citizens."[76]

EPILOGUE

> Our fifty years' struggle for the women's vote was not actuated
> by our setting any extraordinary value on the mere power
> of making a mark on a voting paper once in every three or
> four years. We did not, except as a symbol of free citizenship,
> value it as a thing good in itself; we valued it [. . .] for the sake
> of the equal laws, the enlarged opportunities, the improved
> status for women which we knew it involved.
> —Millicent Garrett Fawcett[1]

Once the Representation of the People Act became law, the National
Union made the pivot many of its leaders had always planned,
broadening its mission beyond the vote to securing full equality for
women in all walks of life. For a while, its members kept the organization's
original name; Fawcett thought it was like the affection veteran soldiers
feel for their regimental flag.[2] In 1919, though, they changed its name
to the National Union of Societies for Equal Citizenship to more closely
reflect the sweeping changes they sought, including equal pay for women,
the reform of divorce laws, and the opening of the professions to women.[3]

Soon after women got the vote, they achieved some of their other
goals. In 1919, Parliament passed the Sex Disqualification (Removal)
Act, opening the professions to women and enabling them to serve as
magistrates and jurors. And in 1923, the Matrimonial Causes Act replaced
the longstanding double standard in grounds for divorce, making these
the same for both men and women. Other goals, like gender equality in
pay, have proven much more difficult to attain.

Fawcett's elder sister and fellow campaigner for gender equality,
Elizabeth Garrett Anderson, passed away in 1917 without ever being able

to cast a vote in a government election. During her career, though, in addition to being the first English woman to qualify as a doctor and being one of the first women elected to a school board, she was the founder of the first English hospital staffed by women, the first woman dean of a medical school, and in 1908, England's first woman mayor.[4]

Elizabeth's friend since childhood, Emily Davies, did get to vote in a national election, walking to a polling place on December 14, 1918, at the age of eighty-eight—a petite figure dressed in black, her blue eyes sparkling.[5] She passed away three years later.

By the time women got the vote, Lady Constance Lytton was in very poor health, having suffered a stroke in 1912 that left her partially paralyzed. She followed the Votes for Women campaign closely, though, marking in her notebook: "February 6th, 1918; 4 years later from publication of my Book Ap. [April] 1914 By the Representation of the People Act about 6,000,000 women 30 years of age and over obtained the Parliamentary Vote."[6] Many people had read her book, *Prisons and Prisoners*, and she enjoyed the letters they sent her about it. Had she seen it, though, her greatest pleasure would likely have come from her mother's review, written in the copy Constance had given her: "A human document . . . beautifully written . . . in spite of the acute pain of the whole thing."[7] After her paralysis, Constance returned home to live with her mother at Homewood, the house Victor Lytton had built for their mother on the family estate. Emmeline Pethick-Lawrence, her first and best suffragette friend, remained a loyal and regular visitor until Constance's death in 1923.[8]

As Fawcett and many anti-suffragists predicted, the higher age limit for women voters was relatively short-lived. In 1928, a government bill to equalize the franchise qualifications for men and women passed its second reading by a vote of 387–10 in the Commons, and then by a substantial majority in the Lords. When the Equal Franchise Act became law, Millicent Fawcett, then eighty-one years old, led a group to lay wreaths in John Stuart Mill's memory at a statue of him on the Embankment in London.[9] In 2018, on the centenary of British women's getting the vote, a statue of Fawcett joined those of David Lloyd George, Winston Churchill, Benjamin Disraeli, and eight other men in Parliament Square.

Disasters the anti-suffragists warned about didn't come to pass. In the years since women gained the vote, they have continued to show their mettle, as Fawcett would likely have put it. And Victorian ideas about the inferiority of women have been discredited as thoroughly as those about imperialism and racial supremacy.

IV

Robbery with Violence

Core Elements of Supremacist Belief Systems

They were conquerors, and for that you want only brute force—
nothing to boast of, when you have it, since your strength is
just an accident arising from the weakness of others. They
grabbed what they could get for the sake of what was to be
got. It was just robbery with violence, aggravated murder on
a great scale, and men going at it blind—as is very proper
for those who tackle a darkness. The conquest of the earth,
which mostly means the taking it away from those who have a
different complexion or slightly flatter noses than ourselves, is
not a pretty thing when you look into it too much.—**Charles
Marlow** in Joseph Conrad's *Heart of Darkness*[1]

In the remarks made to SS leaders mentioned in the Introduction,
Heinrich Himmler was unusually frank when he discussed the Nazis'
genocidal plans. Although senior Nazi officials continued to state publicly
that their policy was to evacuate Jews, Himmler said their real goal was
extermination. He went on to caution his audience that although what
they were doing was "a page of glory" in their history, they must keep it a
secret among themselves.[2]

This honesty was a rare departure from the standard Nazi practice
of hiding the murders they were committing with code words. One

Holocaust scholar, Raul Hilberg, recalled examining tens of thousands of Nazi documents without once encountering the German word for "kill" (*töten*) until, after many years, he finally came across the word in an edict concerning dogs.[3] As mentioned earlier, *Sonderbehandlung* was one of many euphemisms the Nazis used for killing—they gave their victims "special handling." Hilberg once listed more than a dozen other terms used instead of "kill" or "murder."[4]

When senior Nazi officials spoke among themselves, though, the camouflage was no longer necessary. At the Wannsee Conference, for instance, they debated various ways to murder all of the eleven million Jewish people who lived in Europe—whether to shoot their victims, work them to death, or kill them with carbon monoxide from an internal combustion engine.[5] In Adolf Eichmann's minutes, though, this became a discussion about "various possible kinds of solution,"[6] and the extermination plan itself was referred to as "the Final Solution of the European Jewish question."[7]

Like the Nazis, Hungarian fascists used code words to describe the implementation of the Final Solution in their country. Jewish people who had been rounded up and forced to go to Auschwitz were referred to as "resettled," the homes they had been made to leave were called "abandoned apartments," and the contents of their homes and businesses were described as "property left behind."[8]

In addition to linguistic camouflage, Nazis used secrecy to hide what they were doing. Every SS officer who worked in a concentration camp was sworn to silence.[9] Himmler selected Auschwitz as the site for the Birkenau extermination camp partly because the Germans could hide it among the many labor camps in the area.[10] And Himmler's mobile killing squads tried to commit massacres out of public view, unless they were intended to frighten the local population.[11]

The secrecy and euphemisms the Nazis used to conceal their murders from others also shielded them from what Raul Hilberg called "the censuring gaze" of their own conscience.[12] Christian moral codes, of course, include a commandment against homicide, so engaging in murder created an internal conflict the Nazis had to resolve in some way.[13] To do that, they came up with several rationalizations and justifications. A common one was that Jewish people weren't fully human—they were subhuman (*Untermenschen*)—so the moral rules that usually protected humankind didn't apply to them.[14] In the remarks to senior SS officers mentioned above, Himmler referred to non-Germanic people as "human animals."[15]

Because Jews were thought to be less than human, the Nazis believed it was all right to treat Jewish people—and other targets of their venom, including Roma and Slavs—like animals. And they did. They shipped Jews to Auschwitz in cattle wagons and killed most with Zyklon-B, a pesticide. In the 1940 Nazi propaganda film *The Eternal Jew*, the filmmaker juxtaposed images of rats with those of Jewish people. A narrator explained the connection: just as rats were the vermin of the animal kingdom—spreading diseases like cholera, typhoid fever, and dysentery—Jews were the vermin of the human race. Considering the peril, it wasn't just permissible for Germans to eradicate European Jewry, it was a matter of self-protection, like exterminating rats.[16]

That wasn't the only excuse Nazis came up with for committing mass murder. Flipping truth on its head, they projected their aggressive impulses and greed upon their victims, claiming that "international Jewry" was plotting to rule the world and destroy Germany and German life. *The Eternal Jew* concluded with footage of Hitler saying, in a 1939 speech to the German Reichstag: "If international-finance Jewry inside and outside of Europe should succeed once more in plunging nations into another world war, the consequences will not be the Bolshevization of the earth and thereby the victory of Jewry, but the annihilation of the Jewish race in Europe."[17]

Individual murderers and thieves often came up with their own rationalizations to avoid feeling guilty for their misdeeds. A common one, used even by senior Nazi officials, displaced responsibility onto others. They told themselves they were only acting under orders. Adolf Eichmann was the most notorious example. At his trial in Jerusalem, Eichmann said of the 1942 conference, in which senior Nazis discussed the plan to exterminate European Jewry: "I felt something of the satisfaction of Pilate, because I felt entirely innocent of any guilt. The leading figures of the Reich at the time had spoken at the Wannsee Conference, the 'Popes' had given their orders; it was up to me to obey, and that is what I bore in mind over the future years."[18]

They also soothed their consciences by telling themselves that they hadn't acted out of hatred or vindictiveness, or that what they had done was entirely legal under their laws, or that they couldn't have stopped the slaughter even if they had tried.[19]

* * *

Supremacists in Leopold's Congo Free State and Victorian England followed the same pattern. Whether supremacist ideologies are based on ethnicity, race, or gender, they have the same core elements:

1. Supremacists want something that belongs to members of a group they dominate.

Jewish people had two things the Nazis wanted: their property and their labor. At Auschwitz alone, Nazis looted an estimated 142,996,769 Reichsmarks (about $800 million in today's value) from the belongings prisoners had taken with them to the camp[20] and another 60 million Reichsmarks (about $340 million today) from selling their labor to private companies.[21]

Living in a pre-industrial society, people in the Congo Basin didn't own personal property of great value to a European monarch. They did, however, have two things Leopold craved: land and labor. The Nazis' forced labor camps in Europe, massive as they were, didn't hold a candle to the mammoth slave colony Leopold set up in the Free State. As mentioned earlier, according to Félicien Cattier's calculations, by 1906, Leopold had extracted more than 70 million francs ($350 million in today's value) from his private estate in the Congo.[22]

Men didn't enslave women in nineteenth-century England but dominated and exploited them. As mentioned earlier, a woman usually earned half as much as a man for doing the same work.[23] As a result, working-class women were fortunate if they earned enough to pay for the bare necessities.[24] After someone in the crowd shouted to Constance Lytton and the other suffragettes in a deputation headed toward Parliament, "Go home and do your washing!" Lytton thought of the washerwomen who, perhaps distraught with worry about how to get by from day to day, had washed the white collars and shirt fronts of members of Parliament. She told herself that she would speak on their behalf if she managed to find a way past the phalanx of police blocking her way to the Houses of Parliament, and thus became a spokesperson for the deputation.[25]

2.   Supremacists use violence and coercion to dominate members of a weaker group and take what they want.

Socially dominant groups commonly use systematic violence and coercion to oppress and exploit members of subordinate groups.[26] Leopold's Force Publique soldiers used extreme violence to dominate and coerce Congolese natives. A commission he appointed to investigate reports of government-sponsored atrocities found that when people living in a village failed to come up with the rubber or provisions the government required, soldiers often went on a murderous rampage, massacring villagers and setting huts afire.[27] They also took women as hostages, whom they held in conditions so deficient that many died.[28] As E. D. Morel said, Leopold's philanthropy in the Congo was actually "legalized robbery enforced by violence."[29]

The coercion nineteenth-century English men used to dominate women was usually less lethal.[30] Economic and social pressures induced most women to marry[31] and, once married, to continue living with a husband even if he was abusive. A woman could only obtain a divorce if she proved her husband had engaged in cruelty, incest, or bestiality and had been adulterous as well. And if she left her husband without getting a divorce, a woman forfeited all claims to the custody of her children.[32]

What happened to Caroline Norton, a prominent poet and novelist, showed the coercive power of Victorian child custody laws. After Norton left a husband who had repeatedly beaten her, he was given sole custody of their sons and rarely allowed her to see them. Once, he failed to tell her that her youngest son had fallen ill until the boy was on his deathbed. She rushed to see her son and anxiously asked a woman whom she met in the town where he lived whether he had gotten any better, only to have the woman tell her: "No, he is not better, he is dead."[33]

Sometimes, the coercion men used was more obvious. In late-nineteenth-century London, wife beating was described as "normal" when used as a disciplinary measure, and some industrial parts of England and Scotland were known as "kicking districts" due to the great frequency with which husbands assaulted their wives.[34] In an 1853 debate in the House of Lords about a bill to increase the penalties for wife battering, Earl Granville lamented the continuing effect of an old English proverb—"a woman, a dog, and a walnut tree, the more they are beaten, the better they'll be."[35]

3. Supremacists usually try to hide the harm they inflict.

E. D. Morel began to suspect that Leopold's activities in the Free State weren't as benign as he was making them out to be when a Free State official berated Morel's employer for disclosing that a shipment of goods to the Congo consisted largely of war materiel—information that he insisted must be kept secret.[36] Leopold refused to give the Belgian Parliament access to the Free State's financial records when it was considering annexation,[37] and had the records burned after it annexed the Free State from him.[38]

Some of those who opposed women's suffrage worried that enfranchisement would remove the veil of privacy that surrounded British households and intrude into the sacred precinct of family life, as William Ewart Gladstone once wrote in a letter to a colleague explaining his opposition to a women's suffrage bill.[39]

4. **Supremacists disguise their wrongdoing with euphemisms and code words.**

Leopold's officers in the Congo hid their domination and exploitation of the Congolese with doublespeak and euphemisms. A native kidnapped from his village to serve as a soldier or a porter was called "a volunteer" or "a liberated man."[40] The officers also misappropriated language from a legitimate practice to lend an aura of respectability to their illegitimate one.[41] When they chained Congolese men together and forced the men to carry goods and materiel without pay, it was a "porterage tax"; when they coerced women in villages into providing food for their soldiers, it was a "foodstuffs tax"; when they made men go into the jungle and harvest rubber for them, it was a "rubber tax."[42] The Congolese received almost no services from the government for payment of these "taxes." It was, as Professor Cattier concluded, not a state at all, just a predatory business.[43]

Victorian English men also used verbal camouflage to hide (and justify) the force they used to coerce women. They called wife battering "domestic chastisement"[44] and spousal rape "the exercise of conjugal rights."[45]

5. **Supremacists justify their exploitation by claiming that members of a group they exploit are inferior, so ordinary social rules don't apply.**

The three European jurists Leopold appointed to investigate reports that government soldiers had committed atrocities in the Congo decided it would be unfair to judge the soldiers by European standards of civilized behavior because the natives were so uncivilized.[46] They didn't doubt that coercion was necessary to civilize a people "still in large measure savages."[47]

Among the reasons anti-suffragists gave for opposing women's suffrage was that women were intellectually inferior to men.[48] They usually expressed this in a more gentlemanly way, though, saying that women were guided too much by emotion and too little by reason,[49] or as Tennyson put it: "Man with the head, and woman with the heart."[50]

In a 1913 letter to the *Times*, the playwright George Bernard Shaw mocked one claim Prime Minister Asquith had made regarding his opposition to enfranchising women:

> In the debate on the Dickinson Bill Mr. Asquith for the first time opposed the franchise for women on the ground that woman is not the female of the human species, but a distinct and inferior species, naturally disqualified from voting as a rabbit is disqualified from voting—A man may object to the proposed extension of the suffrage for many reasons. [. . .] [I]t is one thing to follow a Prime Minister who advances all, or some, or any of these reasons for standing in the way of votes for women. It is quite another to follow a Prime Minister who places one's mother on the footing of a rabbit.[51]

6. **In extreme cases, supremacists claim people from another group aren't fully human and treat them like animals.**

One way supremacists legitimize the violence used to exploit people from other groups is to divest them of human qualities or attribute to them characteristics usually associated with animals.[52] Because of the belief that humans are superior to all other animals, supremacists consider the others to be less than human.[53] So, their thinking goes, they can treat these others inhumanely, even slaughter them.[54]

Well into the twentieth century, the most common slur Europeans in the Congo used when referring to Congolese people was "macaques." In 1960, after a Belgian king made remarks in Leopoldville that heaped praise on what Leopold had done in the Congo, Prime Minister Lumumba was furious. He responded by accusing the Belgians of having presided over "a regime of injustice, suppression, and exploitation," adding with a snarl, "We are no longer your 'monkeys.'"[55]

Reformers in Victorian England worked to pass laws to limit the severity of "correction" a husband could mete out to his wife. In 1853, one of them urged his colleagues to extend to women the same protection they had given "to poodle dogs and donkeys" when they had passed the Cruelty to Animals Act four years earlier.[56] And, as mentioned earlier, when Constance Lytton saw townspeople jeer and laugh at a sheep, it occurred to her that men in Victorian and Edwardian England treated women much the same way.[57]

7. Supremacists devise stereotypes and rationalizations to justify the privileges they receive.

While the justifications vary from culture to culture depending on the groups involved, they all support a dominant group's claim that inequality is fair, legitimate, natural, or moral.[58] In some cases, supremacists claim their dominance is just a law of nature, as an MP did in an 1873 debate on a women's suffrage bill, arguing: "Man in the beginning was ordained to rule over the woman, and this is an Eternal decree which we have no right and no power to alter."[59]

Supremacists often generate several different stereotypes about members of a subordinate group. Leopold's commissioners believed that the Congolese had no sense of morality,[60] were bloodthirsty,[61] and needed to learn the value of work,[62] all of which legitimized their domination by Europeans. In some cases, the stereotypes contradict each other. At times, British anti-suffragists claimed that women were so obstinate that giving them the vote would lead to endless family discord, and at other times said they were so easily influenced that letting them vote would effectively give a second vote to their favorite male relative or clergyman.[63] Either way, they were unfit to vote.

Sometimes, members of a dominant group say that although they place limits on members of a less powerful group, they only do that to protect this weaker group. A leading expert on the common law of England, Justice William Blackstone, said the constraints placed upon Victorian women were intended only for their protection—advantages granted to them because they were such great favorites under the laws of England.[64]

* * *

These, then, are the red flags that supremacists are at work. It begins benignly enough, with people's pride in their own group, their heritage, and even their strongly held political beliefs.

Pride becomes pathological, though, when members of a group begin to believe they are superior to other groups and should be able to rule over everyone else. Claims of group superiority and the use of violence against those from less powerful groups are markers of exploitation. Other markers are supremacists' use of secrecy and doubletalk to hide what they are doing, as well as rationalizations to legitimize what would otherwise be seen (and condemned) as wrong. At times, the euphemisms they use to camouflage their villainy serve as justifications too. They often claim their group is exceptional. Of course, exceptionalists rarely believe that their group is exceptionally bad or inferior. They arrive at the same pathological place as other supremacists, convinced that commonly accepted moral rules don't apply to them because they are superior.

Turning attention now to exceptionalists who believe that "human beings stand at the pinnacle of the moral hierarchy,"[65] let's return to the question asked in the Introduction: Do the reasons these exceptionalists give for believing that humans deserve unique moral status have merit? To begin answering this question, the next chapter will consider the reasons people commonly give for believing that humans are different from and superior to all other animals.

V

Of Human Chauvinism

Many of the protective ditches, moats, and minefields painstakingly dug to separate us from the other animals have now been bridged or flanked. Those driven to preserve for us some unique, unambiguous, defining characteristic are tempted to shift the definitions once again and erect a final line of defense around our thoughts. [. . .] For example, we might point to our knowledge that all of us will someday die, or that sex is the cause of babies. [. . .] Perhaps no ape has ever glimpsed these important truths. Perhaps some have. We do not know. But standing alone on such homiletic pinnacles is a hollow victory for the human species. These occasional insights are minor matters compared to the vaunted distinctions of humanity that have crumbled into dust as we have learned more about the other animals. At so fine a level of detail, the motives of those who would define us by this or that idea seem suspect, the human chauvinism manifest.

—Carl Sagan and Ann Druyan[1]

Humans have long had a chauvinistic streak.

In Aristotle's day, the Greeks believed that Earth was the center of not only our solar system but also the entire universe, that the sun and planets and all the stars revolved around them and their world. After it became clear that the sun didn't travel around the Earth but instead the opposite was true, people consoled themselves with the belief that at least the sun—their sun—was the center of the universe. When they learned that the cosmos didn't rotate around the sun, they hoped that at least the solar system was at the center of our galaxy, the Milky Way. Now, we know that isn't true either.[2]

On Valentine's Day, 1990, the Voyager 1 spacecraft had traveled beyond Neptune, more than three and a half billion miles from Earth, when it took a final series of family portraits of our solar system. In one portrait, shown below, Earth appears as a tiny bluish-white dot in a band of sunlight.

For Carl Sagan, the pale blue dot provided this perspective:

> The Earth is a very small stage in a vast cosmic arena. Think of the rivers of blood spilled by all those generals and emperors so that, in glory and triumph, they could become the momentary masters of a fraction of a dot. Think of the endless cruelties visited by the inhabitants of one corner of this pixel on the scarcely distinguishable inhabitants of some other corner, how frequent their misunderstandings, how eager they are to kill another, how fervent their hatreds. Our posturings, our imagined self-importance, the delusion that we have some privileged position in the Universe, are challenged by this point of pale light. [. . .]
>
> There is perhaps no better demonstration of the folly of human conceits than this distant image of our tiny world.[3]

Fig. 13. Pale Blue Dot

More than a century and a half earlier, Charles Darwin had a similar idea, writing in a notebook: "Man in his arrogance thinks himself a great work worthy [of] the imposition of a deity. More humble and I think truer to consider him created from animals."[4] At the time, most biologists were as chauvinistic as everyone else. Many took his theory—that humans were not a unique creation but the product of the same evolutionary forces that impartially shaped all other animals—as a personal insult.

As if Darwin hadn't wounded humankind's vanity enough with his ideas about human evolution, in *The Descent of Man and Selection in Relation to Sex*, he challenged the widespread belief that our extraordinary mental capacities made us unique in the animal kingdom. First, he listed many of the arguments people made about human uniqueness:

> [T]hat man alone is capable of progressive improvement; that he alone makes use of tools or fire, domesticates other animals or possesses property; that no animal has the power of abstraction, or of forming general concepts, is self-conscious and comprehends itself; that no animal employs language; that man alone has a sense of beauty, is liable to caprice, has the feeling of gratitude, mystery & c.; believes in God, or is endowed with a conscience.[5]

Then he cited evidence to disprove each of these claims, one by one, concluding: "[T]he difference in mind between man and the higher animals, great as it is, certainly is one of degree and not of kind."[6]

Since Darwin's time, we've learned a great deal more about nonhuman animals, their ability to make and use tools, their intelligence, moral sense, culture, and capacity for language—abilities once thought to justify giving humans a superior place in the moral universe, above all other animals.

These are some of the things we've learned.

1. The ability to make and use tools

Humans' ability to make tools was once thought so exceptional that in 1949, a British anthropologist published a book about stone axes and other tools early humans had made—titled *Man the Tool Maker*. In the fall of 1960, Jane Goodall, then a twenty-six-year-old protégé of the prominent anthropologist Louis Leakey, saw a chimpanzee in Tanzania—whom she later named David Greybeard—fish termites out of a mound with a long stalk of sword grass he had trimmed for the purpose.[7] At the time, Leakey, like most other scientists, believed that making tools was a uniquely human activity. When Goodall sent him a copy of her field notes, which contained entries about how chimpanzees had pruned a stalk of grass or stripped leaves off a twig to use to probe deep into a mound and fish out termites, Leakey replied, "Now we must redefine tool, redefine Man, or accept chimpanzees as humans."[8]

A primatologist who worked with Goodall, Geza Teleki, learned how difficult it was to fish for termites when he worked for several months under the tutelage of an adept termite fisher, a chimpanzee called Leakey. Teleki spent hours inserting a probe into termite mounds, waiting for termites to attach themselves to it, and then pulling it out without getting any of the insects. In time, he realized that he had to dexterously guide the probe through a twisting tunnel to the optimal depth and gently vibrate it until termites bit onto it. If he failed to pull the probe out at the right time, the termites could chew right through it; if he pulled it out too rapidly or clumsily, the termites were often scraped off on the sides of the tunnel, leaving nothing but a shredded probe. After months of practice, Teleki thought he had become as proficient at fishing for termites as a four- or five-year-old chimp.[9]

Once scientists learned that chimpanzees fashioned tools from natural objects, some continued to maintain that humans' use of tools was unique, either because only humans possessed kits of different tools for different purposes, or were dependent on tools for their survival, or used them to gain access to underground food sources. Subsequent research has discredited all of these claims.[10] Two researchers disproved a final claim—that humans were the only species to combine many tools to reach a single goal—when they found that chimpanzees in central Africa used sets containing as many as five different tools to extract honey from bees' hives. This led them to the Darwinian conclusion that the difference in tool use between chimpanzees and humans might be quantitative, not qualitative.[11]

Primates aren't the only animals who make and use tools. Field studies have shown that crows living on New Caledonian islands in the South Pacific make and use hooked tools to extract insects and worms from trees.[12] Scientists working at Oxford University wondered whether captive New Caledonian crows would use tools like these in a laboratory experiment. They provided a couple of crows with two pieces of wire—one straight and the other with a hook at one end—to see if they would use the wire with the hook to lift food in a small bucket out of a plexiglass tube. One crow, Abel, promptly took the hooked wire and flew off to another part of the aviary, but the other crow, Betty, proceeded to bend the straight piece of wire into a hook and use it to pull up the bucket. When the researchers gave Betty another straight piece of wire to see if the first time was a fluke, she bent it into a hook too and used it to extract the bucket.[13]

Making and using tools are still thought to be rare in the animal world, and humans, of course, have made far more sophisticated and specialized tools than any other animal. But a few other species besides chimpanzees and crows are now known toolmakers, including elephants and woodpecker finches.[14] The primatologist Frans de Waal said of these studies: "So much for man the tool-maker."[15]

2. The capacity to use language

Two years after Darwin published *On the Origin of Species*, a German linguist, Max Müller, addressed the similarities between humans and other animals in a lecture at the Royal Institution in London:

> Where, then, is the difference between brute and man? What is it that man can do, and of which we find no signs, no rudiments, in the whole brute world? I answer without hesitation: the one great barrier between the brute and man is *Language*. Man speaks and no brute has ever uttered a word. Language is our Rubicon, and no brute will dare to cross it.[16]

In a discussion of what set humans apart from other animals, Mary Midgley, a British moral philosopher, called language "the key to the human castle" because it provided such compelling evidence of our extraordinary mental abilities, like self-awareness and abstract thinking.[17] That was why, she said, people were so upset when, a century after Müller's lecture at the Royal Institution, American researchers tried to teach a young female chimpanzee named Washoe American Sign Language (ASL). Washoe, Midgley said, "took to it like a duck to water," acquiring a vocabulary of about 150 ASL signs and understanding another 200.[18] When researchers placed four other chimps with Washoe, the chimps constantly used sign language to communicate with one another, signed to themselves, and, without having been taught, swore. Their favorite curse word was the ASL sign for "dirty."[19] When Roger Fouts, a graduate student working with Washoe, refused to give her a second slice of cake at a party, Washoe signed: "dirty Roger."[20]

As Frans de Waal noted, many of those who claimed the capacity to use language was uniquely human had originally defined language as symbolic communication. Once they learned that apes could use sign language, "they realized that the only way to keep these interlopers out was by dropping the symbol claim and stressing syntax instead."[21] They said that even if chimpanzees were able to learn and communicate using sign language, the chimpanzees couldn't follow grammatical rules or create a sentence the way people did.[22] Other defenders of the castle said that the ASL-signing chimps weren't using language at all, because they didn't use negative terms or interrogatives. When skeptics learned that chimps used negatives and asked questions, they then pointed to some other aspect of human language not present in chimpanzee communication, and that became the essential feature of language—a strategy De Waal referred to as "moving the goalposts."[23]

By now, in addition to evidence that chimpanzees can acquire and use sign language, researchers have completed similar studies of gorillas and bonobos with much the same results.[24] Compared to humans' linguistic abilities, all apes studied so far have fallen far short. But some have learned small vocabularies of hand signals or computerized symbols and have used them effectively to communicate their needs and desires.[25]

3. Intelligence

An individual's awareness that he or she is separate from the environment is thought to be a sign of intelligence. The mirror self-recognition test— in which researchers observe whether an animal who looks in a mirror appears to recognize the reflection as his or her own self or behaves as though it is an image of another animal—once provided the most reliable evidence of an animal's self-awareness. Before ape language research, scientists believed that chimpanzees lacked self-awareness because they didn't seem to recognize the image they saw in a mirror as their own.[26]

Once chimpanzees learned sign language, though, researchers gained a more direct source of information about self-awareness: they could ask the animal about his or her reflection in a mirror. After Washoe had become familiar with mirrors, a researcher asked, "Who is that?" (referring to her image in a mirror), and she signed back, "Me, Washoe."[27] A few years later, an elegant version of the mirror self-recognition test confirmed that some other chimpanzees were also able to recognize their reflection in a mirror as their own image.[28] The American psychologist who conducted this study, Gordon Gallup, commented that "these data [showed] that contrary to popular opinion and preconceived ideas, man [might] not have a monopoly on the self-concept. Man [might] not be evolution's only experiment in self-awareness."[29]

Humans were also thought to have a monopoly on another facet of intelligence—the ability to remember past events. In 1920, the American philosopher John Dewey expressed a common belief:

> With the animals, an experience perishes as it happens, and each new doing or suffering stands alone. But man lives in a world where each occurrence is charged with echoes and reminiscences of what has gone before, where each event is a reminder of other things.[30]

Scientists working with Washoe found that Dewey's impression was mistaken. By the early 1980s, it had been more than ten years since she had seen Allen and Beatrix Gardner, a couple who had cared for her when she was an infant and had taught her sign language. When they visited her after this long absence, Washoe looked dumbfounded at first. Then she signed, "Come, Mrs. G" to Beatrix Gardner and took her into an adjoining room, where they began to play a game they hadn't played together for many years.[31,32]

Some chimpanzees can remember detailed information for a short period of time too. When nine university students and three young chimpanzees were briefly shown five numbers between 1 and 9 on a touch-screen monitor and asked to touch the location on the monitor where each number had appeared, the chimpanzees scored better than the students, especially when the numbers were displayed for a very short time.[33] One of the chimpanzees, Ayumu, had a photographic memory. When shown the numerals for just a fifth of a second (about the time it takes to blink an eye), he could quickly tap the correct order of the numbers about 80 percent of the time—a feat no human has ever equaled.[34]

Other animals far removed from chimpanzees on the tree of evolution have remarkable memories too. In the late summer and fall, nutcrackers bury seeds they will need for food during the following winter and spring. In one study, a nutcracker stored some 32,000 pine seeds in more than 7,000 different caches and then successfully returned to retrieve more than 70 percent of them, even though the bird had buried the seeds before the first snowfall and often recovered them through deep snow.[35]

American crows have excellent memories too, but not for the locations of buried seeds; they can remember a person's face. Whenever John Marzluff, a wildlife biologist, walked around the campus at the University of Washington after having captured and banded many crows there, groups of crows would scold and dive-bomb him, suggesting that they recognized him as a threatening person. To determine if the crows actually recognized an individual person and, if so, whether the recognition was based on the person's face or other characteristics, two people trapped and banded birds on the campus while wearing "caveman" masks. Then other people participating in the study walked slowly around the area, wearing either a "caveman" mask, a neutral mask, or no mask at all.[36] For more than two years, the crows consistently scolded only those who wore "caveman" masks,[37] suggesting that the birds not only recognized an individual human face but continued to remember it for some time.[38]

Since the time of Aristotle, humans have thought we were the only ones who had the capacity to reason and understand principles of cause and effect—another aspect of intelligence.[39] That belief began to be challenged when Goodall discovered that David Greybeard fashioned tools for termite fishing. Since then, scientists have found that chimpanzees use tools for other tasks too. For example, researchers studying chimpanzees in a West African forest found that the chimpanzees ate five different kinds of nuts and selected tools to crack them open according to the hardness of the nut, using harder and heavier tools to crack harder nuts.[40]

Other research has shown that New Caledonian crows also have some understanding of the properties a tool needs to have. In one study, researchers placed some meat out of a bird's reach and placed a stick within reach that was too short to get the meat but could be used to get a second stick long enough to reach it. All seven crows who were tested used the short stick to get the long one, and then used the latter to get the meat. The researchers concluded that the crows had used reasoning to solve the problem.[41]

Other studies with New Caledonian crows showed that one of Aesop's fables—in which a thirsty crow dropped stones into a pitcher to raise the water level enough so that he could drink—might not have been entirely fictional. When tested with a block of meat floating in a Plexiglas tube, crows learned to drop stones into the tube until the water level was high enough for them to reach the meat with their bills.[42] When Frans de Waal did a similar test with chimpanzees using a shelled peanut floating in a tube as a reward, a chimp named Lisa kicked and shook the tube at first but then went to a water bubbler several times, filled her mouth with water, and spat it into the tube until the peanut came within her reach.

Other chimps weren't as successful. One tried to urinate into the tube. De Waal commented that "she had the right idea even though the execution was flawed."[43]

In summarizing the research that compared the performance of apes and children on tasks involving different aspects of intelligence such as memory, understanding of causality, and tool use, De Waal concluded that the apes performed at about the level of a two-and-a-half-year-old child.[44] Tying this to Darwinian principles of evolution, he wrote that instead of a gap between the cognition of humans and other animals, there is "a gently sloping beach created by the steady pounding of millions of waves. Even if human intellect [was] higher up on the beach, it was shaped by the same forces battering the same shore."[45]

4. Moral sense

David Oderberg, a moral philosopher, believes it is the ability to make ethical decisions that sets humans apart from all other animals. The critical difference to him is that humans can choose between right and wrong, whereas "[a]nimals, from the smallest single-celled organism to the most human-like ape, are governed purely by *instinct*."[46] Studies showing that animals engaged in complex behaviors like toolmaking, social-group formation, or mutual assistance were beside the point, as he argued in 2000: "No experiment that has ever been conducted into animal behaviour has demonstrated that animals know *why* they do what they do, or are *free* to choose one course of action over another."[47]

Research has shown, however, that some animals have empathy, an appreciation of reciprocity, and a sense of fairness—capacities that are widely considered to be the building blocks of human morality.[48] In a series of experiments conducted in 1964, researchers wanted to see whether rhesus monkeys who became familiar with a device that delivered a food pellet to them when they pulled a chain would continue to pull the chain if they saw that pulling it also gave an electric shock to a monkey in a compartment next to them. The researchers found that most of the monkeys would go hungry if it meant that getting food would cause another monkey to experience pain. Further, monkeys who had been shocked themselves in a previous experiment were even less likely to pull the chain to get a food pellet if they saw it would cause another monkey to get a shock.[49]

An incident that happened between Washoe and one of the people who worked with her, Kat Beach, provided another piece of evidence of an animal's capacity for empathy. As Roger Fouts recounted in his memoir:

> In the summer of 1982 Kat was newly pregnant, and Washoe doted over her belly, asking about her BABY. Unfortunately, Kat had a miscarriage, and she didn't come into the lab for several days. When she finally came back Washoe greeted her warmly but then moved away and let Kat know she was upset that she'd been gone. Knowing that Washoe had lost two of her own children, Kat decided to tell her the truth.
>
> MY BABY DIED, Kat signed to her. Washoe looked down to the ground. Then she looked into Kat's eyes and signed CRY, touching her cheek just below her eye. That single word, CRY, Kat later said, told her more about Washoe than all of her longer, more grammatically perfect sentences. When Kat had to leave that day, Washoe wouldn't let her go. PLEASE PERSON HUG, she signed.[50]

Another time, Washoe saw a chimpanzee drowning in a moat surrounding the island where the chimps were kept. Although she had known the chimp only for a few hours, Washoe vaulted over an electrified barrier at the edge of the moat, stepped out onto the slippery mud at the water's edge, and pulled the flailing chimpanzee to safety.[51]

De Waal also studied whether chimpanzees engaged in reciprocal exchanges, another element of human morality, by conducting experiments in which bundles of food were thrown into a group of chimps shortly after one chimp had been seen spontaneously grooming another. Observers then kept track of how often each chimp shared food with every other chimp. They found that chimps were more likely to share food with one who had groomed them than with the others, and were more likely to resist requests for sharing by those who hadn't groomed them.[52] De Waal considered these behaviors to be compelling evidence that chimpanzees engaged in reciprocal exchanges in what he called "the chimpanzee service economy."[53]

In 2003, De Waal and a doctoral student also studied capuchin monkeys' sense of fairness.[54] They placed two monkeys in cages next to each other and trained the monkeys to trade pebbles for pieces of cucumber. The monkeys seemed quite content, handing over a pebble each time and eating the cucumber they received in return. Then the researchers introduced inequity, giving one of the monkeys a grape—a snack the monkeys preferred—while continuing to give the other one a piece of cucumber. As soon as the monkey who got the cucumber noticed that a companion was getting a tasty grape for performing the same task, the monkey rebelled, discarding the morsel of cucumber or throwing it back at the researcher.[55]

Some primates, then, behave as though they have at least a rudimentary sense of right and wrong.[56] It's unlikely, though, that their moral world is as complex as ours—that they weigh their interests against the rights of others, develop a vision of the greater social good, or feel lifelong guilt about something they shouldn't have done.[57]

5. Culture

Reminiscent of Müller's remark that the capacity to use language set humans apart from all other animals, De Waal referred to the issue of whether other animals transmitted behavior from one generation to another through culture as "the last rubicon."[58] In September of 1953, primatologists saw Imo, a one-and-a-half-year-old female Koshima snow monkey, dunk sweet potatoes in a nearby brook to rinse off sand from the beach where they had been dumped instead of painstakingly brushing them off as others in her troop did. The following year, Imo's mother and two of Imo's playmates were seen washing potatoes in the stream. After years, more than half of the monkeys in the troop were doing the same thing.[59]

Then Imo had what Carl Sagan called her second epiphany.[60] Scientists studying the monkeys also dropped kernels of wheat on the beach as food for them. The monkeys ate the wheat with great difficulty, picking the sand off one grain at a time. Then researchers saw Imo take a handful of wheat to the same brook where she washed potatoes and throw it in the water. After the sand sank, she ate the wheat when it floated back to the surface. Slowly, more and more monkeys on the island adopted this technique too.[61] More than a half-century later, the snow monkeys on the island where Imo had lived were still washing the sand off sweet potatoes even though none of them had ever known Imo.[62]

The Koshima snow monkeys aren't the only primates who transmit behavior from one generation to another; chimpanzees do too. Roger Fouts saw that happen while working with Washoe. After one of Washoe's infants died, Fouts managed to acquire a ten-month-old male chimpanzee named Loulis from a research center and placed him with Washoe to ease her grief. To see if Loulis would learn signs from Washoe, researchers made sure not to use sign language when he was present. After just eight days, Loulis made the sign for one of the people taking care of him. When he was twenty-nine months old, he was using at least seventeen different signs; by the time he was six, he had learned fifty-one signs.[63]

Over the years, Jane Goodall and other field researchers noted that many socially transmitted behavior patterns—such as grooming practices, tool use, and courtship behaviors—were present in some chimpanzee troops but not others. In 1999, they published an article in the journal *Nature*, listing thirty-nine of the socially transmitted behaviors they had discovered in the course of seven long-term field studies.[64] Two weeks after the article was published, a prominent American biologist, Stephen Jay Gould, wrote an article in the *New York Times* discussing how our need to see ourselves as separate from and superior to all other animals led us to erect "golden barriers" that marked an unbridgeable gap between them and us. He summarized the history of the barriers this way:

> Thus, we have proposed many varied criteria—and rejected them, one
> by one. We tried behavior—the use of tools, and upon failure of this
> broad standard, the use of tools explicitly fashioned for particular tasks.

(Chimps, after all, strip leaves off twigs, and then use the naked sticks for extracting termites out of nests.) And we considered distinctive mental attributes—the existence of a moral sense, or the ability to form abstractions. All have failed as absolutes of human uniqueness (while a complex debate continues to surround the meaning and spread of language and its potential rudiments).

The evidence presented in the *Nature* article, he said, proved that chimpanzees had complex cultures. He went on to conclude: "The development of 'culture'—defined as distinct and complex behavior originating in local populations and clearly passed by learning, rather than genetic predisposition—has persisted as a favored candidate for a 'golden barrier' to separate humans from animals, but must now be rejected as well."[65]

* * *

It turns out that we aren't unique. Of course, making a tool to extract termites from a nest is not as complex as building a spacecraft and having it send back a photo of our solar system while it heads into interstellar space. A monkey foregoing a food pellet so that another monkey won't suffer an electric shock isn't morally equivalent to the sacrifice Father Kolbe made when he volunteered to take the place of another prisoner sentenced to a starvation cell at Auschwitz. And Washoe learning a few hundred signs didn't enable her to communicate with anything close to the fluency of most older children, much less the adults who taught her the signs. But, as Darwin said, evidence shows that the differences between other animals and us are ones of degree, not of kind.

As James Rachels pointed out, animals are enough like us that they deserve the same basic protections as we do,[66] and we can use principles of human morality as a starting point in making moral decisions about the way we treat them. Rachels described how we could do that:

First we might select a right that we are confident humans have. Then we can ask whether there is a relevant difference between humans and animals that would justify us in denying that right to animals while granting it to humans. If not, then the right is possessed by the animals as well as by the people.[67]

According to Rachels, the belief that it's wrong to cause another person to suffer pain without a good reason is a cardinal principle of moral philosophy.[68] Using the capacity to suffer pain as a moral guideline in our treatment of animals isn't a new idea. The utilitarian philosopher Jeremy Bentham suggested it more than two hundred years ago. Noting that France had abolished slavery in her colonies, he wrote:

> The day *may* come, when the rest of the animal creation may acquire those rights which never could have been withholden from them except but by the hand of tyranny. The French have already discovered that the blackness of the skin is no reason why a human being should be abandoned without redress to the caprice of a tormentor. It may come one day to be recognized, that the number of the legs, the villosity of the skin, or the termination of the *os sacrum*, are reasons equally insufficient for abandoning a sensitive being to the same fate. [. . .] [T]he question is not, Can they *reason?* nor, Can they *talk?* but, Can they *suffer?*[69]

The capacity to feel pain as an ethical criterion has several advantages over those commonly used in the past, which were based on abilities such as intelligence, moral sense, or the use of language. First, these traditional guidelines aren't impartial, because they're chauvinistically weighted toward human strengths. Second, decisions about whether an animal is sensitive to pain can be based on objective facts, including physiological and behavioral evidence. Finally, there is general agreement among biologists about which species of animals can feel pain.

To decide whether the way we commonly treat animals is ethical or not, it will be necessary to look closely at the treatment in question.

People around the world use animals for many different purposes: for food, clothing, scientific research, as beasts of burden, among many others. It won't be possible to consider all of those purposes here, so the next two chapters will discuss the most common way we use animals— as food—to see whether the reasons people give for using them this way justify the pain they suffer.

VI

On Factory Farms, Money Talks but in Obscenities

Industry standards for production systems and animal care are generally guided by economics. Welfare issues, such as animal stress and suffering, might be considered in rearing, but only in the context of how they impact performance, efficiency, or profitability. Industrial livestock production systems have often deleteriously affected the welfare of virtually every species of farm animal in the United States [. . .] and raise serious ethical questions regarding the way in which these animals are treated.—Pew Commission on Industrial Farm Animal Production[1]

Let's begin with the most common form of animal agriculture: industrial animal production. Deciding whether people have good enough reasons to justify eating meat from factory farms will require answering three questions: Can the animals kept there suffer pain?[2] If so, how substantial is their pain? And are the reasons people give for eating meat good enough to justify eating the products of these farms, considering the pain the animals suffer?

If animals kept on farms could talk like Wilbur in *Charlotte's Web* or Old Major in *Animal Farm*, we could answer the first question by asking them whether they feel pain. That not being possible, we can use the physiological and behavioral changes that occur when people are in pain and see if an animal undergoes comparable changes, treating any similarity as evidence that the animal is experiencing pain.

In 1991, eighteen scientists, medical researchers, and philosophers on a committee formed by the British Institute of Medical Ethics suggested using four physiological conditions and three behaviors associated with human pain to determine whether an animal had the capacity to suffer pain. Among the physiological conditions they identified was the presence of sensory neurons called nociceptors, which recognized damaging or potentially damaging stimuli, and an internal opioid system, which could be triggered to reduce pain. Among the behaviors identified were the attempt to avoid stimuli that also caused pain in humans, as well as a response to analgesic medications similar to humans'.[3] Applying these criteria, the committee concluded that all vertebrate animals could probably feel pain.[4] The authors of several other comprehensive assessments of animals' capacity to feel pain reached the same conclusion.[5]

Since the Institute of Medical Ethics published its criteria, many scientists have used similar ones to assess the extent to which four species commonly raised in intensive food animal production operations[6]—chickens, turkeys, pigs, and cows[7]—can suffer pain. Often, they studied the effect of analgesic medications on an animal's behavior. In one study, researchers separated chickens raised for meat (called "broilers" in the industry) into two groups depending on whether the animals showed evidence of lameness. Then they allowed each animal to choose between two different feeds, one of which contained an analgesic compound. The researchers found that the birds who didn't appear lame usually preferred the feed without the analgesic, perhaps because they didn't like the taste of the medication.[8] The lame birds, in contrast, selected the feed with the analgesic more often, and their walking ability improved when the amount of analgesic in their blood increased. The researchers concluded that the birds were in pain and sought relief from their distress.[9] In a previous study, many of the same researchers had found that lame broilers took about thirty-four seconds to cross an obstacle course to a feeder, but after ingesting feed with an analgesic, they only took about eighteen seconds.[10]

To investigate the extent to which animals undergoing surgical procedures like castration or the removal of their horn buds with a hot iron suffered pain, other researchers administered different types of pain-relief treatment to those who underwent the procedures and compared their behavior to that of other animals who had the surgery without receiving any treatment for pain. In one study, calves who had been dehorned without receiving anti-inflammatory medication frequently flicked their ears for the first twenty-four hours after the surgery, suggesting that they were in pain. Those who had received medication showed very few ear flicks, much like the calves in the control groups, who had gone through a simulated procedure but hadn't been operated upon.[11]

In other studies, scientists investigated the effectiveness of different types of treatment in reducing the pain piglets felt when castrated. One group of researchers found that when piglets weren't given any anesthesia or analgesia, their squeals were longer, louder, and higher than those of piglets in control groups, who had received some form of treatment for pain.[12]

Dozens of other assessments of pain levels in farmed animals could be added to these, but that seems unnecessary. It's readily apparent that chickens, turkeys, pigs, and cows can suffer pain.

* * *

Turning now to the question of whether the pain these animals suffer on factory farms is substantial or not, we will first consider pigs. In intensive confinement operations, producers commonly welcome piglets into the world by mutilating them. Farmers clip or grind down their teeth, amputate part of their tails, and castrate males not kept for breeding. In one study, researchers identified three types of vocalizations piglets made when castrated: grunts, squeals, and screams. They found that those who had been castrated without receiving a local anesthetic screamed in pain an average of twenty-five times after the procedure, almost twice as often as those who had been given an anesthetic.[13]

In intensive operations, cows are painfully mutilated in several ways too. They're branded and dehorned, and the males not used for breeding are also castrated.

All chickens raised for meat suffer acute pain shortly before their death, when slaughterhouse workers clamp their legs into metal shackles and hang them upside down before killing them.[14] By then, many chickens have become lame. In 1992, when British researchers compared rates of gait abnormality in three breeds of chickens used in modern broiler production to that in a control group that had been randomly bred for eleven generations, they found the randomly bred chickens had almost perfect gait scores. In contrast, 26 percent of the birds intensively selected for high growth rates had problems moving around, as shown by a limp, unsteadiness, or a severe splaying of one foot. The selection practices led to many of the birds growing so big so fast that their developing legs couldn't support them.[15]

Artificial selection for faster growth rates isn't the only practice that has caused the exacerbation of lameness in modern strains of broilers. To make more money, producers have increased the density of birds kept in a broiler shed. The author of an article in a 1975 broiler industry publication suggested that "more pounds of live broiler [could] be produced per square foot if floor space per bird [was] reduced."[16] According to the author, if five birds were raised in two square feet of floor space (leaving each bird with a space about the size of an eight-inch square), profits would be more than double what they would be if each bird was allowed a single square foot of floor space. Although a higher and higher percentage of birds would die as the stocking density increased, he said, the economic losses from their deaths would be more than offset by the profits generated from increasing the stocking density.[17] In other words, although increased densities would drive the welfare of the birds down, they would drive the producer's profits up. (See Chart 1.)

To increase profits, in recent years, producers have also selected chickens who can more efficiently convert feed and gain more weight. To assess the impact that intense selection had had on the growth rate

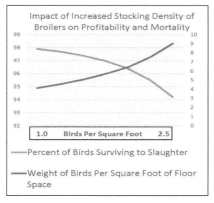

Chart 1. Impact of Stocking Density of
Broilers on Profits & Mortality

and body size of broilers, in 2014, Canadian researchers raised strains of birds that had been commonly used in broiler operations in 1957, 1978, and 2005—all under the same conditions. When the birds were fifty-six days old, those from the 1978 strain were almost twice as heavy as their 1957 counterparts, and birds from the strain used in 2005 were more than four times heavier than those from the 1957 strain.[18] Increased body size joined with faster growth and increased stocking density to create a perfect storm. The result was what John Webster—a founding member of the British government's Farm Animal Welfare Advisory Committee— called a long and depressing list of pathological conditions of bones, joints, tendons, and skin, euphemistically called "leg weakness."[19]

Producers often claim that the optimal welfare of the animals goes hand in hand with optimal productivity: "If they weren't happy, their performance would suffer." In John Webster's opinion, though, the lameness of chickens in intensive broiler operations disproves that claim.[20] The health of industrially produced broilers is so compromised that producers have them slaughtered when they are only six weeks old. If, for any reason, the date of slaughter is postponed for as little as two weeks, the birds begin to die spontaneously "at a rate that would alarm even the coldest of accountants," as Webster said.[21] Noting in 1994 that a quarter of the heavy strains of broilers used in intensive operations were in chronic pain for about a third of their lives, he said that this "must constitute, in both magnitude and severity, the single most severe, systematic example of man's inhumanity to another sentient animal."[22]

Thirteen years after Webster's condemnation of the broiler industry, researchers assessed the walking ability of 51,000 birds in British intensive production operations to see if any progress had been made in reducing the incidence or severity of the broilers' lameness. The answer was none. They found that 27.6 percent of the chickens had an impaired gait, as shown by limping, unsteadiness, or severe splaying of one leg, and 3.3 percent were almost unable to walk at all. The authors concluded: "[M]odern husbandry and genotypes, biased toward economics of production, have been detrimental to poultry welfare in compromising the ability of chickens to walk."[23]

The same two practices—selection for fast growth and selection for weight gain—have resulted in an even higher incidence of painful leg disorders in turkeys raised industrially. Forty years of intensive selection have led to broad-breasted adult males weighing over sixty-six pounds (thirty kilograms), almost four times heavier than unselected birds.[24] In one study of male breeding turkeys, it was found that more than half were lame and all showed gait abnormalities.[25] In another study, postmortem analysis showed that all seventy adults of a heavy breed had degenerative hip disorders.[26]

Plainly, animals suffer significant pain on factory farms. Even though the pain is often severe and prolonged, that doesn't necessarily mean that eating meat from these producers is wrong. As mentioned at the start of the chapter, the next question is whether people have good enough reasons to justify doing so. To answer it, let's consider the reasons people commonly give for eating meat.

1. **We need to eat meat to be healthy. We can't get the protein and other nutrients our bodies need without eating some meat.[27]**

In a recent study, this was the most common reason people gave for eating meat.[28] Forty years ago, many dieticians and nutritionists believed that people who didn't have meat in their diets were at much higher risk of not getting necessary nutrients compared to those who did. Not anymore. Beginning in the 1980s, a paradigm shift happened after epidemiological studies began showing that vegetarians were less likely to suffer from many chronic degenerative diseases and tended to live longer.[29] Commenting on the results of these studies, the American Dietetic Association stated in 1997: "Scientific data suggest positive relationships between a vegetarian diet and reduced risk for several chronic degenerative diseases and conditions, including obesity, coronary artery disease, hypertension, diabetes mellitus, and some types of cancer."[30]

Much of the first wave of research on vegetarian diets compared the incidence of disease in people who followed different diets. A second wave of studies aggregated the data from earlier ones and analyzed the cumulative results to test the reliability of conclusions from the first wave. For instance, researchers in a study of six thousand vegetarians and five thousand non-vegetarians found that, after adjusting for other factors thought to affect death rates, the vegetarians enjoyed a significant reduction in mortality from coronary artery disease.[31] A study in the second wave analyzed the data from that study together with data from four other large-scale studies and arrived at the same conclusion: the vegetarians were significantly less likely to die from coronary artery disease.[32]

A subsequent study of more than five hundred thousand American men and women compared a wide range of levels of meat intake on risk of death from several chronic diseases. The researchers used a 124-item food-frequency questionnaire to break the respondents into five groups, or quintiles, depending on the amount of meat in their diets. The impact of red meat consumption on overall death rates was striking. After adjusting for many variables known to affect death rates—such as age, smoking, and Body Mass Index—researchers found that men in the fifth of the population that ate the most red meat (Q5 on the chart below) had a significantly higher risk of dying during the period of the study than did men in the group that ate the least red meat (Q1). It was the same for women: those who ate the most red meat (Q5) had a much higher death rate than those who ate the least (Q1). Quintile by quintile, as red meat consumption increased, the overall death rate increased along with it.[33]

An important lesson has emerged from these studies. Meat isn't a health food. Just the opposite. The widespread belief that people must eat at least some meat to be healthy is mistaken.

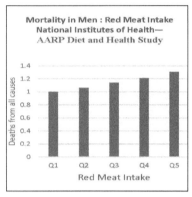

Chart 2. Mortality in Men and Red Meat Consumption

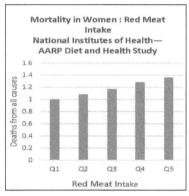

Chart 3. Mortality in Women and Red Meat Consumption

2. In nature, animals eat other animals to survive. We're animals too, so it isn't wrong for us to eat other animals.[34]

This rationale brings to mind a story Benjamin Franklin told about how, after having been a vegetarian for many years, he began to eat fish again:

I believe I have omitted mentioning that, in my first voyage from Boston, being becalm'd off Block Island, our people set about catching cod, and hauled up a great many. Hitherto I had stuck to my resolution of not eating animal food, and on this occasion I considered [. . .] the taking [of] every fish as a kind of unprovoked murder, since none of them had, or ever could do us any injury that might justify the slaughter. All this seemed very reasonable. But I had formerly been a great lover of fish, and, when this came hot out of the frying pan, it smelt admirably well. I balanc'd some time between principle and inclination, till I recollected that, when the fish were opened, I saw smaller fish taken out of their stomachs; then thought I, "If you eat one another, I don't see why we mayn't eat you." So I din'd upon cod very heartily and continued to eat with other people, returning only now and then occasionally to a vegetarian diet. So convenient it is to be a *reasonable creature*, since it enables one to find or make a reason for everything one has a mind to do.[35]

It's not all right for us to do something just because other animals do it. After all, some male animals kill infants they haven't sired or have sex with an unwilling partner.[36] As John Stuart Mill once pointed out: "Either it is right that we should kill because nature kills; torture because nature tortures; and ruin and devastate because nature does the like; or we ought not to consider what nature does, but what is good to do."[37]

3. **People everywhere eat meat. Something almost everyone does can't be wrong. It's normal.**[38]

This is a cousin to the "eating meat is natural" justification and is equally invalid. Even if people all over the world have done something for a long time, that hasn't made it right.

Slavery is as old as civilization and was practiced all over the world.[39]

When Leopold asked representatives of other Western nations to let him acquire "a slice of the magnificent African cake," they didn't tell him that would be wrong. Instead, each country, even tiny Portugal, worked to get a slice of its own. Thirty years later, they had carved up almost the entire continent and divided it among themselves.

In the same way, for centuries, men used their strength to dominate and exploit women.

We now know that slavery, colonialism, and the exploitation of women were wrong. Just because they were common for so long didn't make them right. Even though people everywhere eat meat, that doesn't make it right.

4. **I enjoy the taste of meat.**

This is the last of the "four Ns" people gave to justify eating meat in the study mentioned earlier (i.e. that it's **n**ecessary, **n**atural, **n**ormal, and **n**ice).

The "meat tastes nice" rationale is as illogical as the "it's natural" and "it's normal" rationalizations. The taste of food has nothing to do with whether the way it is produced is ethical or not. Take white veal production. According to John Webster, it abuses all of the Five Freedoms—including freedom from hunger and freedom to express normal behavior—which underlie the European Union's standards for the protection of farmed animals.[40] He once denounced white veal production as "one of the most bizarre and . . . unequivocally cruel forms of livestock production."[41] Still, some people savor the taste of veal.

5. **If I didn't eat meat from factory farms, the animals raised there would still suffer just as much, so eating meat from these farms isn't wrong.**

Some people believe that one person's decision not to eat meat from factory farms won't make any difference to the number of animals these farms produce. The supply chain is so long, their argument goes, with payments going from the consumer to a retailer to a distributor to a middleman and then finally to the producer, that it's unlikely that any consumer's purchasing decisions will even register with a producer. Although some industrial producers' practices are morally wrong, they say, consumers don't share responsibility for that wrongdoing when they eat meat from these farms, because if they didn't, animals would still suffer just as much.[42]

Although the industrial meat production system is massive and complex, an economist who has studied it, Steven McMullen, has pointed out that products of animal agriculture are still subject to the economics of supply and demand like other products:

> The market response to consumer choices is clear: When people decide to shift their consumption away from animal products, the result will be fewer animals raised and fewer animals killed. This result comes from four effects: the direct effect, the supply chain effect, the network effect, and the impact of economies of scale. Many of these results are difficult to see immediately, and some are never visible to the consumer, but they are real nevertheless.[43]

The direct effect occurs, according to McMullen, when people substitute veggie burgers for ground beef. At first, the supermarket probably puts the excess meat on sale and sells it to other people. In time, the supermarket begins placing smaller orders with the meat distributor, and the distributor, in turn, places smaller orders with the producer. Because of the way the market for agricultural products operates and because of its low profit margins, any changes in demand are ultimately reflected in the amount sold.[44]

In addition to having direct and supply chain effects, a consumer's purchasing decisions spill over and affect other people's decisions through network effects. For example, McMullen explained, if consumers switch purchases from meat to tofu, stores respond by having bigger displays for and stocking more varieties of tofu. If consumption grows enough, products that were once found only in specialty stores make their way into supermarkets. Then, as more and more of these products are sold, economies of scale bring their prices down and consumption increases even more, as has happened with organic food and gluten-free products. Over time, the effects of a single person's purchasing decisions can have a substantial impact.[45] In the case of a decision to adopt a vegetarian diet, McMullen cited one estimate that in 2015, the average vegetarian in the United States saved between 371 and 582 animals, including 23 chickens, 139 shellfish, and more than 200 fishes, many of whom would have been ground up and fed to other animals.[46]

Even if the meat production market were too mammoth and complex for one person's purchasing decisions to affect it (which appears doubtful), becoming a vegetarian could have other welcome consequences. Vegetarians have a lower incidence of many debilitating diseases, including coronary heart disease,[47] diabetes,[48] and obesity.[49]

The benefits of a plant-based diet extend far beyond the person who follows it. Producing food from animals rather than from plants takes more of the planet's finite resources, so a person who consumes less meat and fewer dairy products makes it possible for more food to be grown and more people to nourish themselves.

Take energy. On average, eleven times more fossil fuel is needed to produce protein from animals than from plants.[50]

Meat-based food production is also much less efficient when it comes to water, an increasingly scarce resource.[51] It takes a hundred times more water to produce protein from animals than from grain.[52]

The same is true for land, another resource used to produce almost all food. On average, it takes between six and seventeen times more land to produce protein from animals than from soybeans.[53]

Increasing the efficiency of our food production systems has become critically important. More than eight hundred million people now suffer from hunger,[54] and that number will continue to grow if, as experts project, we need to produce food for two billion more people by mid-century.[55] The worldwide consumption of meat is projected to double by 2050,[56] putting food security on a collision course with population growth. We can avoid the collision, though, if large segments of the world's population consume less meat and fewer dairy products.[57]

A shift toward plant-based food production would greatly benefit the environment too. Livestock production is a major cause of global warming, responsible for 15–18 percent of all human-generated greenhouse gas emissions.[58] Plant-based food production generates much lower levels of emissions. A 2014 study found that a person who frequently ate meat was responsible for about twice the level of greenhouse gas emissions as someone who followed a plant-based diet.[59] And scientists from the United Nations Environmental Programme concluded that we wouldn't be able to substantially reduce agriculture's adverse impact on the environment without a worldwide dietary shift away from animal products.[60]

Considering all of the consequences mentioned above, adopting a vegetarian diet is far from futile. Those who claim that it is appear to be "reasonable creatures" like Benjamin Franklin—who come up with a reason to justify whatever they have a mind to do.

VII

On Family Farms, Money May Not Swear, but It Still Talks Too Loud

> The moral case for family farms is much stronger than for factory farms. Still, in the final analysis, the institution of family farming and our financial support of it seem ethically indefensible.—David DeGrazia[1]

J ames Rachels isn't the only moral philosopher who thought that people should stop eating meat from factory farms. After weighing the harm suffered by intensively produced animals against the reasons for eating their meat, David DeGrazia concluded: "Factory farming is an ethically indefensible institution."[2] As mentioned in the quotation above, though, for him, the question was closer regarding traditional family farms, where the animals might suffer less because they weren't reared as intensively.

This chapter will consider several related questions: Is meat from animals raised on family farms unacceptably tainted by economic decisions like in industrial operations? Does economics also taint food like eggs, milk, or cheese that can be produced from animals without taking their lives? And what about fishes—is it wrong to eat them?

In the last chapter, the only moral principle we used to decide whether it's wrong to eat meat from industrial operations was our duty not to inflict pain on others without a good reason. The pain animals suffer on factory farms is so severe that there was no need to consider any other duty. The answer was obvious, as James Rachels put it.[3] Some of that pain comes from being confined in close quarters with so many other animals. The case may be different, though, in a lower-density operation like a small family farm.

The duty to avoid inflicting unjustified pain isn't the only ethical duty we have though. Let's return for a moment to Rachels's suggestion that we can make moral decisions about how to treat animals by selecting a right we are confident people have and asking whether there is a relevant difference between people and animals that justifies denying them the same right. People everywhere agree that murder is wrong and that all humans have a right to life. Do some other animals have a right to life too? Rachels stated the ethical principle succinctly: "[A]n individual has a right to life if that individual has a life."[4] By that, he meant that the individual isn't only alive but has mental, social, and emotional experiences that make up what we think of as a life.[5]

Some nonhuman animals clearly have these kinds of experiences. As we've seen, chimpanzees and some other primates have intelligence, live in social groups guided by a rough sense of fairness, and experience strong emotions. Each animal has a life of his or her own, with its pleasures and sorrows, with family, friends, and competitors.

To decide whether it's wrong to eat meat produced less intensively, we'll need to determine whether cows, chickens, pigs, and turkeys have lives too. If so, it would be wrong to take their lives from them without a good reason. Their lives belong to them.

Let's consider each species in turn, beginning with cows.

Cows

It can be challenging to determine what any animal is thinking or feeling. That's especially true with the stoic and enigmatic cow. Temple Grandin, an expert on farmed animals who has consulted extensively with livestock producers, believes that beneath their calm exteriors, cows are often torn by curiosity and fear—that they're "curiously afraid."[6]

D. H. Lawrence saw this one morning when he milked a black cow named Susan while wearing a pair of white pants she had never seen. As he described it:

> [S]he wheels away as if the devil was on her back. I have to go behind her, talk to her, stroke her, and let her smell my hand; and smell the white trousers. She doesn't know they are trousers. She doesn't know that I am a gentleman on two feet. Not she. Something mysterious happens in her blood and her being, when she smells me and my nice white trousers.[7]

Cows have other strong emotions too. Lawrence thought Susan seemed to know it made him mad when she swatted him in the face with her tail while he was milking her, but as he recounted:

> Sometimes she swings it, just on purpose: and looks at me out of the black corner of her great, pure-black eye, when I yell at her. And when I find her away down the timber, when she is a ghost, and lost to the world, like a spider dangling in the void of chaos, then she is relieved. She comes to, out of a sort of trance, and is relieved, trotting up home with a queer, jerky cowy gladness.[8]

Cows can solve problems and seem to enjoy it when they do. In one study, researchers divided heifers into two groups: those in the experimental group could press a panel that opened a gate leading to food; others in the control group were put behind a separate gate that opened and allowed them to get food whenever a heifer in the first group pressed the panel. Researchers found that when a cow in the first group discovered how to open the gate, her heart rate went up. Some even jumped up in the air in what the researchers called a "eureka moment."[9] The heifers in the control group didn't show the same excitement when their gate opened even though it meant they, too, had gained access to food.[10]

Cows also have a complex social life, forming strong and lasting bonds with family members and herd mates.[11] Calves usually seek the companionship of other calves, romping with them and play-fighting.[12] Mothers are especially close to their calves and try to protect them. In one study, researchers riding in an unfamiliar utility vehicle approached pairs of cows and newborn calves. As the vehicle got closer, 99 percent of the cows placed themselves between it and their calves, often lowering their heads in a defensive posture.[13]

As mentioned in the last chapter, cows can suffer pain. They also seek pleasure. They show this, according to John Webster, "when they lie with their heads raised to the sun on a perfect English summer's day."[14]

Turkeys

Much like the way cows protect their calves, turkey hens protect their broods. Mark Twain saw this once on a hunting trip he made with his uncle:

> The hunter concealed himself and imitated the turkey-call by sucking the air through the leg-bone of a turkey which had previously answered a call like that and lived just long enough to regret it. There is nothing that furnishes a perfect turkey-call except that bone. Another of Nature's treacheries, you see. She is full of them; half the time she doesn't know which she likes best—to betray her child or protect it. In the case of the turkey she is badly mixed: she gives it a bone to be used in getting into trouble, and she also furnishes it with a trick for getting itself out of the trouble again. When a mamma-turkey answers an invitation and finds she has made a mistake in accepting it, she does as the mamma-partridge does—remembers a previous engagement and goes limping and scrambling away, pretending to be very lame; and at the same time she is saying to her not-visible children, "Lie low, keep still, don't expose yourselves; I shall be back as soon as I have beguiled this shabby swindler out of the country."[15]

Much like cows, turkeys enjoy basking in the sunshine.[16] While the adults are resting, youngsters will sometimes begin to play, one bird strutting up to another. Others may join the strutting, punctuated by hops and short bursts of running around.[17]

Contrary to the widespread belief that they're dimwitted, turkeys have the intelligence to maintain relationships in a complex social hierarchy. They recognize many flock mates and remember even flock mates they've been separated from for several months.[18] They also pay close attention to details in their home range. A naturalist who spent a season foraging with wild turkeys found that they often noticed snakes long before he did. One day, a hen traveling behind him gave an alarm call for a snake. He recalled what he saw when he looked in the direction she was craning her head:

> Lying within some thick grass is a one-inch-diameter stick approximately twenty-four inches long and alternately curving. Thinking what a silly mistake for an almost grown wild turkey to make, especially considering the amount of exposure she has had to snakes, I proceed to tell her how silly she is as she continues to alarm putt and crane at the stick. I decide to pull the stick out of the grass to show her how ridiculous she has been and how embarrassed we all are for her. Just as I reach for the stick, something tells me to reconsider. Withdrawing my hand, I peer carefully into the grass, and there within inches of the stick is a rattlesnake in a tight little coil. The hen looks at me and walks away voicing several more putts that sound a little to me like "tsk, tsk."[19]

Chickens

Cows and turkey hens may be very devoted mothers, but we call people who are extremely protective of others "mother hens." The belief that hens are models of maternal care goes back centuries. More than five hundred years ago, an Italian naturalist wrote about the sacrifice hens made to protect their chicks from harm:

They follow their chicks with such great love that, if they see or spy at a distance any harmful animal, such as a kite or a weasel, the hens first gather them under the shadow of their wings, and with this covering they put up such a very fierce defense—striking fear into their opponents in the midst of a frightful clamor, using both wings and beak—that they would rather die for their chicks than seek safety in flight, leaving them to the enemy.[20]

Recent studies have confirmed that mother hens attend to the welfare of their chicks and respond to chicks in distress. In one study, when some chicks looked distressed after being hit by a puff of air, mothers separated from the chicks by a clear panel seemed to share their chicks' discomfort; their heart rates jumped and they clucked maternally to their broods—changes that didn't occur when they themselves were hit with a puff of air. Researchers concluded that the hens shared their chicks' emotional state—a building block of empathy.[21]

Research has also shown that chickens are more intelligent than previously thought.[22] They use memory and a type of logical reasoning to keep track of their group's social hierarchy and navigate through it.[23] When researchers introduced hens to a stranger whom they had seen defeat a bird who was above them in their group's pecking order, they usually decided not to challenge the stranger. If they saw a dominant bird defeat a stranger, though, half of the time they challenged the stranger themselves, suggesting that they understood they had a chance of defeating the new bird.[24]

Pigs

Like cows, turkeys, and chickens, mother pigs are very protective of their young. If a piglet becomes separated from their mother and squeals in distress, she responds by vocalizing herself and going to the piglet.[25]

As they grow older, piglets form social bonds with some littermates. They scamper around and play rough-and-tumble games like the ones chimpanzees play. Often, these shared experiences turn into long-lasting friendships.[26]

In *Animal Farm*, George Orwell repeats the widely held belief that pigs are the most intelligent of all farmed animals; he writes: "The work of teaching and organizing the others fell naturally upon the pigs, who were generally recognized as being the cleverest of the animals."[27] Recent research on cognition in pigs has provided some support for this belief. In one study, pigs who knew the location of a small baited food bucket were released with a dominant pig who had no idea where the food was located. The subordinate pig usually avoided arriving at the bucket at the same time as the dominant pig and sometimes led the latter away from the food.[28]

A pig's social nature can extend to people. Lyall Watson, an ethologist, lived for nine months on a small island in the Indian Ocean, spending much of his time with a pig who answered to the name of Babi (Indonesian for "pig"). He found that Babi had a sweet personality:

> Babi loved to be groomed. Anywhere on her neck or ears was heaven. It turned her legs to jelly and would end with her leaning heavily on me with her eyes closed. And if I moved, she would roll over with all four trotters in the air, waiting to have her belly rubbed. [. . .]
>
> But the thing I found most endearing about this pig was her very real pleasure in being alive. [. . .] Babi was impossibly good-hearted. She was cheerful about absolutely everything, greeting everyone and everything with the same happy grunt. "Hah," I realized, was not just my morning call but an all-purpose salutation, something like "Howzit?" or "What's happening?" She used it on the villagers, on dogs she met on the beach, or on a coconut that fell to earth nearby. It was her affirmation of life taking place. Wherever she was, was the best of all possible worlds. She was an incurable optimist.[29]

It seems unnecessary to add more examples of the emotional, social, and mental lives of these animals. They have pleasures and sorrows, successes and frustrations; they experience curiosity and fear. They're social animals who enjoy the company of family and friends. The young play together. The adults challenge rivals and may try to outwit them.

Clearly, all these animals have lives of their own—lives they try to lead as best they can.

* * *

As we apply James Rachels's ethical principle that one who has a life deserves not to have it taken from them without a good reason, it'll be critical to keep in mind that the quality of life someone enjoys is important, but so is its quantity. Most people think that if the staff at an animal shelter put a young, healthy dog or cat to death—even if they take the animal's life painlessly—that raises moral concerns. Animals raised for food on farms have lives that belong to them, just as dogs and cats do, and taking the life of a young, healthy farmed animal raises similar concerns. As before, let's consider each kind of farmed animal in turn to see if less intensive producers allow animals to enjoy a full, natural life before they are killed.

Chickens

Small-scale farms can provide chickens with a more enriched life than factory farms. For example, this is how a farmers' cooperative in southwest England described the way in which its farmers raised chickens:

> The Devonshire Red™ is a slow growing chicken that has been specially selected for our West Country Free Range Chicken. They are reared using traditional farming methods on small West Country, family run farms. They have access to tree-planted fields, which encourages them to roam and show natural foraging behaviour such as scratching, preening and dust bathing. This allows the chicken to live a fuller, more active and enriched life.[30]

Chickens raised on a small farm, foraging in tree-lined pastures with family and friends and taking dust baths, may have a good quality of life. The brevity of their lives, though, is what raises moral concerns. Although slow-growing breeds of chickens raised for meat are allowed to live twice as long as the fast-growing ones raised on factory farms, they're still slaughtered in their youth, at only about twelve weeks old.[31]

Turkeys

Farmers sometimes raise slower-growing varieties of turkeys not prone to the compromised welfare of the broad-breasted turkeys described in the last chapter. Even if they were raised according to the most humane standards, though, the economics of production would still lead producers to cut their lives short. According to the Livestock Conservancy, an advocacy group that tries to preserve heritage varieties and breeds of livestock, farmers who raise heritage turkeys usually slaughter turkeys when they're only seven months old—a fraction of their natural lifespan.[32]

Pigs

Just as some chickens and turkeys lead more enriched lives on family farms, some pigs lead better lives than do those raised on industrial hog farms. For example, pigs living on Paul Willis's free-range pig farm in Thornton, Iowa, graze or root around with family members and other pigs whose company they enjoy and, if the weather is warm enough, wallow in the mud.[33]

Their enjoyment of life is cut short, though, when they're slaughtered in their youth. Their lot is like the one Old Major tried to warn the young pigs about in *Animal Farm*:

> [E]ven the miserable lives we lead are not allowed to reach their natural span. For myself I do not grumble, for I am one of the lucky ones. I am twelve years old and have had over four hundred children. Such is the natural life of a pig. But no animal escapes the cruel knife in the end. You young porkers who are sitting in front of me, every one of you will scream your lives out at the block within a year.[34]

Cows

Some calves raised for beef have a better quality of life than do most farmed animals. They're allowed to be suckled by and to graze alongside their mothers, play with other calves, and generally enjoy their lives. They're usually slaughtered, though, at only one and a half years old— about a tenth of their natural lifespan.[35]

In all meat production systems, economic factors usually determine when an animal is slaughtered. Even on family farms, producers take animals' lives from them when they're young because that is when they are worth the most. Even if less intensive farmers give animals relatively better lives than do industrial producers, they still take the best part of the animals' lives. Money may not swear on family farms like it does on factory farms, but it talks loudly enough to taint the meat produced.

Dairy and Eggs

It may seem that it would be a different story for cows raised to produce milk, that farmers would try to keep them healthy throughout their lives so they would keep producing milk for as long as possible. And dairy cows are usually allowed to live longer than cattle raised for beef. As Old Major warned, though, they're worked "to the last atom of their strength."[36]

Modern milk production systems place extreme metabolic demands on the cows, partly due to the high yield for which most commercial breeds have been selected. John Webster calculated that one would have to jog for at least six hours a day, day after day, to equal the work rate of a modern dairy cow.[37] Producers work cows so hard that they break down. Even if they haven't broken down yet, they're often sent to slaughter when they've stopped being as productive as younger cows. For example, between 2003 and 2011, dairy cows in an Italian province were slaughtered, on average, shortly after they turned six years old—about a third of their natural lifespan.[38]

Not only do most dairy cows have their lives taken from them when they are young but, to add insult to injury, they're killed after having been repeatedly bred and having had their calves taken from them.[39] Economics drives this practice too. The milk that a calf would nurse from his or her mother is worth more to the producer than the cost of milk replacer and dry feed provided to that calf. Calves not kept for breeding are sold for beef or veal. As Jonathan Balcombe commented: "If we heard of an alien civilization that takes babies away from mothers, eats the babies, and also consumes the mother's milk, we would probably not want to meet them."[40]

People may also eat eggs, believing there's no bloodshed in egg production. That isn't true either. Every year, millions of male chicks born to laying hens are killed shortly after they emerge from their shells because they neither produce eggs nor have the build of the breed that provides the most meat.

Old Major didn't warn the laying hens on Manor Farm about their fate, but it's much like that of dairy cows. They, too, are worked long and hard, then killed when they're worn out, having lived a fraction of their natural lifespan. After laying an egg a day for a year or two, many hens are emaciated and poorly feathered.[41] As they are of little economic value anymore, farmers often just kill them and dispose of their bodies—referring to them, with brutal realism, as "spent."[42] Temple Grandin, the meat industry consultant mentioned earlier, was horrified when she visited a large egg production operation and saw the condition of hens who had reached the end of their productive lives. She remarked in a paper presented at the National Institute of Animal Agriculture in 2001: "The more I learned about the egg industry the more disgusted I got. Some of the practices that had become 'normal' for this industry were overt cruelty. Bad had become normal. Egg producers had become desensitized to suffering."[43]

Fishes

Let's turn now to the issue of whether it's ethical to eat fish;[44] the threshold question, as with terrestrial farmed animals, is whether fishes have the capacity to feel pain. Consistent with the analysis developed by the British Institute of Medical Ethics (mentioned in the last chapter as a reliable way to determine whether an animal can experience pain), in 1999, a professor at the University of London's Royal Veterinary College suggested that three questions had to be answered to decide whether fishes feel pain: Do they have the type of neurological equipment other species use to transmit information about pain levels and to modulate pain? Do they respond to stimuli thought to be painful by acting to avoid said stimuli? And if they take steps to avoid painful stimuli, do they still do that after receiving analgesic medication?[45] To answer these questions, he summarized the research that had been done up to that time, including studies that had found that goldfishes who received a mild electric shock swam in an agitated manner, but after they received a dose of morphine, their agitation disappeared. He also mentioned research that had found that after a goldfish who had similarly been shocked and given morphine received naloxone, an analgesic inhibitor, the analgesic effects of morphine were reversed, and the fish resumed swimming in an agitated way. He concluded: "The appropriate question appears not to be 'do fish feel pain?' but rather, 'what types of pain do fish experience?'"[46]

Studies conducted since then have provided additional evidence of fishes' capacity to suffer pain. In 2003, researchers from the University of Edinburgh located twenty-two nociceptors on the head and face of the rainbow trout. They also found that fishes who received an injection of an irritant in their lips rocked from side to side while resting at the bottom of the tank and rubbed their lips in the gravel there.[47] Another study by one of these researchers, Lynne Sneddon, found that when the fishes received a dose of morphine after an injection of an irritant, they rocked and rubbed their lips much less—evidence that the morphine acted as an analgesic.[48]

Another method scientists use to determine whether animals can suffer pain is to see if, in order to gain access to pain-killing medication, they're willing to do something they normally avoid. This was the method used in the study mentioned earlier, in which researchers allowed chickens to choose between two different feeds—one of which contained a somewhat bitter-tasting analgesic—and found that lame chickens tended to select the feed with the analgesic whereas the birds who weren't lame tended to choose the other feed. Sneddon performed a similar experiment with zebrafishes. She found that, when given a choice, they preferred to spend time in a chamber enriched with gravel, plants, and a view of fishes in an adjacent tank rather than a barren, brightly lit chamber. After Sneddon injected an irritant into the lips of the fishes in one group and added an analgesic to the water in the barren chamber, though, the fishes who received the injection tended to shift their preference to that chamber whereas the others usually continued to prefer the enriched chamber.[49]

Some skeptics argue that fishes can't experience pain, claiming that only animals with a human-like neocortex can become aware of pain.[50] Most scientists do not share this view.[51] In 2005, John Webster assessed the evidence this way:

> [A] powerful portfolio of physiological and behavioural evidence now exists to support the case that fish feel pain and that this feeling matters. In the face of such evidence, any argument to the contrary based on the claim that "fish do not have the right sort of brain" can no longer be called scientific. It is just obstinate.[52]

The pain fishes suffer when caught varies with the method used to capture them. In longline fishing, the pain begins when live fishes are impaled on hooks attached to lines that are set in the water. When other fishes take the bait, they become impaled themselves and languish there for hours, even days, until the lines are hauled in. All the while, they may be attacked by sharks and other predators.[53] As the lines are drawn in toward the boat, marlin, tuna, salmon, and other large fishes may be stabbed with a sharp hook on a pole and lifted aboard.

When trawlers are used, fishes are squeezed together at the tail end of a bag-shaped net dragged behind the boat. Many suffocate in the crush when their gill covers are pressed against the netting or other fishes and they can't breathe. Others die when the compression disrupts their blood flow. In one study, it was found that 29 percent of the fishes were dead when brought aboard a trawler after a two-hour trawl and 61 percent after a four-hour trawl.[54] Many fishes suffer a similar fate when a school is encircled by a seine net hauled behind a boat and they are crushed at the end of the net when it is drawn together and hauled to the surface.[55]

Fishes suffer a different type of injury when netting designed to capture fishes of a certain size is dropped in the sea. When fishes of that size swim into a gill net, they get trapped. They're only able to get their heads through openings in the net and become ensnared as they try to back out. When they struggle to escape, filaments of the net cut through their skin.[56] Like in longline fishing, they remain trapped there, perhaps for days, until a ship returns and the net is hauled in.

In short, every method of capture inflicts great suffering on wild-caught fish.

The same is true of the ways they're slaughtered. In 2011, the most common way commercial fishermen slaughtered fishes was to take them out of the water and let them suffocate.[57] The time it takes for that to happen depends on the species of fish and the temperature. For example, it takes a rainbow trout about ten minutes to lose brain function after being removed from the water when the air temperature is near freezing, but only 2.6 minutes when the temperature is 20°C/68°F.[58]

Salmon, tuna, and other large fishes are often killed by exsanguination. After they're caught, fishermen cut their gills and leave them to bleed to death, which takes several minutes.[59] Evisceration is widely practiced on commercial fishing boats too. Depending on the species, the fish is cut open and some organs or parts of organs are removed. It takes twenty minutes or more for a fish to die that way.[60]

Fishes raised on fish farms often fare little better. Sometimes, workers kill them by cutting their gills and letting them bleed to death. Other times, a worker smashes a fish on the head with a wooden or polypropylene club, or drives a spike into the fish's brain and twists it.[61]

Fish farm operators are working to develop less brutal methods of slaughter. Even if they succeed in developing a method that inflicts no pain or suffering on a fish, the inhumane methods used to capture and kill wild fishes taint farmed fishes too, as they're fed fishmeal and fish oil made from wild-caught fishes—a process known as "fish in, fish out" (i.e.

wild-caught fishes in, farmed fishes out). In 2020, for instance, about a quarter of a kilogram of wild-caught fish was consumed by fishes in the aquaculture industry for every kilogram of farmed fish produced.[62]

Plainly, fishes suffer more pain when slaughtered than most farmed animals do. Victoria Braithwaite, a former colleague of Sneddon's at the University of Edinburgh, noted the disparity in her book, *Do Fish Feel Pain?*:

> We tend not to think too hard about the way we capture fish at sea—it isn't very pretty. We wouldn't accept killing chickens by throwing them into a tank of water and waiting for them to drown, so why don't we object to fish suffocating on trawler decks?[63]

CONCLUSION

We're now ready to return to the question of whether the way we commonly treat animals is justified by the differences between them and us, or is an example of a dominant group exploiting innocent members of a weaker one. To decide, let's see if the treatment has the core features of a supremacist ideology identified in Chapter IV:

1. **Supremacists want something that belongs to members of a group they dominate.**

Throughout human history, people have wanted many things from animals: their labor to work our farms and build our cities, their fur to clothe us, and their bodies to benefit our scientific research. And most people want their flesh as food.

2. **Supremacists use violence and coercion to dominate members of a weaker group and take what they want.**

People so often use violence and coercion to dominate animals that it doesn't seem necessary to discuss this at length. Regarding animal agriculture, for example, almost all farmed animals meet a violent death at an early age after having been confined throughout their life.

3. Supremacists usually try to hide the harm they inflict.

Besides minimizing and trying to evade responsibility for the damage they cause, human supremacists often try to hide it too.[64] Meat producers may have considered Paul and Linda McCartney's prediction—that "if slaughterhouses had glass walls, everyone would be vegetarian"—when deciding to place meat production and processing facilities in remote locations. Although many other factors likely influence such a decision, producers' resistance to disclosing where and how farmed animals are raised,[65] and their attempts to make it a crime to record or publicize what takes place on an industrial farm, suggest that concealment is a significant factor in their decisions.

4. Supremacists disguise their wrongdoing with euphemisms and code words.

We shroud meat consumption with many euphemisms. People eat "pork," "beef," "veal," and "bacon"—not the flesh of pigs or cattle. "Meat" is itself a euphemism for the flesh of an animal. Borrowing a term from plant agriculture, meat producers say that farmed animals are "harvested," not "slaughtered."

In some cases, the euphemism is intended to conceal what actually takes place. For instance, in an editorial titled "Let's Kill 'Slaughtering,'" a meat industry journal once advised readers to call places where animals are slaughtered a "meat plant" or "meat factory," not a "slaughterhouse."[66]

5. Supremacists justify their exploitation by claiming that members of a group they exploit are inferior, so ordinary social rules don't apply.

As Stephen Jay Gould recounted in the chapter on human chauvinism, our need to believe we are superior has led us to erect a series of "golden barriers" that set us apart from and above all other animals. This need is reflected in our use of language. When we speak of "animals," the word usually doesn't include us. And even when we know an animal's gender, we usually refer to the animal as "it"—as if he or she were something, not someone.

The "golden barriers" have changed over the years to accommodate changes in the prevailing moral philosophy. When moral standing was based on having a soul, religious leaders assured people that animals didn't have souls. When the capacity to reason became determinative, Cartesian scientists said other animals lacked rationality.[67] They also assured people like Jeremy Bentham—who believed our moral obligations to others depended on their capacity to suffer—that other animals were machine-like creatures, incapable of feeling or suffering.[68] Although the barriers changed, the result remained the same: whether the ethical rule prohibited harming one who had a soul or rationality or sentience, the rule didn't apply to animals.

6. **In extreme cases, supremacists claim people from another group aren't fully human and treat them like animals.**

As is the case at Manor Farm during Napoleon's reign,[69] we treat all animals equally (as inferior to ourselves) but treat some more equally than others. As Melanie Joy put it, we love dogs, eat pigs, and wear cows.[70]

Farmed animals tend to have a lower moral status than many other animals just because they're used for food. Animals considered food are seen as having reduced mental capacities and are stripped of their known capacities to suffer and to experience emotions.[71] Although few people dispute that these animals can suffer,[72] some adjust their beliefs about whether an animal is sentient when they have a mind to.[73] In one study, some Americans who were unfamiliar with tree kangaroos were told that the animals were cooked as food by Papua New Guineans. People in the control group, who hadn't been told that, ended up attributing more capacity to suffer to the kangaroos than did those in the group who had been told they were food animals.[74]

In some cases, farmed animals' lesser moral status is stated explicitly. For example, an Ohio animal cruelty law provides that it's against the law to keep animals in an enclosure without providing them with wholesome exercise and change of air—unless they are cattle, poultry, pigs, sheep, or goats.[75]

7. Supremacists devise stereotypes and other justifications for the privileges they receive.

In 2003, an American psychologist listed some statements people were making about animals:

> Animals are often described as benefiting from being used, as being content with their lot, as being insensitive to pain, unintelligent, unaware, or wanting to be used. Animal use is frequently described as natural, economically necessary, or inevitable.

As he noted, these statements are strikingly similar to those white supremacists once made to justify slavery.[76] They also bring to mind some claims male supremacists made to legitimize the domination of women. And if they seem familiar, that may be because, as mentioned earlier, they're among the most common reasons people give when asked why they eat meat.

* * *

It turns out that human supremacism is like white supremacism or male supremacism. It, too, springs from a penchant to dominate and exploit members of a weaker group and is wrong in the same way these other supremacist ideologies are.

VIII
Overcoming Supremacism

It almost never feels like prejudice. Instead, it seems fitting and just—the idea that, because of an accident of birth, *our* group (whichever one it is) should have a central position in the social universe. Among Pharaonic princelings and Plantagenet pretenders, children of robber barons and Central Committee bureaucrats, street gangs and conquerors of nations, members of confident majorities, obscure sects, and reviled minorities, this self-serving attitude seems as natural as breathing. It draws sustenance from the same psychic wellsprings as sexism, racism, nationalism, and all the other deadly chauvinisms that plague our species.—**Carl Sagan**[1]

We return to the question of how people can justify harming others, even when what they do is monstrous. In March of 1944, Heinrich Himmler explained why it was necessary to kill Jewish women and children in a speech to senior Nazi officials:

Now I want you to listen carefully to what I have to say here in this select gathering, but never to mention it to anybody. We had to deal with the question: what about the women and children?—I am determined in this matter to come to an absolutely clear-cut solution. I would not feel entitled merely to root out the men—well, let's call a spade a spade, for "root out" say kill or cause to be killed—well I just couldn't risk merely killing the man and allowing the children to grow up as avengers facing our sons and grandsons.[2]

As Himmler understood, when supremacists exploit those they dominate, it often starts an endless cycle of revenge and retaliation, which both sides justify by pointing to what the other has done.

It need not be that way. Robert Schuman, for example, could have dedicated his life to exacting revenge on Germans after the Nazis imprisoned him when he was a member of the French Chamber of Deputies and held him captive for almost a year, first in France and then in Germany. As soon as he escaped and made his way back to France, though, he began putting together a postwar plan to rebuild Europe. While on the run from the Nazis, he surprised a man who was helping him hide by talking about the need for France to work with Germany to rebuild Europe after the war. As the man recalled later:

> One must have lived through those days of struggle and resistance, the daily secret combat and ceaseless threat of confiscation, of concentration camp, perhaps death, to understand how much this project could appear then as an illusion, a mirage, an impossible dream, almost a Utopia. And yet Schuman, in his place of concealment from the Gestapo, was already thinking big, of the necessary reconstruction of this Europe "which we must all make together."[3]

Schuman's chance to help reconcile France and Germany came in 1950, while he was the French minister of foreign affairs. After World War I, the victorious Allies had made their enemies cede resource-rich territories to them, leaving the losers with bitterness and resentment that provided fuel for the next war. Schuman worried that the victors were committing the same mistake after World War II by forcing the Germans to give up control over the coal-rich Saar and Ruhr regions.[4]

To avoid yet another war, Schuman believed Europeans had to put aside all the inflammable hatred, jealousy, and mistrust that had accumulated over the years.[5] He and the head of the French Planning

Fig. 14. Robert Schuman

Commission, Jean Monnet, decided that one way to begin doing that would be to establish a common market for French and West German coal and steel. If successful, it could avoid conflicts about the steel both countries needed to rebuild after the war. However, under Schuman and Monnet's plan, unlike treaties or trade agreements between countries, a group of independent appointees would control the production and sale of coal and steel—matters previously within the sovereignty of each country. This arrangement would not only address the Germans' complaints about their loss of control over coal and steel production in their own country, it would also greatly increase the chance of peace's being maintained, as coal and steel were then vital resources for waging war.

Schuman's ultimate goal, though, was much more ambitious than avoiding conflicts about coal and steel: he wanted to bring about the peaceful unification of Europe. As he explained in a speech he gave in May of 1949, when the Council of Europe was established:

We are carrying out a great experiment, the fulfilment of the same recurrent dream that for ten centuries has revisited the peoples of Europe: creating between them an organization putting an end to war and guaranteeing an eternal peace.[6]

He hoped that the establishment of the European Coal and Steel Community would initiate a step-by-step process of increasing unification—fostered by cultural exchange programs and increased trade and travel between different countries, all of which would lead people to "create a brotherhood that [transcended] all boundaries."[7]

As Schuman had hoped, the six countries that had formed the Coal and Steel Community in 1951 joined together six years later to establish the European Economic Community, a broad common market and customs union that ultimately led to the founding of the European Union in 1993.

* * *

After World War II, many social scientists started searching for ways to reduce group conflicts that can burst into mass violence. Their research yielded insights that have become especially valuable in a time of resurgent nationalism,[8] xenophobia, trade disputes, and violence-stained campaigns by religious and ethnic groups.

Among their most valuable findings are the following:

1. Contact between people from different groups can reduce conflicts between them.

In 1946, an American educator, Theodore Brameld, completed a study about relations between white American students and their African American, Mexican American, and Japanese American peers. He concluded: "[W]here people of various cultures and races freely and genuinely associate, these tensions and difficulties, prejudices and confusions, dissolve; where they do not associate, where they are isolated from one another, there prejudice and conflict grow like a disease."[9]

Eight years later, an American social psychologist, Gordon Allport, wrote a book that was destined to become a classic, *The Nature of Prejudice*, about the beneficial impact of contact between people from different ethnic, racial, or religious groups. Allport mentioned the link between ignorance and discrimination, quoting a wit who defined prejudice as "being down on something you're not up on."[10] Under the right conditions, Allport said, contact can reduce friction and potential misunderstandings between groups. The situations that yield the greatest benefits involve cooperation between people of equal status from different groups, ideally on projects in which they work together to achieve common goals.[11]

Since *The Nature of Prejudice* was published, social scientists from all over the world have studied prejudice and the level of contact between people from different groups to see if the two are related in any way. By 2001, hundreds of such studies, involving a quarter of a million people from thirty-eight countries, had been completed. Using sophisticated statistical tools, two social psychologists conducted a meta-analysis of the data from these studies similar to the analyses of cumulative data from diet-related studies mentioned earlier. They found that contact between people from different groups frequently reduces levels of ethnic, religious, and racial prejudice as Allport said, and can also reduce discrimination based on sexual orientation, mental disability, and physical disability.[12]

Another analysis of these data by the same two researchers shed light on how intergroup contact works to reduce prejudice. The researchers found it likely that prejudice diminishes because people become less anxious about the threats posed by members of the other group and have more empathy for them.[13] Although contact usually improves relations between people from different groups, evidence showed it isn't powerful enough to resolve all conflicts that arise.[14] It may not be able to stop a violent conflict that has begun to rage. However, once the violence is quelled, it can help bring about a measure of reconciliation, as studies of post-conflict contact in Rwanda and Sri Lanka have shown.[15] Intergroup contact isn't the only tool needed in the armory to fight intergroup conflict, in other words, but it is an essential one.

2. **Supranational and global organizations can significantly reduce the harms inflicted by nationalist,[16] ethnic, religious, and political[17] supremacists.**

As mentioned earlier, Robert Schuman and other founders of the first supranational organizations—such as the Coal and Steel Community and the European Economic Community—designed them as an antidote to the nationalist rivalries and resentments that had sparked recurrent European wars and the two world wars.[18] They succeeded. By removing barriers to trade, employment, and travel, European supranational organizations have reduced conflicts between people from different countries—even those who were "hereditary enemies," like France and Germany[19]—to the point that wars between them seem "unthinkable," as Schuman hoped.[20]

Experience has shown that the creation of a supranational identity need not extinguish national or local ones.[21] For instance, a 2017 survey found that although nine out of every ten citizens of the European Union felt attached to their city, town, or village and to their country, more than half said they also felt attached to the union.[22] Schuman was a good example. Although he devoted much of his life to the unification of Europe, he said his strongest ties were to Lorraine, where his ancestors had lived for centuries.[23]

International organizations can help overcome group-based supremacism too. When supranational organizations like the European Union require one form of governance as a condition of membership, international organizations that don't limit membership in that way— such as the United Nations—can have a much broader membership and can foster contact and trade between people from countries with different systems of government. When conflicts between groups erupt into violence, international organizations can help restore peace through mediation, like the initiatives the United Nations undertook to end the civil wars in Sierra Leone and El Salvador.

Finally, global organizations can help solve problems that are beyond the power of any country or supranational organization to solve—such as global warming, pandemics, and the proliferation of nuclear weapons. As Allport pointed out, projects in which people work together on issues of shared concern are among the most beneficial types of intergroup contact because they can help people from different groups recognize they have common interests and a shared humanity.[24]

3. **Supremacists tend to have a "supremacist syndrome" of beliefs and attitudes.**
Gordon Allport was among the first to suggest that prejudicial beliefs and attitudes are often generalized to many outgroups: "If a person is anti-Jewish, he is likely to be anti-Catholic, anti-Negro, anti any outgroup."[25] Four decades later, American researchers developed an instrument called the Social Dominance Scale, which has shed some light on the roots of generalized prejudice. To measure the extent to which a person preferred inequality and hierarchy, the researchers asked respondents to indicate whether they agreed or disagreed with inequality- and dominance-related statements, such as "Some groups of people are simply not the equals of others" and "To get ahead in life, it is sometimes necessary to step on others." Respondents were also asked whether they agreed with contrary statements like "In an ideal world, all nations would be equal" and "If people were treated more equally we would have fewer problems in this country."[26] The initial studies found that those who expressed support for group-based social inequality and dominance were more likely to endorse racist and sexist beliefs too, as well as to support the nationalist belief that people from their country were better than those from other countries and should be able to dominate everyone else.[27,28]

Consistent with Allport's hypothesis about generalized prejudice, subsequent research has shown that people who are prejudiced against one group tend to be prejudiced against other disfavored groups as well. A person's support for group-based dominance and inequality has been found to predict prejudiced attitudes toward a wide array of denigrated groups, including poor people, Latinos, Asians, foreigners, gays, women, Arabs, Muslims, Blacks, Jews, immigrants, and refugees.[29] Other studies have found that social dominants tend to have "supremacist syndrome"—beliefs and attitudes that extend beyond generalized prejudice to encompass a broad range of political opinions usually including support for nationalism[30] and restrictive immigration policies,[31] and opposition to international diplomacy.[32]

Due to the wide range of their dominance-related social and political attitudes, supremacists cause a wide range of harm. Donald Trump's attitudes and beliefs are a timely example of the supremacist syndrome. In addition to his own sexist and racist beliefs and conduct, his administration endorsed nationalism, implemented policies hostile to immigrants, and withdrew from international agreements and treaties, including the Iran Nuclear Agreement, the Paris Climate Agreement, and the Intermediate-Range Nuclear Forces Treaty.

4. Supremacists' penchant for dominance and hierarchy extends to animals and the natural world.

Considering Donald Trump's dismissal of research showing that human activities have contributed to causing global warming, it isn't surprising that, under his administration, the United States withdrew from the Paris Climate Agreement. At first glance, that would appear to be unrelated to his supremacist worldview; in the same way, his administration's weakening of rules protecting the environment and endangered species may seem unrelated.

Studies have shown, however, that people who are prejudiced against disfavored ethnic groups are more likely to have negative attitudes toward animals and to be willing to exploit them for human benefit.[33] The desire to dominate and be superior often leads them to favor exploiting the natural world in unsustainable ways, because their penchant for dominance extends to the human domination of nature.[34]

Because a willingness to exploit the natural world is often linked to prejudice against historically oppressed groups of people, efforts to combat one type of bias can have implications for combating others.[35] Studies have shown that programs that draw attention to the capacities animals share with humans can expand children's moral concern for not only animals but also other people.[36] One study found that a program that emphasized the similarities between animals and humans led Canadian college students to be more concerned about the welfare of immigrants.[37] And a study of 2,255 first- and second-grade students in China found that those who had completed a program of animal- and nature-related activities displayed significantly more prosocial[38] behaviors toward other children than did students who hadn't gone through the program.[39] Encouraging people to be more concerned about the welfare of animals can lead them to be more concerned about the well-being of other people too.[40]

* * *

It may seem like so much pie in the sky to suggest that we can overcome supremacist ideologies that have been the source of so much conflict and bloodshed throughout human history. After all, people have worked for generations to abolish social inequality, but "systems of group-based social inequality continue . . . to maintain their grip around the throats of democratic and egalitarian aspirations."[41] And the recent resurgence of xenophobia, trade wars, nationalism, and harsh reactions to human migration warns that the supremacists' grip may be getting even stronger.

Making the task even more difficult (and critical) to solve is the fact that global warming will increase the pressures that spawn conflict and violence. We're already experiencing levels of international migration never witnessed before,[42] numbers that will grow as the climate warms. A World Bank study estimated that by 2050, there will be 140 million "climate refugees" from sub-Saharan Africa, Latin America, and South Asia.[43]

Considering all of this, eradicating supremacism may seem impossible. It's not. For one thing, we now have a much better understanding of how group-dominance ideologies work than we did even a generation ago. Social scientists have identified and refined tools we can use to reduce intergroup strife and violence. Although increased rates of migration and competition for limited resources will push the pressure points between people from different groups, we now have a better understanding of how positive contact between them can reduce those pressures.[44]

European history suggests that even where supremacist ideologies had driven deep roots, they could be uprooted. Consider, too, the history told in the first three chapters of this book. In the past century and a half, people favoring egalitarian societies have overcome group-dominance ideologies based on nationalism, racism, and sexism. To rephrase a saying attributed to Martin Luther King, Jr., the moral arc of the planet is bending toward equality.[45]

Although governments and large organizations have been able to create more equitable societies, it may seem that one person can't make much of a difference. In a speech Senator Robert Kennedy gave to South African students in 1966—when white supremacists ruled the country and the prospect of change was bleak—he warned against the sense of futility that could come from the "belief that there [was] nothing one man or woman [could] do against the enormous array of the world's ills." He continued:

> Few will have the greatness to bend history itself; but each of us can work to change a small portion of events, and in the total of all those acts will be written the history of this generation. [. . .] It is from numberless diverse acts of courage and belief that human history is shaped. Each time a man stands up for an ideal, or acts to improve the lot of others, or strikes out against injustice, he sends forth a tiny ripple of hope, and crossing each other from a million different centers of energy and daring those ripples build a current which can sweep down the mightiest walls of oppression and resistance.[46]

When Kennedy gave this speech, Nelson Mandela was imprisoned by white supremacists. Twenty-eight years later, he was sworn in as the president of South Africa.

WHAT WE CAN DO

Here are some things each of us can do to bend our world toward equality and away from a cutthroat, supremacist-dominated dystopia:

1. **Participate in and support programs that foster positive contact between people from different groups.**
The founders of the United Nations believed that sustaining peace after World War II depended on increasing contact between people from different groups to dispel the suspicion and mistrust that could arise when they were unfamiliar with each other's ways. As expressed in the constitution of the United Nations Educational, Scientific, and Cultural Organization (UNESCO):

> That since wars begin in the minds of men, it is in the minds of men that the defences of peace must be constructed;
>
> That ignorance of each other's ways and lives has been a common cause, throughout the history of mankind, of that suspicion and mistrust between the peoples of the world through which their differences have all too often broken into war;
>
> That the great and terrible war which has now ended was a war made possible by the denial of the democratic principles of the dignity, equality and mutual respect of men, and by the propagation, in their place, through ignorance and prejudice, of the doctrine of the inequality of men and races.[47]

Since that time, hundreds of studies undertaken all over the world have consistently shown that contact between people from different groups can indeed be a powerful tool to reduce levels of prejudice and conflict.[48] Skeptics' belief that intergroup contact isn't powerful enough to affect the attitudes of the most biased people has proven to be mistaken. Studies have shown that even intolerant ideologues can benefit from contact between groups at least as much as less prejudiced people.[49] They've also shown that the beneficial effect of intergroup contact holds true across different cultures and that intergroup contact can reduce prejudice directed at many different groups.[50]

Analyses of data from these studies revealed that contact reduces prejudice the most under the conditions Gordon Allport identified in *The Nature of Prejudice*. Other studies have added another requirement. For the optimal reduction of intergroup bias and conflict, the contact must be more than just a pleasant experience; it must address (and potentially redress) the social inequality[51] that can inflame members of dominated groups. Whenever people from an elite group get more than their fair share of valued resources, those who get less tend to resent it,[52] not unlike the capuchin monkeys in Frans de Waal's inequity study, who protested when they saw a peer get a grape for performing the same task they had, for which they had only received a piece of cucumber. Although contact between groups can scale back prejudice, it seems to be not powerful enough to make members of dominated groups forget the discrimination and inequality they've suffered. Reducing levels of prejudice can, however, lead groups to work together to eradicate the underlying inequality.

Things we can do: To foster positive contact between groups, we can participate in cultural exchange programs, join intercultural activities in our community, or simply become friends with people from other groups.

2.   Support humanitarian policies and programs for refugees.

People in record numbers are now fleeing their homeland to escape from violence and persecution. The vast majority of refugees flee to a country near their own. This has resulted in some countries with limited resources providing a place for millions of refugees to live, while others with much more ability to help welcome relatively few. According to statistics compiled by the United Nations, in 2016, people living in countries that provided shelter to more than eight million international refugees had only 2.5 percent of the world's income, while the United States—with more than 25 percent of global income—hosted fewer than 300,000.[53,54]

This isn't fair. Or sustainable.

Although some refugees can return to their country of origin, while others manage to make a permanent home in the country where they've found asylum, the best option for many refugees is resettlement in a third country. In 2017, more than 1.2 million refugees needed resettlement, but only 6 percent of them found a country that welcomed them.[55] People living in countries that provide homes for an equitable share of international refugees not only enrich themselves by increasing contact with people from other groups, they also encourage countries hosting large numbers of refugees to keep borders open by sharing the responsibility to help refugees.

Things we can do: We can help refugees living in our community and financially support organizations like the United Nations Refugee Agency and nongovernmental refugee assistance organizations. If our own country isn't resettling its fair share of refugees, we can work to get it to do that.

3. Support environmental and humane education programs for children.

As mentioned earlier, studies have found that people who endorse social inequality and dominance by one group are also more likely to support the exploitation of the natural environment in unsustainable ways.[56]

Programs that include animal- and nature-related activities can have a beneficial spillover effect on a child's relationships with other children, as shown by the program mentioned earlier that increased the prosocial behavior of first- and second-grade students in China.[57] Another study found that Australian college students who expressed the most concern for the welfare of animals tended to have more empathy for the welfare of other people too, prompting the study's authors to suggest that humane education programs could be used to break cycles of antisocial behavior and engender empathy between people.[58]

Things we can do: We can work to make sure environmental and humane education programs that emphasize the capacities other animals share with humans are part of every young person's education.[59] Positive contact with farmed animals through activities and visits to farm sanctuaries may prove especially valuable.[60]

4. **Support public officials who work to establish egalitarian policies and programs, and discourage those who don't.**

Overcoming supremacism begins with recognizing that supremacist ideologies aren't only wrong but endanger all of us by igniting conflict and violence that can spread like wildfire. The most durable rejection of supremacism occurs when public officials repudiate the exploitation of one group by a stronger one, as the Belgian Parliament did when it took over governance of the Congo region from Leopold, and as the British Parliament did when it enfranchised women.

Politicians don't often admit it when they prefer social inequality and their own group's dominance,[61] but there are often several telltale behaviors that betray their real attitudes and beliefs. Those high in social dominance can suffer from a supremacist syndrome that leads them to have racist[62] and sexist beliefs,[63] support exploitation of the natural world in unsustainable ways,[64] deny the climate crisis,[65] and support nationalist policies.[66] Officials who favor egalitarian policies and programs can reduce conflict by fighting racism and sexism, working to stop human exploitation of the natural world, and supporting multilateral organizations.

Things we can do: We can work for and financially support officials and candidates who support and implement egalitarian programs; in contrast, we can work against those who support inequality and dominance by an elite group.

5. **Reduce our own carbon footprint.**

The climate crisis is irrefutable evidence that when it comes to our planet's future, we're all in this together. Because people living in less prosperous countries usually contribute less to the continued warming of the Earth, they usually have fewer opportunities to mitigate it.[67] Those of us who live in countries that are better off can (and need to) do our part. Global warming can serve as a spark that ignites social kindling by causing groups to compete for increasingly scarce resources—like water, food, and arable land.[68] However, our shared fate can also bring us together in cooperative initiatives to fight the climate crisis. Individual countries can help a great deal by exceeding the targeted levels of carbon-footprint reduction they agreed to reach under the Paris Climate Agreement. We all can make it easier for our country to do that by reducing our own carbon footprint.

Things we can do: We can recycle what we use; we can reduce our use and waste of energy, water, and food; and we can refrain from consuming meat, eggs, and dairy products. As Michael Pollan said: "The wonderful thing about food is you get three votes a day. Every one of them has the potential to change the world."[69]

Afterword
Beyond Supremacism

Human beings are not wicked by nature. We have enough intelligence, goodwill, generosity, and enterprise to turn Earth into a paradise both for ourselves and for the biosphere that gave us birth. We can plausibly accomplish that goal, at least be well on the way, by the end of the present century. The problem holding everything up thus far is that *Homo sapiens* is an innately dysfunctional species. [. . .]

Our species' dysfunction has produced the hereditary myopia of which we are all uncomfortably familiar. People find it hard to care about other people beyond their own tribe or country, and even then past one or two generations. It is harder still to be concerned about animal species—except for dogs, horses, and others of the very few we have domesticated to be our servile companions.—Edward O. Wilson[1]

Supremacism is a product of the human myopia Edward O. Wilson was writing about. We have a natural affinity for those like us, for our kin and others close to us. Until recently, though, what we knew about our family history only extended back a few generations. Once we began to understand the genetic code, though, we became able to trace our history back to the dawn of life on our planet. Now, we know that we're related to every other animal who lives with us on Earth—that, as Richard Dawkins said, "we are all cousins."[2]

Some of our cousins are closer to us than others. To use another of Dawkins's metaphors, about twenty-five million generations ago, we and cows shared great-grandparents, whose descendants we now slaughter for food.[3]

We don't have to be time travelers, though, to see how closely related we are to other species and how much we owe to our common ancestors; we need only look at our own bodies. For example, 175 million generations ago,[4] evolution produced fishes with skeletal structures that we've inherited. As Neil Shubin, an American biologist and paleontologist, put it: "[T]he earliest creature to have the bones of our upper arm, our forearm, even our wrist and palm, also had scales and fin webbing. That creature was a fish."[5]

To move beyond supremacism, we need not forsake our loyalty to those we see as our kin but can just update our family tree in light of our new knowledge. It won't be the first time we've done this. At the dawn of history, we were loyal to our family and those who lived and traveled with us. Over time, though, we've slowly expanded the boundary of our group to include first the tribe, local community, and country, then supranational and international communities in recent years. We can see our history as a slowly dawning awareness that despite vast differences in culture, religion, and forms of government, people everywhere want and

---

The Mismeasure of Animals

We patronize them for their incompleteness, for their tragic fate of having taken form so far below ourselves. And therein we err, and greatly err. For the animal shall not be measured by man. In a world older and more complete than ours they move finished and complete, gifted with extensions of the senses we have lost or never attained, living by voices we shall never hear. They are not brethren, they are not underlings; they are other nations, caught with ourselves in the net of life and time, fellow prisoners of the splendor and travail of the earth.—Henry Beston[6]

need the same things: nutritious food for themselves and their family, clean air and water, effective medical care, freedom from oppression, and a community free of violence and war.

Our myopia has also led us to believe that we are exceptional because our cleverness enables us to do things no other animal can. Although that cleverness may seem unique, it's not. As Stephen Jay Gould wrote: "[E]ach species is unique in its own way: shall we judge among the dance of the bees, the song of the humpback whale, and human intelligence?"[7] If having an exceptional capacity entitles a species to special moral status, all of our cousins deserve that status too.

We're also beginning to appreciate that life itself is exceptional. We now know that our sun is just one of quadrillions, that there are more stars in the universe than grains of sand on our beaches.[8] And we haven't found evidence of life anywhere else.

Carl Sagan once commented that leaders of major religions could have responded to discoveries about the immensity and elegance of the universe by saying, "This is better than we thought! The Universe is much bigger than our prophets said, grander, more subtle, more elegant." Instead, they said, "No, no, no! My god is a little god and I want him to stay that way."[9]

The same could be said regarding recent discoveries about our family tree. Rather than respond by saying, "Our family is a close-knit little family and we want it to stay that way!" we should say, "This is better than we thought! Although our universe seems barren and desolate, our home planet teems with life. And everyone who lives here is related to us. So we'll take care of them and treat them with the respect they deserve. After all, they're family!"

Notes

Introduction

1   William Graham Sumner, *Folkways: A Study of the Sociological Importance of Usages, Manners, Customs, Mores, and Morals* (Boston: Ginn and Company, 1906), 11.

2   Roger Manvell and Heinrich Fraenkel, *Heinrich Himmler: The Sinister Life of the Head of the SS and Gestapo* (New York: Skyhorse Publishing, 2007), 132.

3   Peter Longerich, *Heinrich Himmler*, translated by Jeremy Noakes and Lesley Sharpe (Oxford: Oxford University Press, 2012), 304.

4   Lawrence Rees, *Auschwitz: A New History* (New York: Public Affairs, 2005), 45–46; Timothy Snyder, *Black Earth: The Holocaust as History and Warning* (New York: Tim Duggan Books, 2015), 172–173.

5   Martin Gilbert, *The Holocaust: A History of the Jews of Europe During the Second World War* (New York: Henry Holt, 1985), 191.

6   Ibid., 192.

7   Raul Hilberg, *The Destruction of the European Jews* (Chicago: Quadrangle Books, 1967), 619.

8   Gilbert, *The Holocaust: A History of the Jews of Europe*, 678.

9   Rudolf Höss, *Death Dealer: The Memoirs of the SS Kommandant at Auschwitz*, edited by Steven Paskuly and translated by Andrew Pollinger (New York: Da Capo Press, 1996), 159.

10 Albert Bandura, *Moral Disengagement: How People Do Harm and Live with Themselves* (New York: Worth Publishers, 2016), 1–3.

11 *Nazi Conspiracy and Aggression* (Washington: U.S. Government Printing Office, 1946), Volume IV, 559.

12 While some Nazis claimed there is an "Aryan" race, that is a fiction. Any belief that people can be validly separated into racial groups is mistaken, too. However, for brevity's sake, the term "race" will be used in this book to refer to such a belief.

13 For simplicity's sake, Leopold II will be referred to as Leopold.

14 Arthur Conan Doyle, *Crime of the Congo* (London: Hutchinson & Co., 1909), 55.

15 Ch. Didier Gondola, *The History of Congo* (Westport, Connecticut: Greenwood Publishing Group, 2002), 75.

16 The ninth edition of James Rachels's *The Elements of Moral Philosophy* was published in 2018 by McGraw-Hill. Rachels wrote the first four editions. Since his death in 2003, his son, Stuart, has periodically updated the book.

17 James Rachels, *Created from Animals: The Moral Implications of Darwinism* (Oxford: Oxford University Press, 1990), 129.

I.1. The Holocaust in Hungary: Mission Impossible

1 Henryk Świebocki, "Prisoner Escapes," in *Anatomy of the Auschwitz Death Camp*, edited by Yisrael Gutman and Michael Berenbaum (Indianapolis: Indiana University Press, 1994), 503.

2 Rudolf Vrba and Alan Bestic, *I Cannot Forgive* (New York: Grove Press, 1964), 194–195.

3 Martin Gilbert, *The Holocaust: A History of the Jews of Europe During the Second World War* (New York: Henry Holt, 1985), 658–659.

4 Martin Gilbert, *Auschwitz and the Allies* (New York: Holt, Rinehart, and Winston, 1981), 341.

5 Raul Hilberg, *The Destruction of the European Jews*, 3rd edition (New Haven: Yale University Press, 2003), 1038.

6 Gideon Hausner, *Justice in Jerusalem* (New York: Shocken Books, 1968), 166.

7 Gilbert, *The Holocaust: A History of the Jews of Europe*, 686.

8 Vrba and Bestic, *I Cannot Forgive*, 198–200.

9 Rudolf Höss, *Death Dealer: The Memoirs of the SS Kommandant at Auschwitz*, edited by Steven Paskuly and translated by Andrew Pollinger (New York: Da Capo Press, 1996), 113.

10 Świebocki, "Prisoner Escapes," 503–504.

11 Vrba and Bestic, *I Cannot Forgive*, 214–215.

12 Höss, *Death Dealer*, 113–114; Lawrence Rees, *Auschwitz: A New History* (New York: Public Affairs, 2005), 141.

13 Vrba and Bestic, *I Cannot Forgive*, 214–215.

14 Ibid., 154–163.

15 Ibid., 137–147.

16 Rees, *Auschwitz: A New History*, 45–46; Timothy Snyder, *Black Earth: The Holocaust as History and Warning* (New York: Tim Duggan Books, 2015), 42.

17 The prisoner Father Kolbe offered to replace, Franciszek Gajowniczek, survived Auschwitz. Świebocki, "Prisoner Escapes," 505.

18 Vrba and Bestic, *I Cannot Forgive*, 202–205.

19 Rudolf Vrba and Alfréd Wetzler, "Report of Rudolf Vrba and Alfred Wetzler," in *London Has Been Informed: Reports by Auschwitz Escapees*, edited by Henryk Świebocki (Oświścim: The Auschwitz-Birkenau State Museum, 1997), 177–178.

20 Vrba and Bestic, *I Cannot Forgive*, 201–202.

21 Ibid., 221.

22 Ibid., 222.

23 Ibid., 225.

24 Ibid., 225–226.

25 Ibid., 226–228.

26 Ibid., 232.

27 Ibid., 230–234.

28 Ibid., 235.

29 Ibid., 238.

30 Rudolf Vrba, "The Preparations for the Holocaust in Hungary: An Eyewitness Account," in *The Nazis' Last Victims: The Holocaust in Hungary*, edited by Randolph L. Braham and Scott Miller (Detroit: Wayne State University Press, 1998), 74.

31 Vrba and Bestic, *I Cannot Forgive*, 239–241.

32 Ibid., 241–242.

33 Ibid., 246–247.

34 Henryk Świebocki, "Auschwitz: What Did the World Know During the War?" in *London Has Been Informed*, 39.

35 Randolph L. Braham, *The Politics of Genocide: The Holocaust in Hungary* (New York: Columbia University Press, 2016), 961.

36 Vrba and Wetzler, "Report of Rudolf Vrba and Alfred Wetzler" in *London Has Been Informed*, 244–245.

37 Braham, *The Politics of Genocide*, 961.

38 Ibid., 962.

39 Vrba and Bestic, *I Cannot Forgive*, 250.

40 Ibid.

41 Ibid., 251.

42 Before joining a Slovakian partisan unit fighting the Nazis, Rosenberg (by then having adopted the name on his false identification papers, Rudolf Vrba) went to see his mother, who lived in a small city in western Slovakia. She did

not know that he had been imprisoned at Auschwitz and reprimanded him for not having written to her or sending her his address. She quickly rattled off questions: Where had he been living? Did he have a job? Who did his laundry? As soon as he could get a word in edgewise, Rosenberg quietly said, "Please, Mama, sit down for a moment. I've a good deal to tell you." Vrba and Bestic, *I Cannot Forgive*, 255–256.

I.2. The Holocaust in Hungary: The Master of Mass Murder Arrives in Hungary

1   David Cesarani, *Becoming Eichmann: Rethinking the Life, Crimes, and Trial of a "Desk Murderer"* (New York: Da Capo Press, 2004), 165.

2   Thomas L. Sakmyster, Hungary's *Admiral on Horseback: Miklos Horthy, 1918–1944* (Boulder, Colorado: East European Monographs, 1994), 310–311.

3   Ibid., 311.

4   Ibid., 320.

5   Randolph L. Braham, *The Politics of Genocide: The Holocaust in Hungary* (New York: Columbia University Press, 2016), 263.

6   Ibid., 282.

7   Sakmyster, *Hungary's Admiral on Horseback*, 308.

8   Ibid.

9   Ibid., 400.

10 Braham, *The Politics of Genocide*, 284–285.

11 Raul Hilberg, *The Destruction of the European Jews* (Chicago: Quadrangle Books, 1967), 309.

12 Christopher R. Browning, *The Path to Genocide: Essays on Launching the Final Solution* (Cambridge: Cambridge University Press, 1995), 17.

13 Martin Gilbert, *The Holocaust: A History of the Jews of Europe During the Second World War* (New York: Henry Holt, 1985), 168.

14 Gideon Hausner, *Justice in Jerusalem* (New York: Shocken Books, 1968), 65.

15 Hilberg, *The Destruction of the European Jews* (1967), 263.

16 Ibid.

17 Debórah Dwork and Robert Jan van Pelt, *Holocaust: A History* (New York: W.W. Norton, 2002), 281.

18 Hilberg, *The Destruction of the European Jews* (1967), 265.

19 Mark Roseman, *The Villa, the Lake, the Meeting: Wannsee and the Final Solution* (London: Penguin, 2002), 111, 113, 118.

20 Ibid., 1.

21 Braham, *The Politics of Genocide*, 457.

22 Ibid., 434.

23   Ibid., 431, 433.

24   Ibid., 1508.

25   Sakmyster, *Hungary's Admiral on Horseback*, 336.

26   Braham, *The Politics of Genocide*, 459.

27   Ibid., 474.

28   Ibid., 477.

29   Ibid., 442.

30   C. A. Macartney, *October Fifteenth: A History of Modern Hungary, 1929–1945* (Edinburgh: Edinburgh University Press, 1956), 2:246, quoted in Braham, *The Politics of Genocide*, 442.

31   Braham, *The Politics of Genocide*, 469.

32   Ibid., 470.

33   Roger Manvell and Heinrich Fraenkel, *Heinrich Himmler: The Sinister Life of the Head of the SS and Gestapo* (New York: Skyhorse Publishing, 2007), 135.

34   See *Eichmann in Hungary: Documents*, edited by Jeno Levai (Budapest: Panama Press, 1961), 202–205.

35   Jeno Levai, *Black Book on the Martyrdom of Hungarian Jewry* (Zurich: Central European Times Publishing Co., 1948), 108.

36   Braham, *The Politics of Genocide*, 523–529.

37   Ibid., 618.

38   Ibid., 617.

39   Braham, *The Politics of Genocide*, 494.

40   Ibid.

41   Zoltán Vági, László Csösz, and Gábor Kádár, *The Holocaust in Hungary: Evolution of a Genocide* (Lanham, Maryland: AltaMira Press, 2013), 82.

42   Randolph L. Braham, *Eichmann and the Destruction of Hungarian Jewry* (New York: Twayne Publishers, Inc., 1961), 24–25.

43   Braham, *The Politics of Genocide*, 775.

44   Ibid., 775.

45   *Eichmann in Hungary: Documents*, edited by Jeno Levai, 126.

46   Martin Gilbert, *The Routledge Atlas of the Second World War* (New York: Routledge, 2009), 148, 153.

47   Zoltán Szabó, "The Auschwitz Reports: Who Got Them and When?" in *The Auschwitz Reports and the Holocaust in Hungary*, edited by Randolph L. Braham and William J. vanden Heuvel (Columbia University Press, 2011), 112–113; Braham, *The Politics of Genocide*, 1018.

48   Lawrence Rees, *Auschwitz: A New History* (New York: Public Affairs, 2005), 45–46; Timothy Snyder, *Black Earth: The Holocaust as History and Warning*

(New York: Tim Duggan Books, 2015), 242.

49 Martin Gilbert, *Auschwitz and the Allies* (New York: Holt, Rinehart, and Winston, 1981), 341.

50 Ibid., 233.

51 Braham, *The Politics of Genocide*, 1019.

52 Sakmyster, *Hungary's Admiral on Horseback*, 350.

53 Braham, *The Politics of Genocide*, 1019.

54 Ibid., 964.

55 Ibid., 972.

56 Sakmyster, *Hungary's Admiral on Horseback*, 349.

57 Braham, *The Politics of Genocide*, 1020.

58 Levai, *Black Book on the Martyrdom of Hungarian Jewry*, 243.

59 Braham, *The Politics of Genocide*, 775, 1704.

60 Ibid., 1026–1027.

61 Miklós Horthy, *Admiral Miklós Horthy: Memoirs*, annotated by Andrew L. Simon (Safety Harbor, Florida: Simon Publications, 2000), 272.

62 Braham, *The Politics of Genocide*, 1027.

63 Ibid., 1028.

64 Deborah S. Cornelius, *Hungary in World War II: Caught in the Cauldron* (New York: Fordham University Press, 2011), 311.

65 Ibid., 311–312.

66 Braham, *The Politics of Genocide*, 1704–1705.

67 Randolph Braham, "Hungary: The Controversial Chapter of the Holocaust," 13 November 2011, accessed on September 2, 2019, https://www.youtube.com/watch?v=fy0URzSpjaM.

68 Gilbert, The *Routledge Atlas of the Second World War*, 151.

69 Braham, *The Politics of Genocide*, 1703.

I.3. The Holocaust in Hungary: Reprieve

1 Guido Knopp, *Hitler's Hitmen*, translated by Angus McGeoch (Stroud, Gloucestershire: Sutton Publishing, 2006), 35.

2 Bengt Jangfeldt, *The Hero of Budapest: The Triumph and Tragedy of Raoul Wallenberg*, translated by Harry D. Watson and Bengt Jangfeldt (London: I. B. Tauris, 2014), 153.

3 Alex Kershaw, *The Envoy: The Epic Rescue of the Last Jews of Europe in the Desperate Closing Months of World War II* (Cambridge, Massachusetts: Da Capo Press, 2010), 59.

4   Paul A. Levine, *Raoul Wallenberg in Budapest: Myth, History and Holocaust* (London: Vallentine Mitchell, 2010), 107.

5   Ibid., 137.

6   Jangfeldt, *The Hero of Budapest*, 131.

7   Ibid., 136.

8   Ibid.

9   Levine, *Raoul Wallenberg in Budapest*, 143.

10 Ibid., 142–143.

11 Ibid., 155.

12 Randolph L. Braham, *The Politics of Genocide: The Holocaust in Hungary* (New York: Columbia University Press, 2016), 1033.

13 Ibid., 1041.

14 Zoltán Vági, László Csösz, and Gábor Kádár, *The Holocaust in Hungary: Evolution of a Genocide* (Lanham, Maryland: AltaMira Press, 2013, 140–141.

15 Jeno Levai, *Black Book on the Martyrdom of Hungarian Jewry* (Zurich: Central European Times Publishing Co., 1948), 257.

16 Braham, *The Politics of Genocide*, 1042.

17 Ibid., 1043.

18 Jangfeldt, *The Hero of Budapest*, 171.

19 Per Anger, *With Raoul Wallenberg in Budapest: Memories of the War Years in Hungary*, translated by David Mel Paul and Margareta Paul (Washington, D.C.: Holocaust Library, 1981), 38–39.

20 Jangfeldt, *The Hero of Budapest*, 171.

21 Ingrid Carlberg, *Raoul Wallenberg: The Heroic Life and Mysterious Disappearance of the Man Who Saved Thousands of Hungarian Jews from the Holocaust*, translated by Ebba Segeberg (New York: MacLehose Press, 2015), 234.

22 Elenore Lester, *Wallenberg: The Man in the Iron Web* (New York: Prentice Hall Direct, 1984), 89.

23 Anger, *With Raoul Wallenberg in Hungary*, 35.

24 Lester, *Wallenberg: The Man in the Iron Web*, 89.

25 Levine, *Raoul Wallenberg in Budapest*, 228–229.

26 Ibid., 108.

27 Lester, *Wallenberg: The Man in the Iron Web*, 89.

28 Levine, *Raoul Wallenberg in Budapest*, 230.

29 Carlberg, *Raoul Wallenberg*, 267.

30 Lester, *Wallenberg: The Man in the Iron Web*, 89–90.

31   Levine, *Raoul Wallenberg in Budapest*, 185.
32   Randolph L. Braham, *Eichmann and the Destruction of Hungarian Jewry* (New York: Twayne Publishers, Inc., 1961), 31.
33   Thomas L. Sakmyster, *Hungary's Admiral on Horseback: Miklos Horthy, 1918–1944* (Boulder, Colorado: East European Monographs, 1994), 357.
34   Ibid.
35   Ibid., 358.
36   Guido Knopp, *Hitler's Hitmen*, 37.
37   Braham, *The Politics of Genocide*, 1063.
38   Vági, Csösz & Kádár, *The Holocaust in Hungary: Evolution of a Genocide*, 141–142.
39   Ibid., 142.
40   Sakmyster, *Hungary's Admiral on Horseback*, 359–360.
41   Levine, *Raoul Wallenberg in Budapest*, 208.
42   Ibid., 236.
43   Braham, *The Politics of Genocide*, 1058.
44   Lester, *Wallenberg: The Man in the Iron Web*, 91–92.
45   Ibid., 92.
46   Braham, *The Politics of Genocide*, 1066.
47   Ibid., 1067.
48   Ibid., 1067–1068.
49   Sakmyster, *Hungary's Admiral on Horseback*, 360.
50   Ibid.
51   Braham, *The Politics of Genocide*, 1069.
52   Ibid., 1070.
53   Ibid., 1069.
54   Jeno Levai, *Black Book on the Martyrdom of Hungarian Jewry* (Zurich: Central European Times Publishing Co., 1948), 243.
55   Levine, *Raoul Wallenberg in Budapest*, 260.
56   Jangfeldt, *The Hero of Budapest*, 191.

I.4. The Holocaust in Hungary: The Bloodhound Returns

1   Tommy Lapid in John Bierman, *Righteous Gentile: The Story of Raoul Wallenberg, Missing Hero of the Holocaust* (New York: Viking Press, 1981), 89.
2   Randolph L. Braham, *The Politics of Genocide: The Holocaust in Hungary* (New York: Columbia University Press, 2016), 1069.
3   Ibid., 1100.
4   Ibid., 1104.

5   Ibid., 1103.

6   Ibid., 1107.

7   Ibid., 1108.

8   Thomas L. Sakmyster, *Hungary's Admiral on Horseback: Miklos Horthy, 1918–1944* (Boulder, Colorado: East European Monographs, 1994), 378.

9   Ibid., 379–380.

10 Bengt Jangfeldt, *The Hero of Budapest: The Triumph and Tragedy of Raoul Wallenberg*, translated by Harry D. Watson and Bengt Jangfeldt (London: I. B. Tauris, 2014), 207.

11 Ibid., 208.

12 Paul A. Levine, *Raoul Wallenberg in Budapest: Myth, History and Holocaust* (London: Vallentine Mitchell, 2010), 306.

13 Elenore Lester, *Wallenberg: The Man in the Iron Web* (New York: Prentice Hall Direct, 1984), 105.

14 *Eichmann in Hungary: Documents*, edited by Jeno Levai (Budapest: Panama Press, 1961), 146.

15 Braham, *The Politics of Genocide*, 1115.

16 "*Judenrein*" was a term Nazis used to describe an area "cleansed" of Jews.

17 Braham, *The Politics of Genocide*, 1114.

18 Levine, *Raoul Wallenberg in Budapest*, 305.

19 Ibid., 308.

20 Jangfeldt, *The Hero of Budapest*, 213.

21 Ibid., 212.

22 Ibid.

23 Braham, *The Politics of Genocide*, 1123.

24 Zoltán Vági, László Csösz, and Gábor Kádár, *The Holocaust in Hungary: Evolution of a Genocide* (Lanham, Maryland: AltaMira Press, 2013), 156.

25 Bierman, *Righteous Gentile*, 82.

26 Ibid., 83–84.

27 Bettina Stangneth, *Eichmann Before Jerusalem: The Unexamined Life of a Mass Murderer*, translated by Ruth Martin (New York: Alfred A. Knopf, 2014), 264.

28 David Cesarani, *Becoming Eichmann: Rethinking the Life, Crimes, and Trial of a "Desk Murderer"* (New York: Da Capo Press, 2004), 191.

29 Jangfeldt, *The Hero of Budapest*, 241.

30 Ibid., 244; Sharon Linnéa, *Raoul Wallenberg: The Man Who Stopped Death* (Philadelphia: The Jewish Publication Society,1993), 95–96.

31 Jeno Levai, *Black Book on the Martyrdom of Hungarian Jewry* (Zurich: Central European Times Publishing Co., 1948), 379.

32 Raoul Wallenberg, *Letters and Dispatches: 1924–1944* (New York: Skyhorse Publishing, 1987) 265–267.

33 Ingrid Carlberg, *Raoul Wallenberg: The Heroic Life and Mysterious Disappearance of the Man Who Saved Thousands of Hungarian Jews from the Holocaust*, translated by Ebba Segeberg (New York: MacLehose Press, 2015), 328–329.

34 Braham, *The Politics of Genocide*, 1157.

I.5. The Holocaust in Hungary: The Inferno

1 Randolph L. Braham, *The Politics of Genocide: The Holocaust in Hungary* (New York: Columbia University Press, 2016), 1440.

2 Ibid., 1161.

3 Kristián Ungváry, *The Siege of Budapest: 100 Days in World War II*, translated by Ladislaus Löb (New Haven: Yale University Press, 2002), 284–285.

4 Braham, *The Politics of Genocide*, 1162.

5 Ibid., 1163.

6 Bengt Jangfeldt, *The Hero of Budapest: The Triumph and Tragedy of Raoul Wallenberg*, translated by Harry D. Watson and Bengt Jangfeldt (London: I. B. Tauris, 2014), 279.

7 Ibid., 230.

8 Ungváry, *The Siege of Budapest*, 300.

9 Jangfeldt, *The Hero of Budapest*, 278.

10 Alex Kershaw, *The Envoy: The Epic Rescue of the Last Jews of Europe in the Desperate Closing Months of World War II* (Cambridge, Massachusetts: Da Capo Press, 2010), 145–146.

11 Braham, *The Politics of Genocide*, 1167.

12 Jangfeldt, *The Hero of Budapest*, 240.

13 Braham, *The Politics of Genocide*, 1388.

14 Ibid., 1168.

15 Ibid.

16 John Bierman, *Righteous Gentile: The Story of Raoul Wallenberg, Missing Hero of the Holocaust* (New York: Viking Press, 1981), 115.

17 Ungváry, *The Siege of Budapest*, 302.

18 Braham, *The Politics of Genocide*, 1170.

19 Ungváry, *The Siege of Budapest*, 86.

20 Braham, *The Politics of Genocide*, 1170.

21 Ungváry, *The Siege of Budapest*, 303.

22 Kershaw, *The Envoy*, 153–154.

23   Jangfeldt, *The Hero of Budapest*, 301.
24   Ibid., 249.
25   Ibid., 250.
26   Jangfeldt, *The Hero of Budapest*, 301.
27   Braham, *The Politics of Genocide*, 1507.
28   Ibid.; Jeno Levai, *Black Book on the Martyrdom of Hungarian Jewry* (Zurich: Central European Times Publishing Co., 1948), 474.

I. The Holocaust in Hungary: Epilogue

1   Martin Gilbert in the Foreword to *Alfred Wetzler, Escape from Hell: The True Story of the Auschwitz Protocol*, edited by Péter Várni and translated by Ewald Osers (New York: Berghahn Books, 2007), vii.
2   Thomas L. Sakmyster, *Hungary's Admiral on Horseback: Miklos Horthy, 1918–1944* (Boulder, Colorado: East European Monographs, 1994), 382.
3   Randolph L. Braham, *The Politics of Genocide: The Holocaust in Hungary* (New York: Columbia University Press, 2016), 1183, footnote 133.

II.1 King Leopold's Congo: A Slice of Magnificent African Cake

1   Leopold II to Baron Solvyns, 17 November 1877, Archives du Palais Royal, Fonds Congo 100/1, quoted in Thomas Pakenham, *The Scramble for Africa: The White Man's Conquest of the Dark Continent from 1876 to 1912* (New York: Random House, 1991), 22.
2   Wm. Roger Louis and Jean Stengers, *E. D. Morel's History of the Congo Reform Movement* (Oxford: Clarendon Press, 1968), 28–29.
3   Pakenham, *The Scramble for Africa*, 20.
4   Neal Ascherson, *The King Incorporated: Leopold the Second and the Congo* (London: Granta Books, 1963), 94.
5   Arthur B. Keith, *The Belgian Congo and the Berlin Act* (London: Oxford University Press, 1919), 302–304.
6   Martin Ewans, *European Atrocity, African Catastrophe: The Congo Free State and its Aftermath* (London: RoutledgeCurzon, 2002), 101.

II.2. King Leopold's Congo: A Secret Society of Murderers

1   E. D. Morel in Wm. R. Louis and Jean Stengers, *E. D. Morel's History of the Congo Reform Movement* (Oxford: Clarendon Press, 1968), 42.
2   Catherine Cline, *E. D. Morel 1873–1924: The Strategies of Protest* (Belfast, Blackstaff Press, 1980), 24.

3   E. D. Morel, *King Leopold's Rule in Africa* (London: Heinemann, 1904), 103.

4   Louis and Stengers, *E. D. Morel's History of the Congo Reform Movement*, 29.

5   Morel, *King Leopold's Rule in Africa*, 56.

6   Frederick Seymour Cocks, *E. D. Morel: The Man and His Work* (London: George Allen & Unwin, Ltd., 1920), 72.

7   Louis and Stengers, *E. D. Morel's History of the Congo Reform Movement*, 48.

8   Martin Ewans, *European Atrocity, African Catastrophe: The Congo Free State and its Aftermath* (London: RoutledgeCurzon, 2002), 184.

9   Cline, *E. D. Morel*, 37.

10 Donald Mitchell, *The Politics of Dissent: A Biography of E. D. Morel* (Bristol: SilverWood Books, 2014), 35.

11 Louis and Stengers, *E. D. Morel's History of the Congo Reform Movement*, 128–129.

12 Hansard, 20 May 1903, 4:122, 1297–1298.

13 Ewans, *European Atrocity*, 191.

14 Hansard, 20 May 1903, 4:1331–1332.

II.3. King Leopold's Congo: "Poor People, Poor, Poor People"

1   Wm. R. Louis and Jean Stengers, *E. D. Morel's History of the Congo Reform Movement* (Oxford: Clarendon Press, 1968), 161.

2   Thomas Pakenham, *The Scramble for Africa: The White Man's Conquest of the Dark Continent from 1876 to 1912* (New York: Random House, 1991), 594.

3   Letter, Joseph Conrad to Robert Cunninghame Graham, 26 December 1903, in Joseph Conrad, *Collected Letters of Joseph Conrad Volume 3, 1903–1907*, edited by Frederick R. Karl and Laurence Davies (Cambridge: Cambridge University Press, 1988), 101–102.

4   Martin Ewans, *European Atrocity, African Catastrophe: The Congo Free State and its Aftermath* (London: RoutledgeCurzon, 2002), 193–194.

5   Pakenham, *The Scramble for Africa*, 597.

6   Ibid., 598.

7   B. L. Reid, "A Good Man: Has Had Fever. Casement in the Congo," *Sewanee Review* 82 (3) (1974), 473.

8   Séamas Síocháin and Michael O'Sullivan, *The Eyes of Another Race: Roger Casement's Congo Report and 1903 Diary* (Dublin: University College Dublin Press, 2003), 58–59.

9   Ibid., 119.

10 Joseph Conrad, *Heart of Darkness*, edited by Paul B. Armstrong (New York: W.W. Norton, 2006), 7.

11 Síocháin and O'Sullivan, *The Eyes of Another Race*, 66.

12 Demetrius Charles Boulger, *The Congo State Is NOT a Slave State: A Reply to Mr. E. D. Morel's Pamphlet Entitled "The Congo Slave State."* (London: Sampson, Low, Marston & Co., 1903), 3.

13 Síocháin and O'Sullivan, *The Eyes of Another Race*, 67.

14 Ibid., 88.

15 Pakenham, *The Scramble for Africa*, 600.

16 Síocháin and O'Sullivan, *The Eyes of Another Race*, 16–17.

17 Casement to Governor-General, 12 September 2003; quoted in Ewans, *European Atrocity*, 195.

18 Ewans, *European Atrocity*, 179.

19 Casement to Morel, 2 November 1905, Morel Papers; quoted in William R. Louis, *Ends of British Imperialism*, 2nd edition (London: I. B. Tauris, 2006), 158.

20 Casement to Morel, 14 December 1904, Morel Papers, quoted in Louis, *Ends of British Imperialism*, 158.

21 Ewans, *European Atrocity*, 198.

22 Adam Hochschild, *King Leopold's Ghost: A Story of Greed, Terror, and Heroism in Colonial Africa* (New York: Mariner Books, 1999), 204.

23 Ibid., 203–204.

24 Ewans, *European Atrocity*, 198–199.

25 Louis and Stengers, *E. D. Morel's History of the Congo Reform Movement*, 159.

26 Ibid., 161.

27 Ibid., 162.

28 Hochschild, *King Leopold's Ghost*, 209.

29 Ewans, *European Atrocity*, 206.

30 Louis and Stengers, *E. D. Morel's History of the Congo Reform Movement*, 172.

31 Frederick Seymour Cocks, *E. D. Morel: The Man and His Work* (London: George Allen & Unwin, Ltd., 1920), 99.

32 Ewans, *European Atrocity*, 207.

33 Ibid.

34 Ibid., 207–208.

II.4. King Leopold's Congo: Leopold's Commissioners Journey to the Heart of Darkness

1 *The Congo: A Report of the Commission of Enquiry Appointed by the Congo Free State Government: A Translation*, translated by E. D. Morel (London: G. P. Putnam's Sons, 1906), 163.

2   Ibid., 2–4.

3   Martin Ewans, *European Atrocity, African Catastrophe: The Congo Free State and its Aftermath* (London: RoutledgeCurzon, 2002), 212–213.

4   Ibid., 181.

5   *The Congo: A Report of the Commission of Enquiry*, 9–12.

6   Ewans, *European Atrocity*, 213.

7   *The Congo: A Report of the Commission of Enquiry*, 66.

8   Ibid., 67–68.

9   Ibid., 91.

10   Ibid., 93.

11   Ibid., 96–97.

12   Ibid., 91.

13   Ibid., 164.

14   Ibid., 169.

15   Felicien Cattier, *Étude Sur La Situation de l'État Indépendant Du Congo* (Brussels: Larcier, 1906), 309–310.

16   Ibid., 217.

17   Ibid., 220–240.

18   Ibid., 240–241.

19   Ibid., 341; David Van Reybrouck, *Congo: The Epic History of a People*, translated by Sam Garrett (New York: HarperCollins, 2014), 97.

20   Arthur Vermeersch, *La Question Congolaise* (Brussels: Imprimerie Scientifique, 1906), 50.

21   Ibid., 111–112.

22   Ewans, *European Atrocity*, 218.

23   *Verbatim Report of the Five Days' Congo Debate in the Belgian House of Representatives (February 20, 27, 28; March 1, 2)*, translated by E. D. Morel (Liverpool: John Richardson & Sons, 1906), 31.

24   Ibid., 14.

25   Ibid., 129.

26   E. D. Morel, *King Leopold's Rule in Africa* (London: Heinemann, 1904), 58.

27   *Verbatim Report of the Five Days' Congo Debate*, 100–101.

28   Ibid., 134.

29   Ibid., 137.

30   Ewans, *European Atrocity*, 218.

II.5. King Leopold's Congo: Belgium Takes over the Congo

1   The quotation from American abolitionist William Lloyd Garrison forms the

Frontispiece to E. D. Morel, *Red Rubber: The Story of the Rubber Slave Trade Flourishing in the Congo in the Year of Grace 1906* (New York: Nassau Print, 1906).

2   Wm. R. Louis and Jean Stengers, *E. D. Morel's History of the Congo Reform Movement* (Oxford: Clarendon Press, 1968), 211.

3   Donald Mitchell, *The Politics of Dissent: A Biography of E. D. Morel* (Bristol: SilverWood Books, 2014), 54.

4   Morel's approach was much like that of a woman we will meet in the next chapter, Millicent Fawcett, who believed advocates of women's suffrage should make arguments that appealed to both the heart and mind. See Jane Robinson, *Hearts and Minds: The Untold Story of the Great Pilgrimage and How Women Won the Vote* (London, Doubleday, 2018), 198.

5   Morel, *Red Rubber*, 88–89; quoted in Cline, *E. D. Morel*, 60.

6   Morel, *Red Rubber*, 194.

7   Martin Ewans, *European Atrocity, African Catastrophe: The Congo Free State and its Aftermath* (London: RoutledgeCurzon, 2002), 224.

8   Barbara Emerson, *Leopold II of the Belgians: King of Colonialism* (London: Weidenfeld & Nicolson, 1979), 255.

9   Ewans, *European Atrocity*, 225.

10 Emerson, *Leopold II of the Belgians*, 255.

11 Ewans, *European Atrocity*, 227.

12 Neal Ascherson, *The King Incorporated: Leopold the Second and the Congo* (London: Granta Books, 1963), 272.

13 "Treaty of Cession and Annexation," *The American Journal of International Law* 3 (1) (1909), 74–75.

14 Letter, Roger Casement to E. D. Morel, 16 October 1907; quoted in Louis and Stengers, *E. D. Morel's History of the Congo Reform Movement*, 214.

15 Frederick Seymour Cocks, *E. D. Morel: The Man and His Work* (London: George Allen & Unwin, Ltd., 1920), 123.

16 Ibid.

17 Hansard [Parliamentary records], 26 February 1908, 4:184, 1878.

18 Joseph Conrad, *Heart of Darkness*, edited by Paul B. Armstrong (New York: W.W. Norton, 2006), 118.

19 Emerson, *Leopold II of the Belgians*, 262.

20 Ascherson, *The King Incorporated*, 281.

II.5. King Leopold's Congo: Epilogue

1   United Nations, *Declaration on Race and Racial Prejudice*, 27 November 1978.

2   Quoted in George Martelli, *Leopold to Lumumba: A History of the Belgian Congo 1877–1960* (London: Chapman & Hall, 1962), 186.

3   Letter, Joseph Conrad to Roger Casement, 21 December 1903, *Collected Letters of Joseph Conrad, volume 3; 1903–1907*, 95.

4   Neal Ascherson, *The King Incorporated: Leopold the Second and the Congo* (London: Granta Books, 1963), 298–299.

5   Ibid., 300.

6   Ibid., 11.

7   E. D. Morel, *The Future of the Congo: An Analysis and Criticism of the Belgian Government's Proposals for a Reform of the Conditions in the Congo Submitted to His Majesty's Government on Behalf of the Congo Reform Association* (London: Smith Elder, 1909), 62.

8   Wm. R. Louis and Jean Stengers, *E. D. Morel's History of the Congo Reform Movement* (Oxford: Clarendon Press, 1968), 267.

9   Quoted in Adam Hochschild, *King Leopold's Ghost: A Story of Greed, Terror, and Heroism in Colonial Africa* (New York: Mariner Books, 1999), 121.

10   Ibid.

11   Louis and Stengers, *E. D. Morel's History of the Congo Reform Movement*, 7.

III.1. Votes for Women: "Milly, After Elizabeth. . ."

1   Ray Strachey, *The Cause: A Short History of the Women's Movement in Great Britain* (Middletown, Delaware: Endeavor Press, 2016), 86–87.

2   Ray Strachey, *Millicent Garrett Fawcett* (London: John Murray, 1931), 22–23.

3   For clarity, Millicent Garrett Fawcett will be referred to as Millicent Fawcett or Millicent or Fawcett and her husband as Henry Fawcett.

4   F. B. Smith, *The Making of the Second Reform Bill* (Cambridge: Cambridge University Press, 1966), 139–140.

5   Hansard, 20 May 1867, 3:186, 826.

6   By the time of Mill's remarks, cholera had broken out in East London and Elizabeth Garrett had spearheaded the drive to set up a dispensary in a poor, densely crowded part of the city. At the dispensary's opening ceremony in the summer of 1866, a physician who taught at the London Hospital where Elizabeth Garrett had studied said:

      Not only is the management mainly in the hands of ladies, but in Miss Garrett we have the first legally qualified female practitioner which England can boast. . . . I consider it very important that women who enter the profession should not profess to take medical supervision unless they have had a complete medical examination and training. This is what Miss Garrett has had. . . and what is of more consequence she has the knowledge which will qualify her to practice with skill and success.—*British Medical Journal*, 14 July 1866; quoted in Jo Manton, *Elizabeth Garrett Anderson* (New York: E.P. Dutton, 1965), 174.

7   Millicent Fawcett was thrilled to hear Mill mention her sister's opening of the medical profession to women in his remarks. See Millicent Garrett Fawcett, *What I Remember* (Honolulu: University Press of the Pacific, 2004), 64.

8   After learning of Karslake's remarks, suffragists collected the signatures of 129 women from Colchester on a petition supporting enfranchisement and presented it to him two months later. See Elizabeth Crawford, *The Women's Suffrage Movement: A Reference Guide 1866–1928* (London: Routledge, 1999), 43–44.

9   Hansard, 20 May 1867, 3:187, 833.

10   Ibid., 837.

11   In a debate about a bill that would have extended the franchise to more working men, Gladstone had argued that "every man who is not presumably incapacitated by some consideration of personal unfitness or of political danger is morally entitled to come within the pale of the Constitution." Hansard, 11 May 1864, 3:175, 324.

12   Hansard, 20 May 1867, 3:187, 840.

13   Millicent Garrett Fawcett, *Woman's Suffrage: A Short History of a Great Movement* (London: Forgotten Books, 2014), 19.

14   Gladstone was among those who voted against Mill's motion. See Roger Fulford, *Votes for Women: The Story of a Struggle* (London: Faber and Faber, 1958), 51.

15   The maxim is, "First they ignore you, then they laugh at you, then they fight you, then you win." Sandra Waddock and Pietra Rivoli, "'First They Fight You . . .': The Time-Context Dynamic and Corporate Responsibility," *California Management Review* 53 (2) (2011), 87.

16   *Punch*, 25 May 1867, vol. 22, p. 220.

17   John M. Robson, "Mill in Parliament: The View from the Comic Papers," *Utilitas* 2 (1) (1990), 102–143.

18 One of Millicent Fawcett's most cherished possessions was a first edition of *The Subjection of Women* that Mill had given her. See Fawcett, *What I Remember*, 87.

19 Mill, *The Subjection of Women*, 31.

20 Mill was referring to the English common law principle of coverture, under which married women had no right to own property, and also to the availability of a common law petition for "restitution of conjugal rights" in which a husband could secure a court order requiring a wife who had left him to return to the marital bed and board as long as he had not abused her. Mary Lyndon Shanley, *Feminism, Marriage, and the Law in Victorian England* (Princeton: Princeton University Press, 1989), 158.

21 Mill, *The Subjection of Women*, 6.

22 Ibid., 11.

23 Consistent with Mill's claim that anti-suffragists commonly believed male dominion over women had been ordained by God, Earl Percy argued in an 1873 debate on a women's suffrage bill: "The real fact is that man in the beginning was ordained to rule over the woman, and this is an Eternal decree which we have no right and no power to alter." Hansard, 30 April 1873, 3:215, 1251.

24 Francis Power Cobbe, "Criminals, Idiots, Women, and Minors," in *Criminals, Idiots, Women, & Minors: Victorian Writing on Women by Women*, edited by Susan Hamilton (Peterborough, Ontario: Broadview Press, 2004), 90–91.

25 Ibid., 91.

26 Ibid., 100.

27 Strachey, *The Cause*, 95.

III.2. Votes for Women: The Thin End of the Wedge

1 Frances Power Cobbe, "Criminals, Idiots, Women, and Minors," in *Criminals, Idiots, Women, & Minors*, edited by Susan Hamilton (Peterborough, Ontario: Broadview Press, 2004), 103.

2 Ibid., 101.

3 Millicent Garrett Fawcett, *What I Remember* (Honolulu: University Press of the Pacific, 2004), 88.

4 This was an insult the British politician and writer Horace Walpole hurled at Mary Wollstonecraft after she published *A Vindication of the Rights of Woman* in 1792.

5 Millicent Garrett Fawcett, "Electoral Disabilities of Women," in *Before the*

Vote Was Won: Arguments for and Against Women's Suffrage 1864–1896, edited by Jane Lewis (London: Routledge & Kegan Paul, 1987), 100–117.

6   Frances Power Cobbe, "Our Policy: An Address to Women Concerning the Suffrage," in *Before the Vote Was Won*, 91–92.

7   F. W. Pethick-Lawrence, *Fate Has Been Kind* (London: Hutchinson, 1943), 68.

8   Martin Pugh, *The March of the Women: A Revisionist Analysis of the Campaign for Women's Suffrage, 1866–1914* (Oxford: Oxford University Press, 2000), 73.

9   Ibid., 72.

10 Ray Strachey, *The Cause: A Short History of the Women's Movement in Great Britain* (Middletown, Delaware: Endeavour Press, 2016), 171.

11 Hansard, 19 July 1869, 3:198, 146.

12 Hansard, 4 May 1870, 3:201, 237.

13 Hansard, 12 May 1870, 3:201, 620.

14 Liberal members had provided the bill's margin of victory on the first vote, supporting it by a 39-vote majority. After Gladstone announced his government's opposition, Liberals opposed the bill by a 72-vote majority on the second vote. See Brian Harrison, *Separate Spheres: The Opposition to Women's Suffrage in Britain* (New York: Holmes & Meier, 1978), Table 1, 28.

15 Strachey, *The Cause*, 104.

16 Jo Manton, *Elizabeth Garrett Anderson* (New York: E.P. Dutton, 1965), 203.

17 Thomas Henry Huxley, a well-known biologist who some called Darwin's Bulldog because of his spirited defense of Darwin's theory of evolution, was also a candidate for the first London School Board.

18 Letter, Elizabeth Garrett to Emily Davies, 24 July 1870, Emily Davies' papers; quoted in Patricia Hollis, *Ladies Elect: Women in English Local Government 1865–1914* (Oxford: Oxford University Press, 1987), 74.

19 Ibid., 73.

20 Ibid., 75.

21 Ibid.

22 Ibid., 76.

23 Ibid., 39.

24 Ibid.

25 Letter, Emily Davies to Mr. Tomlinson, 21 Nov. 1870, Davies papers; quoted in Hollis, *Ladies Elect*, 77.

26 Manton, *Elizabeth Garrett Anderson*, 206–207.

27 Hollis, *Ladies Elect*, 77.

28 Ibid., 8.
29 Hansard, 10 June 1884, 3:288, 1963–64.
30 Harrison, *Separate Spheres*, Table 1, 28.
31 Ray Strachey, *Millicent Garrett Fawcett* (London: John Murray, 1931), 97.
32 Fawcett, *What I Remember*, 113.
33 Strachey, *The Cause*, 236.

III.3. Votes for Women: Constance Lytton

1 Olive Schreiner, *Dreams* (London: T. Fisher Unwin, 1900), 75–77.
2 "Suffragette" is a term originally coined by a journalist for the *London Daily Mail* to disparage supporters of women's suffrage in Britain who engaged in civil disobedience, and to distinguish them from "suffragists," who used traditional, "constitutional" methods (Roger Fulford, *Votes for Women: The Story of a Struggle* [London: Faber and Faber, 1958], 121). Accordingly, those who eschewed violence and worked to enfranchise women through methods such as organizing support through meetings, distribution of literature, and lobbying legislators will be referred to as "suffragists" and those whose methods sometimes included violence and law-breaking will be referred to as "suffragettes."
3 For clarity, Constance Lytton will be referred to as Constance Lytton, Lady Constance Lytton, Constance, or Lytton and her brother, Victor, as Lord Victor Lytton, Victor Lytton, or Victor.
4 Martin Pugh, *The Pankhursts: The History of One Radical Family* (London: Vintage Books, 2008), 153–154.
5 Ibid., 139–140.
6 Ibid., 174.
7 Hansard, 28 Feb 1908, 4:185, 244.
8 Elizabeth Crawford, *The Women's Suffrage Movement: A Reference Guide 1866–1928* (London: Routledge, 1999), 176.
9 Fulford, *Votes for Women*, 159.
10 Martin Pugh, *The March of the Women: A Revisionist Analysis of the Campaign for Women's Suffrage, 1866–1914* (Oxford: Oxford University Press, 2000), 193.
11 F. W. Pethick-Lawrence, *Fate Has Been Kind* (London: Hutchinson, 1943), 78.
12 Sylvia Pankhurst, *The Suffragette: The History of the Women's Militant Suffrage Movement* (Mineola, New York: Dover Publications, 1911), 248.
13 Ibid.
14 Fulford, *Votes for Women*, 158.

15   Crawford, *The Women's Suffrage Movement: A Reference Guide*, 739–740.

16   Pugh, *The Pankhursts*, 180.

17   Constance Lytton, *Prisons and Prisoners*, edited by Jason Haslam (Peterborough, Ontario: Broadview Press, 2008), 56.

18   Crawford, *The Women's Suffrage Movement: A Reference Guide*, 535.

19   Ibid., 443.

20   Lytton, *Prisons and Prisoners*, 56.

21   Crawford, *The Women's Suffrage Movement: A Reference Guide*, 320.

22   Lytton, *Prisons and Prisoners*, 57.

23   Lyndsey Jenkins, *Lady Constance Lytton: Aristocrat, Suffragette, Martyr* (London: Biteback Publishing, 2005), 94.

24   Lytton, *Prisons and Prisoners*, 59.

25   Ibid.

26   Constance Lytton, *No Votes for Women: A Reply to Some Recent Anti-Suffrage Publications* (London: A.C. Fifield, 1909), 4.

27   Lytton, Constance. *Letters of Constance Lytton.* Edited by Betty Balfour (Cambridge: Cambridge University Press, 1925), 155.

28   Strachey, *The Cause*, 256.

29   Lytton, *Prisons and Prisoners*, 76.

30   Ibid., 83.

31   Ibid., 85.

32   While her mother and younger sister worried that the family was losing Constance to the suffrage movement, her older sister, Betty, wrote later "[T]his is not quite what had happened; it was only that Con had opened her arms wider, to love and serve many others as if they were her family." *Letters of Constance Lytton*, 159.

33   Lytton, *Prisons and Prisoners*, 88.

34   Ibid., 74.

35   Ibid., 90.

36   Ibid., 92.

37   Pugh, *The Pankhursts*, 145.

38   Ibid., 185.

39   Lytton, *Prisons and Prisoners*, 118; Holloway Prison records secured later by Lytton's sister, Betty, indicated that Constance had suffered from a well-marked heart valve disease for some time. Jenkins, *Lady Constance Lytton*, 135.

40   Lytton, *Prisons and Prisoners*, 135.

41   Jenkins, *Lady Constance Lytton*, 121.

42   Lytton, *Prisons and Prisoners*, 135.

43 Ibid., 159.

44 Lytton, *Prisons and Prisoners*, 159–160.

45 Two years later, Olive Schreiner dedicated a book she wrote, *Women and Labor*, to Constance Lytton.

III.4. Votes for Women: "No surrender!"

1   Constance Lytton, *Prisons and Prisoners*, edited by Jason Haslam (Peterborough, Ontario: Broadview Press, 2008), 238.

2   Elizabeth Crawford, *The Women's Suffrage Movement: A Reference Guide 1866–1928* (London: Routledge, 1999), 741.

3   Joyce Marlow, editor, *Suffragettes: The Fight for Votes for Women* (London: Virago Press, 2013), 92.

4   Ibid.

5   Roger Fulford, *Votes for Women: The Story of a Struggle* (London: Faber and Faber, 1958), 179.

6   Sylvia Pankhurst, *The Suffragette: The History of the Women's Militant Suffrage Movement* (Mineola, New York: Dover Publications, 1911), 392.

7   Ibid., 392–396.

8   Gladstone in the National Archives HO 144/1038/18078271; quoted in Lyndsey Jenkins, *Lady Constance Lytton: Aristocrat, Suffragette, Martyr* (London: Biteback Publishing, 2005), 141.

9   Lytton, *Prisons and Prisoners*, 191–192.

10 In June of 1913, Emily Davison rushed onto the Derby racecourse in the middle of a race, planning to attach a WSPU flag to the bridle of the King's horse, Anmer. She was trampled to death. Lytton was unable to attend her funeral, but sent a book of Whitman's poems to be placed in Davison's coffin. Before Davison was buried, it was put in her lifeless hand, opened to her favorite poem. Jenkins, *Lady Constance Lytton*, 205.

11 Crawford, *The Women's Suffrage Movement: A Reference Guide*, 361.

12 Jenkins, *Lady Constance Lytton*, 145.

13 Crawford, *The Women's Suffrage Movement: A Reference Guide*, 361.

14 Lytton, *Prisons and Prisoners*, 207–212.

15 Henry Brailsford, *The Times*, 19 October 1909; cited in Jenkins, *Lady Constance Lytton*, 149.

16 George Bernard Shaw, *The Times*, 23 November 1909; quoted in Michael Holroyd, "George Bernard Shaw: Women and the Body Politic," *Critical Inquiry* 6 (1) (1979), 26.

17 Hansard, 27 October 1909, 5:12, 1001–1002.

18   Lytton, *Prisons and Prisoners*, 218.

19   Ibid., 219.

20   Ibid., 221–222.

21   Ibid., 231.

22   Ibid., 233.

23   Ibid., 238.

24   Ibid., 241.

25   Jenkins, *Lady Constance Lytton.*, 161.

26   Ibid., 162.

27   Ibid.

28   Ibid., 167–170.

29   Victor Lytton, *The Times*, 10 March 1910; Jenkins, *Lady Constance Lytton*, 167–170.

30   Martin Pugh, *The March of the Women: A Revisionist Analysis of the Campaign for Women's Suffrage, 1866–1914* (Oxford: Oxford University Press, 2000), 80.

31   Martin Pugh, *Electoral Reform in War and Peace 1906–1918* (London: Routledge & Kegan Paul, 1978), 35; Sandra Holton, *Feminism and Democracy: Women's Suffrage and Reform Politics in Britain, 1900–1918* (Cambridge: Cambridge University Press, 2003), 69–70.

32   Martin Pugh, *The Pankhursts: The History of One Radical Family* (London: Vintage Books, 2008), 207.

33   Jenkins, *Lady Constance Lytton*, 173.

34   Pugh, *The March of the Women*, 140.

35   Pugh, *The Pankhursts*, 218.

36   Ibid., 218–219.

37   Brian Harrison, *Separate Spheres: The Opposition to Women's Suffrage in Britain* (New York: Holmes & Meier, 1978), Table 1, 28.

38   Pugh, *The Pankhursts*, 227.

39   Jenkins, *Lady Constance Lytton*, 175.

40   *The Daily Chronicle*, 16 June 1911; quoted in Pugh, *The Pankhursts*, 227.

41   *The Star*, 19 June 1911; quoted in Diane Atkinson, *Votes for Women* (Cambridge: Cambridge University Press, 1988), 31.

42   Pugh, *The March of the Women*, 192.

43   David Lindsay Keir, *The Constitutional History of Modern Britain Since 1485*, 9th edition (London: Black, 1923), 484.

44   *Evening Standard and Globe*, 8 November 1911; quoted in Emmeline Pankhurst, *My Own Story* (London: Eveleigh Nash, 1914), 207.

45   Pankhurst, *My Own Story*, 207.

46 Marlow, editor, *Suffragettes, The Fight for Votes for Women*, 148–149.

47 Emmeline Pankhurst argued to WSPU members that window-smashing was a political statement, that "[t]he argument of the broken pane of glass is the most valuable argument in modern politics." Andrew Rosen, *Rise Up, Women! The Militant Campaign of the Women's Social and Political Union 1903–1914* (London: Routledge, 2013), 157.

48 Atkinson. *Votes for Women*, 32.

49 Pugh, *The Pankhursts*, 232.

50 Harrison, *Separate Spheres*, 186.

51 Atkinson, *Votes for Women*, 32.

52 Harrison, *Separate Spheres*, 181.

53 Pugh, *The Pankhursts*, 243.

III.5: Votes for Women: The Great Pilgrimage to the Vote

1 Ray Strachey, *The Cause: A Short History of the Women's Movement in Great Britain* (Middletown, DE: Endeavour Press, 2016), 299.

2 As mentioned in a prior note, those who eschewed violence and worked to enfranchise women through nonmilitant or "constitutional" methods such as organizing support through meetings, distribution of literature, and lobbying legislators will be referred to as "suffragists," while those whose methods sometimes included violence and law-breaking will be referred to as "suffragettes."

3 Hansard, 28 March 1912, 5:36, 715–716.

4 Brian Harrison, *Separate Spheres: The Opposition to Women's Suffrage in Britain* (New York: Holmes & Meier, 1978), 193.

5 David Rubinstein, *A Different World for Women: The Life of Millicent Garrett Fawcett* (Athens: Ohio University Press, 1991), 175.

6 Ray Strachey, *Millicent Garrett Fawcett* (London: John Murray, 1931), 268.

7 John Morley, *The Life of William Ewart Gladstone* (London: Macmillan, 1903), 3:371; quoted in Millicent Garrett Fawcett, *Women's Suffrage: A Short History of a Great Movement* (New York: Dodge Publishing, 2005), 73.

8 Lesley Parker Hume, *The National Union of Women's Suffrage Societies 1897–1914* (New York, Garland Publishing, 1982), 50–51.

9 Hansard, 27 April 1892, 4:3, 1510.

10 Jane Robinson, *Hearts and Minds: The Untold Story of the Great Pilgrimage and How Women Won the Vote* (London, Doubleday, 2018), 151.

11 Hume, *The National Union of Women's Suffrage Societies*, 199.

12 Robinson, *Hearts and Minds*, 219.

13 Ibid., 197–198.

14 Ibid., 197.

15 Ibid., 215.

16 Ibid., 214–215.

17 Ibid., 223.

18 Ibid., 225.

19 Ibid., 225–227.

20 Millicent Garrett Fawcett, *The Women's Victory—and After: Personal Reminiscences* (London: Sidgwick & Jackson, 1920), 57–58.

21 Sandra Holton, *Feminism and Democracy: Women's Suffrage and Reform Politics in Britain, 1900–1918* (Cambridge: Cambridge University Press, 2003), 117.

22 Robinson, *Hearts and Minds*, 231.

23 Ibid., 233.

24 Martin Pugh, *Electoral Reform in Peace and War* (London: Routledge & Kegan Paul, 1978), 138.

25 Holton, *Feminism and Democracy*, 135.

26 Rubinstein, *A Different World for Women*, 214.

27 *The Common Cause*, 7 August 1914, 376; quoted in Rubinstein, *A Different World for Women*, 214.

28 Rubinstein, *A Different World for Women*, 215.

29 Fawcett, *The Women's Victory—and After*, 92.

30 Millicent Garrett Fawcett, *What I Remember* (Honolulu: University Press of the Pacific, 2004), 219–220.

31 Holton, *Feminism and Democracy*, 131.

32 Fawcett, *What I Remember*, 219.

33 Fawcett, *The Women's Victory—and After*, 97.

34 Ibid., 116.

35 Ibid.

36 *War Speeches by British Ministers 1914–1916* (London: Fisher-Unwin, 1917), 102–103; quoted in Fawcett, *The Women's Victory—and After*, 115.

37 Hansard, 14 August 1916, 5:85, 1452; quoted in Fawcett, *The Women's Victory—and After*, 133.

38 Fawcett, *The Women's Victory—and After*, 136–137.

39 Pugh, *Electoral Reform in Peace and War*, 72–73.

40 David Rolf, "Origins of Mr. Speaker's Conference During the First World War," *History* 64: 210 (1979), 43.

41 Fawcett, *The Women's Victory—and After*, 138.

42 *Manchester Dispatch*, 31 January 1917; *cited* in Pugh, *Electoral Reform in Peace and War*, 76.

43 Edward Grey had been given a knighthood in 1912.

44 Letter, Sir Edward Grey to James Bryce, 13 October 1916, Grey papers, 236/5; quoted in Pugh, *Electoral Reform in Peace and War*, 76.

45 Pugh, *Electoral Reform in Peace and War*, 84.

46 Ibid.

47 Ibid.

48 Millicent Fawcett to E. Atkinson, 21 December 1916, Fawcett Library papers; quoted in Pugh, *Electoral Reform in Peace and War*, 84.

49 James William Lowther Ullswater, *A Speaker's Commentaries* (London: Edward Arnold, 1925) 2:197–198; quoted in Pugh, *Electoral Reform in Peace and War*, 84.

50 Pugh, *Electoral Reform in Peace and War*, 85.

51 Ibid., 73.

52 Letter, Willoughby Dickinson to Miss Barry, 20/1/43, Dickinson papers; quoted in Pugh, *Electoral Reform in Peace and War*, 85.

53 Fawcett, *The Women's Victory—and After*, 140–141.

54 The WSPU was no longer active, having suspended its suffrage work at the outset of the war and been dissolved in 1917.

55 Fawcett, *The Women's Victory—and After*, 142–143.

56 Ibid., 142.

57 Strachey, *Millicent Garrett Fawcett*, 311–312.

58 Joyce Marlow, editor, *Suffragettes, The Fight for Votes for Women* (London: Virago Press, 2013), 239–240.

59 Fawcett, *The Women's Victory—and After*, 145.

60 Ibid., 145–146.

61 Strachey, *Millicent Garrett Fawcett*, 312–313.

62 Hansard, 19 June 1917, 5:94, 1645.

63 Ibid., 1648.

64 Ibid., 1702.

65 Fawcett, *The Women's Victory—and After*, 148.

66 Lord Cromer had been the President of the National Society but stepped down in 1912, explaining to Lord Curzon: "I suffer tortures from dyspepsia and I really have not the health, strength, youth, or may I add the temper to go on dealing with these infernal women." See Joyce Marlow, editor, *Suffragettes, The Fight for Votes for Women*, 163.

67 Fawcett, *What I Remember*, 245.

68   Harrison, *Separate Spheres*, 219.
69   Hansard, 9 January 1918, 5:27, 415.
70   Ibid., 416–417.
71   Hansard, 10 January 1918, 5:27, 518.
72   Ibid., 523.
73   Ibid.
74   Fawcett, *The Women's Victory—and After*, 152.
75   Pugh, *Electoral Reform in Peace and War*, 173.
76   Fawcett, *What I Remember*, 247.

III. Votes for Women: Epilogue

1   Millicent Garrett Fawcett, *The Women's Victory—and After: Personal Reminiscences, 1911–1918* (London: Sidgwick & Jackson, 1920), 156.
2   Ibid., 160.
3   Ibid., 161–162.
4   Jo Manton, *Elizabeth Garrett Anderson* (New York: E.P. Dutton, 1965), 335–336.
5   Daphne Bennett, *Emily Davies and the Liberation of Women 1830–1921* (London: Andre Deutsch, 1990), 244.
6   Lyndsey Jenkins, *Lady Constance Lytton: Aristocrat, Suffragette, Martyr* (London: Biteback Publishing, 2005), 215.
7   Ibid., 208.
8   Ibid., 214.
9   Bruce L. Kinzer, Ann P. Robson, and John M. Robson, *A Moralist in and out of Parliament: John Stuart Mill at Westminster 1865–1868* (Toronto: University of Toronto Press, 1992), 148.

IV. Robbery with Violence

1   Marlow in Joseph Conrad's *Heart of Darkness*, edited by Paul B. Armstrong (New York: W.W. Norton, 2006), 7.
2   *Nazi Conspiracy and Aggression*, (Washington: U.S. Government Printing Office, 1946), Volume IV, 563.
3   Raul Hilberg, "Confronting the Moral Implications of the Holocaust," *Social Education* 42, 275 (1978); cited in Robert Jay Lifton, *The Nazi Doctors: Medical Killing and the Psychology of Genocide* (New York: Basic Books, 1986), 445.
4   Raul Hilberg, "The Destruction of the European Jews: Dehumanization and Concealment," in *Understanding Prejudice and Discrimination*, edited by Scott Plous (New York: McGraw-Hill, 2003), 283–284.

5   Mark Roseman, *The Villa, the Lake, the Meeting: Wannsee and the Final Solution* (London: Penguin, 2002), 76.

6   Ibid., 118.

7   Ibid., 109.

8   Randolph L. Braham, *The Politics of Genocide: The Holocaust in Hungary* (New York: Columbia University Press, 2016), 494.

9   Raul Hilberg, *The Destruction of the European Jews* (Chicago: Quadrangle Books, 1967), 619.

10 Rudolf Höss, *Death Dealer: The Memoirs of the SS Kommandant at Auschwitz*, edited by Steven Paskuly and translated by Andrew Pollinger (New York: Da Capo Press, 1996), 27.

11 Hilberg, *The Destruction of the European Jews* (1967), 213.

12 Ibid., 649.

13 Ibid., 8.

14 James Waller, *Becoming Evil: How Ordinary People Commit Genocide and Mass Killing*, 2nd edition (Oxford: Oxford University Press, 2007), 220; David Livingstone Smith, *Less Than Human: Why We Demean, Enslave, and Exterminate Others* (New York: St. Martin's Press, 2011), 15.

15 Peter Longerich, *Heinrich Himmler*, translated by Jeremy Noakes and Lesley Sharpe (Oxford: Oxford University Press, 2012), 309.

16 Smith, *Less Than Human*, 15.

17 Hilberg, *The Destruction of the European Jews* (1967), 257.

18 *Trial of Adolph Eichmann, Record of Proceedings in the District Court of Jerusalem*, 26 June 1961, 4:1423.

19 Hilberg, *The Destruction of the European Jews* (1967), 659–662.

20 Gábor Kádár and Zoltán Vági, *Self-Financing Genocide* (Budapest: Central European University Press, 2001), 129.

21 Franciszek Piper, "The System of Prisoner Exploitation," in *Anatomy of the Auschwitz Death Camp*, edited by Yisrael Gutman and Michael Berenbaum (Indianapolis: Indiana University Press, 1994), 46.

22 Felicien Cattier, *Étude Sur La Situation de l'État Indépendant Du Congo* (Brussels: Larcier, 1906), 217.

23 Diane Atkinson, *Votes for Women* (Cambridge: Cambridge University Press, 1988), 6–7.

24 Mary Lyndon Shanley, *Feminism, Marriage, and the Law in Victorian England* (Princeton: Princeton University Press, 1989), 10.

25 Constance Lytton, *Prisons and Prisoners*, edited by Jason Haslam (Peterborough, Ontario: Broadview Press, 2008), 80–81.

26 Pratto et al., "Social Dominance Orientation and the Legitimization of Inequality Across Cultures," 371.

27 *The Congo: A Report of the Commission of Enquiry Appointed by the Congo Free State Government: A Translation*, translated by E. D. Morel (London: G. P. Putnam's Sons, 1906), 91.

28 Ibid., 67–68.

29 Thomas Pakenham, *The Scramble for Africa: The White Man's Conquest of the Dark Continent from 1876 to 1912* (New York: Random House, 1991), 591.

30 The lesser lethality may be because Victorian English men deemed women to be inferior but still human, deprived of equality but not humanity. See Smith, *Less Than Human*, 54. Some social dominance theorists believe that although coercion and violence are used to maintain gender-based hierarchies, the resulting lethality is usually less than that used to maintain other group-based hierarchies. Felicia Pratto, Jim Sidanius, and Shana Levin, "Social Dominance Theory and the Dynamics of Intergroup Relations: Taking Stock and Looking Forward," *European Review of Social Psychology* 17 (2006), 274.

31 In 1871, nearly 90 percent of all women between forty-five and forty-nine years old were married or had been. Mary Lyndon Shanley, *Feminism, Marriage, and the Law in Victorian England* (Princeton: Princeton University Press, 1989), 9.

32 Ibid.

33 Alan Chedzoy, *A Scandalous Woman: The Story of Caroline Norton* (London: Allison & Busby, 1992), 206.

34 Roderick Phillips, *Untying the Knot: A Short History of Divorce* (Cambridge: Cambridge University Press, 1991), 102.

35 Hansard, 26 May 1853, 3:127, 551.

36 Wm. Roger Louis and Jean Stengers, *E. D. Morel's History of the Congo Reform Movement* (Oxford: Clarendon Press, 1968), 28–29.

37 Martin Ewans, *European Atrocity, African Catastrophe: The Congo Free State and its Aftermath* (London: RoutledgeCurzon, 2002), 228.

38 Adam Hochschild, *King Leopold's Ghost: A Story of Greed, Terror, and Heroism in Colonial Africa* (New York: Mariner Books, 1999), 294–295.

39 Letter, William Gladstone to Samuel Smith, 11 April 1892, quoted in *Before the Vote Was Won*, edited by Jane Lewis, 446.

40 Hochschild, *op. cit.*, 130.

41 Bandura, *Moral Disengagement: How People Do Harm and Live with Themselves* (New York: Worth Publishers), 55.

42 *Verbatim Report of the Five Days' Congo Debate in the Belgian House of Representatives (February 20, 27, 28; March 1, 2)*, translated by E. D. Morel (Liverpool: John Richardson & Sons, 1906), 15–17.

43 Cattier, *Étude Sur La Situation de l'État Indépendant Du Congo*, 341.

44 William Blackstone, *The American Students' Blackstone: Commentaries on the Laws of England*, edited by George Chase (New York: Banks & Brothers, 1884), 159.

45 Shanley, *Feminism, Marriage, and the Law in Victorian England*, 178.

46 *The Congo: A Report of the Commission of Enquiry*, 162–164.

47 Ibid., 163.

48 Millicent Garrett Fawcett, "Electoral Disabilities of Women," in *Before the Vote Was Won: Arguments for and Against Women's Suffrage 1864–1896*, edited by Jane Lewis (London: Routledge & Kegan Paul, 1987), 101.

49 Brian Harrison, *Separate Spheres: The Opposition to Women's Suffrage in Britain* (New York: Holmes & Meier, 1978), 79–80.

50 Alfred Tennyson, "The Princess;" quoted in Lesley Parker Hume, *The National Union of Women's Suffrage Societies 1897–1914* (New York, Garland Publishing, 1982), 2.

51 George Bernard Shaw, *The Times*, 20 June 1913; quoted in *Suffragettes: The Fight for Votes for Women*, edited by Joyce Marlow (London: Virago Press, 2013), 200.

52 Bandura, *Moral Disengagement: How People Do Harm and Live with Themselves*, 3.

53 Smith, *Less Than Human*, 2.

54 Ibid., 251.

55 Robert B. Edgerton, *The Troubled Heart of Africa: A history of the Congo* (New York: St. Martin's Press, 2002), 184.

56 Hansard, 10 March 1853, 3: 124, 1418.

57 Lytton, *Prisons and Prisoners*, 59.

58 Pratto, Sidanius, and Levin, "Social Dominance Theory and the Dynamics of Intergroup Relations: Taking Stock and Looking Forward," 275–276.

59 Hansard, 30 April 1873, 3:215, 1251.

60 *The Congo: A Report of the Commission of Enquiry*, 164.

61 Ibid., 91.

62 Ibid., 41.

63 Fawcett, "Electoral Disabilities of Women," in *Before the Vote Was Won*, 101.

64 Blackstone, *The American Students' Blackstone*, 159.

65 Wesley J. Smith, *A Rat Is a Pig Is a Dog Is a Boy: The Human Cost of the Animal Rights Movement* (New York: Encounter Books, 2010), 238.

V. Of Human Chauvanism

1 Carl Sagan and Ann Druyan, *Shadows of Forgotten Ancestors: A Search for Who We Are* (New York: Random House, 1992), 387.

2 Carl Sagan, *The Varieties of Scientific Experience: A Personal View of the Search for God* (New York: Penguin Press, 2006), 35–37.

3 Carl Sagan, *Pale Blue Dot: A Vision of the Human Future in Space* (New York: Random House, 1994), 9.

4 James Rachels, *Created from Animals: The Moral Implications of Darwinism* (Oxford: Oxford University Press, 1990), 1.

5 Charles Darwin, *The Concise Edition of The Descent of Man and Selection in Relation to Sex*, edited by Carl Zimmer (New York: Penguin Group, 2007), 128.

6 Ibid., 193.

7 Jane Goodall, *My Friends the Wild Chimpanzees* (Washington, D.C.: National Geographic Society, 1967), 31.

8 Jane Goodall, "Learning from the Chimpanzees: A Message Humans Can Understand," *Science* 282 (1998), 2184–2185.

9 Geza Teleki, "Chimpanzee Subsistence Technology: Materials and Skills," *Journal of Human Evolution* 3 (6) (1974), 785–594; quoted in Sagan and Druyan, *Shadows of Forgotten Ancestors*, 392–394.

10 Christophe Boesch, Josephine S. Head, and Martha M. Robbins, "Complex Tool Sets for Honey Extraction in Olango National Park, Gabon," *Journal of Human Evolution* 56 (2009), 560–561.

11 Ibid., 561.

12 Gavin R. Hunt, "Manufacture and Use of Hook-Tools by New Caledonian Crows," *Nature* 249 (1996), 379–381.

13 Alex A. S. Weir, Jackie Chapell, and Alex Kacelnik, "Shaping of Hooks in New Caledonian Crows," *Science* 297 (2002), 981.

14 Thomas Suddendorf, *The Gap: The Science of What Separates Us from Other Animals* (New York: Basic Books, 2013), 147.

15 Frans de Waal, *Our Inner Ape: A Leading Primatologist Explains Why We Are Who We Are* (New York: Riverhead Books, 2005), 179.

16 Frederich Max Müller, *Lectures on the Science of Language Delivered at the Royal Institution of Great Britain*, 3rd edition (London: Longman, Green, Longman, & Roberts, 1862), 360.

17 Mary Midgley, *Beast and Man: The Roots of Human Nature* (London: Routledge, 2002), 206.

18 Ibid.

19 Ibid., 206–207.

20 Philip Lieberman, *The Unpredictable Species: What Makes Humans Unique* (Princeton, New Jersey: Princeton University Press, 2013), 91.

21 de Waal, *Our Inner Ape*, 179.

22 Herbert S. Terrace et al., "Can an Ape Create a Sentence?" *Science* 206 (1979), 891.

23 de Waal, *Our Inner Ape*, 179.

24 Michael D. Hixson, "Ape Language Research: A Review and Behavioral Perspective," *The Analysis of Verbal Behavior* 15 (1998), 17–39.

25 Frans de Waal, *Good Natured: The Origins of Right and Wrong in Humans and Other Animals* (Cambridge, Massachusetts: Harvard University Press, 1996), 210.

26 Robert M. Yerkes and Ada W. Yerkes, *The Great Apes* (New Haven: Yale University Press, 1929), 253.

27 Jane Goodall, *In the Shadow of Man* (London: Collins, 1971), 250–251.

28 Gordon Gallup, "Self-Recognition in Primates: A Comparative Approach to the Bi-Directional Properties of Consciousness," *American Psychologist* 32 (1977), 332–333.

29 Ibid., 333.

30 John Dewey, *Reconstruction in Philosophy* (New York: Henry Holt, 1920), 1; cited in Sagan and Druyan, *Shadows of Forgotten Ancestors*, 369.

31 Roger S. Fouts and Deborah H. Fouts, "Chimpanzees' Use of Sign Language," in *The Great Ape Project: Equality Beyond Humanity*, edited by Paola Cavalieri and Peter Singer (New York: St. Martin's Press, 1993), 37–38.

32 Washoe's ability to remember people's faces was not unique. When Frans de Waal visited a zoo in Holland, a few chimps remembered him from when he worked there more than thirty years earlier, picking his face out of a crowd and greeting him with excited hooting. Frans de Waal, *Are We Smart Enough to Know How Smart Animals Are?* (New York: W. W. Norton, 2016), 70.

33 Sana Inoue and Tetsuro Matsuzawa, "Working Memory of Numerals in Chimpanzees," *Current Biology* 17 (23) (2007), R1005.

34 Tetsuro Matsuzawa, "Symbolic Representation of Number in Chimpanzees," *Current Opinion in Neurobiology* 19 (2009), 95.

35 Diana F. Tomback, "How Nutcrackers Find Their Food Stores," *Condor* 82 (1980), 10–19.

36 The neutral mask looked like Vice President Dick Cheney, prompting Frans de Waal to quip that this mask elicited more negative reactions from the students than the crows. de Waal, *Are We Smart Enough to Know How Smart Animals Are?*, 72.

37 John M. Marzluff et al., "Lasting Recognition of Threatening People by Wild

American Crows," *Animal Behavior* 79 (2010), 703.

38 Ibid., 699.

39 Claudiu Marius Mesaroş, "Aristotle and Animal Mind," *Procedia—Social and Behavioral Sciences* 163 (2014), 186.

40 Christophe Boesch and Hedwige Boesch, "Optimisation of Nut-Cracking with Natural Hammers by Wild Chimpanzees," *Behaviour* 83 (3) (1988), 266.

41 Alex H. Taylor et al., "Spontaneous Meta-Tool Use by New Caledonian Crows," *Current Biology* 17 (2007), 1504.

42 Alex H. Taylor et al., "New Caledonian Crows Learn the Functional Properties of Novel Tool Types," *PLoSONE* 6 (12) (2011), 7.

43 de Waal, *Are We Smart Enough to Know How Smart Animals Are?*, 91–92.

44 Ibid., 141.

45 Ibid., 163.

46 David S. Oderberg, "The Illusion of Animal Rights," *Human Life Review* 26 (2/3) (2000), 42.

47 Ibid., 43; quoted in Wesley J. Smith, *A Rat Is a Pig Is a Dog Is a Boy: The Human Cost of the Animal Rights Movement* (New York: Encounter Books, 2010), 238.

48 Jessica C. Flack and Frans B. M. de Waal, "'Any Animal Whatever': Darwinian Building Blocks of Morality in Monkeys and Apes," *Journal of Consciousness Studies* 7 (2000), 3.

49 Jules H. Masserman, Stanley Wechkin, and William Terris, "'Altruistic' Behavior in Rhesus Monkeys," *American Journal of Psychiatry* 121 (1964), 584.

50 Roger Fouts and Stephen Tukel Mills, *Next of Kin: What Chimpanzees Have Taught Me About Who We Are* (New York: William Morrow, 1997), 291.

51 Ibid., 179–180.

52 Frans B. M. de Waal, "The Chimpanzees' Service Economy: Food for Grooming," *Evolution and Human Behavior* 18 (1997), 384.

53 Ibid., 375.

54 Sarah F. Brosnan and Frans B. M. de Waal, "Evolution of Responses to (Un) fairness," *Science* (17 October 2014), 1–6.

55 Video of a later repetition of the experiment is online; accessed on 12 November 2019, https://www.youtube.com/watch?v=-KSryJXDpzo.

56 By now, it is well-established that some nonhuman animals have a moral sense. "Moral behavior is a successful strategy used by both human and nonhuman animals living in stable, long-lasting social groups (citations omitted)." Donald M. Broom, "Sentience," in *Encyclopedia of Animal Behavior*,

edited by Jae C. Choe (Cambridge, Massachusetts: Academic Press, 2019), 1:132.

57 de Waal, *Good Natured*, 209.

58 Frans de Waal, *The Ape and the Sushi Master: Cultural Reflections of a Primatologist* (New York: Basic Books, 2001), 213.

59 Masao Kawai, "Newly-Acquired Pre-cultural Behavior of the Natural Troop of Japanese Monkeys in Koshima Islet," *Primates* 6 (1) (1965), 3.

60 Sagan and Druyan, *Shadows of Forgotten Ancestors*, 350.

61 Kawai, "Newly-Acquired Pre-cultural Behavior," 12.

62 Frans B. M. de Waal and Kristin E. Bonnie, "In Tune with Others: The Social Side of Primate Culture," in *The Question of Animal Culture*, edited by Kevin N. Laland and Bennett G. Galef (Cambridge, Massachusetts: Harvard University Press, 2009), 20.

63 Roger S. Fouts, Deborah H. Fouts, and Thomas E. Van Confort, "The Infant Loulis Learns Signs from Cross-Fostered Chimpanzees," in *Teaching Sign Language to Chimpanzees,* edited by R. A. Gardner, B. T. Gardner, and T. E. Van Confort (Albany: State University of New York, 1985), 285.

64 Andrew Whiten et al., "Cultures in Chimpanzees," *Nature* 399 (1999), 683.

65 Stephen Jay Gould, "The Human Difference," *New York Times*, July 2, 1999.

66 James Rachels, *The Legacy of Socrates: Essays in Moral Philosophy* (New York: Columbia University Press, 2007), 10.

67 James Rachels, "Do Animals Have Rights?" in *Can Ethics Provide Answers? And Other Essays in Moral Philosophy* (Lanham, Maryland: Rowan & Littlefield, 1997), 82.

68 Rachels, "The Basic Argument for Vegetarianism," in *The Legacy of Socrates*, 3–6.

69 Jeremy Bentham, *An Introduction to the Principles of Morals and Legislation* (Oxford: Clarendon Press, 1823), 311.

VI. On Factory Farms, Money Talks but in Obscenities

1 Pew Commission on Industrial Farm Animal Production, *Putting Meat on the Table—Industrial Farm Animal Production in America* (Executive Summary) (Washington, D.C.: The Pew Charitable Trusts, 2008), 22.

2 A neuropsychologist has argued that while animals may be able to sense pain, unless their brain has a well-developed prefrontal cortex like the one humans have, they would not find it unpleasant. *See* Bob Bermond, "A Neuropsychological and Evolutionary Approach to Animal Consciousness and Animal Welfare," *Animal Welfare* 10 (2001), 47–62. That position is

not widely shared by scientists. Daniel M. Weary et al., "Identifying and Preventing Pain in Animals," *Applied Animal Behavior Science* 100 (1) (2006), 73.

3   Working Party of the Institute of Medical Ethics, *Lives in the Balance: The Ethics of Using Animals in Biomedical Research*, edited by Jane A. Smith and Kenneth M. Boyd (Oxford: Oxford University Press, 1991), 62.

4   Ibid., 66.

5   Gary E. Varner, *In Nature's Interests?: Interests, Animal Rights and Environmental Ethics* (New York: Oxford University Press, 1998), 52.

6   The term "intensive production system" will be used to describe those systems which include a large number of animals per production unit, high stocking density, and a relatively artificial environment. *See* Ian J. H. Duncan, "Animal Welfare Issues in the Poultry Industry: Is There a Lesson to be Learned?" *Journal of Applied Animal Welfare Science* 4 (3) (2001), 207. These production systems will sometimes be referred to as "factory farms."

7   Although the term "cows" technically refers to female cattle who have had at least one calf, for the sake of readability, it will be used to refer to both genders of cattle, regardless of whether a female has given birth.

8   John Webster, *Animal Welfare: Limping Towards Eden* (Oxford: Blackwell Publishing, 2005), 128.

9   T. C. Danbury et al., "Self-Selection of the Analgesic Drug Carprofen by Lame Broiler Chickens," *Veterinary Record* 146 (2000), 310.

10   D. McGeown et al. "Effect of Carprofen on Lameness in Broiler Chickens," *Veterinary Record* 144 (1999), 668.

11   Weary et al., "Identifying and Preventing Pain in Animals," 67.

12   Marion Kluivers-Poodt et al., "Effects of a Local Anesthetic and NSAID in Castration of Piglets, on the Acute Pain Responses, Growth, and Mortality," *Animal* 6:9 (2012), 1474.

13   G. Marx et al., "Analysis of Pain-Related Vocalization in Young Pigs," *Journal of Sound and Vibration* 266 (2003), 696.

14   Lynne U. Sneddon and Michael J. Gentle, "Pain in Farm Animals," in *Animal Welfare and Animal Health: Proceedings of Workshop 5 on Sustainable Animal Production*, edited by Franz Ellendorff, Volker Moennia, Jan Ladewig, and Lorne A. Babink (Braunschweig, Germany: FAL Agricultural Research, 2000), 15.

15   S. C. Kestin et al., "Prevalence of Leg Weakness in Broiler Chickens and Its Relationship with Genotype," *Veterinary Record* 131 (1992), 193.

16   M. O. North, "Some Tips on Floor Space and Profits," *Broiler Industry*

(December 1975), 24; quoted in Jim Mason and Peter Singer, *Animal Factories* (New York: Harmony Books, 1990), 54.

17 North, "Some Tips on Floor Space and Profits," 24.

18 M. J. Zuidhof et al., "Growth, Efficiency, and Yield of Commercial Broilers from 1957, 1978, and 2005," *Poultry Science* 93 (12) (2014), 2973.

19 John Webster, *Animal Welfare: A Cool Eye Towards Eden* (Oxford: Blackwell Publishing, 1994), 156.

20 Ibid., 253.

21 Ibid.

22 Ibid., 156.

23 Toby G. Knowles et al., "Leg Disorders in Broiler Chickens: Prevalence, Risk Factors and Prevention," *PLoS One* 3(2) (2008), e1545, 4.

24 T. Buchwalder and B. Huber-Eicher, "Effect of the Analgesic Butorphanol on Activity Behavior in Turkeys," *Research in Veterinary Science* 79 (2005), 239.

25 S. R. I. Duff, P. M. Hocking, and R. K. Field, "The Gross Morphology of Skeletal Disease in Adult Male Breeding Turkeys," *Avian Pathology* 16 (4) (1987), 635.

26 I. J. H. Duncan et al., "Assessment of Pain Associated with Degenerative Hip Disorders in Adult Male Turkeys," *Research in Veterinary Science* 50 (2) (1991), 117.

27 For the following discussion, the term "meat" will include beef, pork, chicken, lamb, fish, and other types of seafood.

28 Jared Piazza et al., "Rationalizing Meat Consumption: The 4 Ns," *Appetite* 91 (2015), 17.

29 Joan Sabaté, "The Contribution of Vegetarian Diets to Health and Disease: A Paradigm Shift?" *American Journal of Clinical Nutrition* 78 (supp) (2003), 502S-507S.

30 V. K. Messina and K. I. Burke, "Position Statement of the American Dietetic Association: Vegetarian Diets," *Journal of the American Dietetic Association* 97 (11) (1997), 1317; *See also* Diana Cullum-Dugan and Roman Pawlak, "Position of the Academy of Nutrition and Dietetics: Vegetarian Diets," *Journal of the Academy of Nutrition and Dietetics* 115 (5) (2015), 801–810.

31 Paul N. Appleby et al., "The Oxford Vegetarian Study: An Overview," *American Journal of Clinical Nutrition* 70 (supp) (1999), 525S.

32 Timothy J. Key et al., "Mortality in Vegetarians and Non-Vegetarians: A Collaborative Analysis of 8300 Deaths Among 76,000 Men and Women in Five Prospective Studies," *Public Health Nutrition* 1 (1) (1998), 33.

33 Rashmi Sinha et al., "Meat Intake and Mortality," *Archives of Internal Medicine* 169 (6) (2009), 362–371.

34 Dan Lowe, "Common Arguments for the Moral Acceptability of Eating Meat: A Discussion for Students," *Between the Species* 19 (1) (2016), 183.

35 Benjamin Franklin, *Autobiography of Benjamin Franklin*, edited by John Bigelow (Philadelphia: J. P. Lippincott, 1868), 128–129.

36 Lowe, "Common Arguments for the Moral Acceptability of Eating Meat," 183.

37 John Stuart Mill, "On Nature," in *Nature: The Utility of Religion and Theism* (London: Watts, 1904), 18; quoted in Christopher Schlottman and Jeff Sebo, *Food, Animals and the Environment* (New York: Routledge, 2019), 13.

38 Piazza et al. "Rationalizing Meat Consumption: The 4 Ns," 118.

39 David Livingstone Smith, *Less Than Human: Why We Demean, Enslave, and Exterminate Others* (New York: St. Martin's Press, 2011), 106.

40 John Webster, *Animal Husbandry Regained: The Place of Farm Animals in Sustainable Agriculture* (New York: Routledge, 2013), 139.

41 Webster, *A Cool Eye Towards Eden*, 186.

42 Andrew Chignell, "Can We Really Vote with Our Forks?: Opportunism and the Threshold Chicken," in *Philosophy Comes to Dinner: Arguments About the Ethics of Eating*, edited by Andrew Chignell, Terence Cuneo, and Matthew C. Halteman (New York: Routledge, 2016), 182–202.

43 Steven McMullen, *Animals and the Economy* (London: Palgrave Macmillan, 2016), 64.

44 Ibid., 64–65.

45 Ibid., 66–67.

46 Ibid., 66, citing Harish Sethu, "How Many Animals Does a Vegetarian Save?" *Counting Animals: A Place for People Who Love Animals and Numbers* (2012), accessed 4 October 2018, http://www.CountingAnimals.com/how-many-animals-does-a-vegetarian-save/.

47 Luc Dauchet et al., "Fruit and Vegetable Consumption and Risk of Coronary Heart Disease: A Meta-Analysis of Cohort Studies," *The Journal of Nutrition* 136 (2006), 2588.

48 David A. Snowdon and Roland L. Phillips, "Does a Vegetarian Diet Reduce the Occurrence of Diabetes?" *American Journal of Public Health* 75 (1985), 510.

49 Timothy Key and Gwyneth Davey, "Prevalence of Obesity Is Low in People Who Do Not Eat Meat," *British Medical Journal* 313 (1996), 816.

50 David Pimentel and Marcia Pimentel, "Sustainability of Meat-Based and Plant-Based Diets and the Environment," *American Journal of Clinical Nutrition* 78 (supp.) (2003), 661–662S.

51 Almost two-thirds of the world's population is expected to live in water-

stressed basins by 2025. Henning Steinfeld et al., *Livestock's Long Shadow—
Environmental Issues and Options* (*Executive Summary*) (Rome: Food and
Agriculture Organization of the United Nations, 2006), xxii.

52 Pimentel and Pimentel, "Sustainability of Meat-Based and Plant-Based Diets,"
662S.

53 Lucas Reijnders and Sam Soret, "Quantification of the Environmental Impact
of Different Dietary Protein Choices," *American Journal of Clinical Nutrition*
78 (supp.) (2003), 665S.

54 *The State of Food Security and Nutrition in the World: Safeguarding Against
Economic Slowdowns and Downturns* (Rome: Food and Agriculture
Organization of the United Nations, 2019), 6.

55 *World Population Prospects: The 2012 Revision* (*Executive Summary*) (New
York: United Nations, 2013) xv.

56 Steinfeld et al., *Livestock's Long Shadow—Environmental Issues and Options*, xx.

57 Joan Sabaté and Sam Soret, "Sustainability of Plant-Based Diets: Back to the
Future," *American Journal of Clinical Nutrition* 100 (supp.) (2014), 476S.

58 Steinfeld et al., *Livestock's Long Shadow*, xxi; Pierre J. Gerber et al., *Tackling
Climate Change Through Livestock—A Global Assessment of Emissions and
Mitigation Opportunities* (Rome: Food and Agriculture Organization of the
United Nations, 2013), 15.

59 Peter Scarborough et al., "Dietary Greenhouse Gas Emissions of Meat Eaters,
Fish Eaters, Vegetarians and Vegans in the UK," *Climatic Change* 125 (2014),
179.

60 Edgar Hertwich et al., *Assessing the Environmental Impacts of Consumption
and Production: Priority Products and Materials* (New York: United Nations
Environmental Programme, 2010), 82.

VII. On Family Farms, Money May Not Swear, but It Still Talks Too Loud

1 David DeGrazia, *Taking Animals Seriously: Mental Life and Moral Status*
(Cambridge: Cambridge University Press, 1996), 288.

2 Ibid., 285.

3 James Rachels, *The Legacy of Socrates: Essays in Moral Philosophy* (New York:
Columbia University Press, 2007), 4.

4 James Rachels, "The Moral Argument for Vegetarianism," in *Can Ethics
Provide Answers? and Other Essays in Moral Philosophy* (Lanham, MD: Rowan
& Littlefield, 1997), 104.

5 Ibid., 105.

6 Temple Grandin and Catherine Johnson, *Animals Make Us Human: Creating*

the Best Life for Animals (New York: Houghton-Mifflin Harcourt, 2009), 143.

7   D. H. Lawrence, "Love Was Once a Little Boy," in *Reflections on the Death of a Porcupine and Other Essays* (Bloomington: Indiana University Press, 1963), 166–167.

8   Ibid., "Love Was Once a Little Boy," 167.

9   Jonathan Leake, "The Secret Life of Moody Cows," *The Times*, 27 February 2005; Donald M. Broom, "Cognitive Ability and Awareness in Domestic Animals and Decisions About Obligations to Animals," *Applied Animal Behaviour Science* 126 (2010), 6.

10 Kristin Hagen and Donald M. Broom, "Emotional Reaction to Learning in Cattle," *Applied Animal Behaviour Science* 85 (2004), 211.

11 Marie-France Bouissou et al., "The Social Behaviour of Cattle," in *Social Behaviour in Farm Animals*, edited by Linda J. Keeling and H.W. Gonyou (Wallingford, Oxfordshire: CABI International, 2001), 113.

12 Lori Marino and Kristin Allen, "The Psychology of Cows," *Animal Behavior and Cognition* 4 (4) (2017), 481.

13 Cornelia Flörcke et al., "Individual Differences in Calf Defence Patterns in Red Angus Beef Cows," *Applied Animal Behaviour Science* 139 (3–4) (2012), 203.

14 John Webster, *Animal Welfare: Limping Towards Eden* (Oxford: Blackwell Publishing, 2005), 76.

15 Mark Twain, "Hunting the Deceitful Turkey," in *Mark Twain: Collected Tales, Sketches, Speeches & Essays 1891–1910*, edited by Louis J. Budd (New York: Library of America, 1992), 805–806.

16 Joe Hutto, *Illumination in the Flatwoods: A Season Living Among the Wild Turkeys* (Guilford, Connecticut: Lyons Press, 2009), 80.

17 William M. Healy, "Behavior,'" in *The Wild Turkey: Biology and Management*, edited by James G. Dickson (Mechanicsburg, Pennsylvania: Stackpole Books, 1992), 55.

18 Ibid., 64–65.

19 Hutto, *Illumination in the Flatwoods*, 182.

20 Ulisse Aldrovandri, *Aldrovandri on Chickens: The Orinthology of Ulisse Aldrovandri*, translated by L.R. Lind (Norman, Oklahoma: University of Oklahoma Press, 2012), II: 14, 142–143.

21 J. L. Edgar et al., "Avian Maternal Response to Chick Distress," *Proceedings of the Royal Society B* 278 (2011), 3129.

22 Carolynn L. Smith and Jane Johnson, "The Chicken Challenge: What

Contemporary Studies of Fowl Mean for Science and Ethics," *Between the Species* 15 (1) (2012), 93.

23 Lori Marino, "Thinking Chickens: A Review of Cognition, Emotion, and Behavior in the Domestic Chicken," *Animal Behavior and Cognition* 20 (2017), 137.

24 Michèle-E. Hogue, Jacques Beaugrand, and Paul C. Lagüe, "Coherent Use of Information by Hens Observing Their Former Dominant Defeating or Being Defeated by a Stranger," *Behavioural Processes* 38 (3) (1996), 134.

25 Daniel M. Weary and David Fraser, "Calling by Domestic Piglets: Reliable Signals of Need?" *Animal Behaviour* 50 (4) (1995), 1052.

26 A. Stolba and D. G. M. Wood-Gush, "The Identification of Behavioural Key Features and Their Incorporation into a Housing Design for Pigs," *Annals of Veterinary Research* 15 (2) (1984), 296.

27 George Orwell, *Animal Farm* (New York: Houghton Mifflin Harcourt, 1990), 12; cited in Michael Mendl, Suzanne Held, and Richard W. Byrne, "Pig Cognition," *Current Biology* 20 (18) (2010), R798.

28 Suzanne Held, Jonathan J. Cooper, and Michael Mendl, "Advances in the Study of Cognition, Behavioural Priorities and Emotions," in *The Welfare of Pigs*, edited by Jeremy N. Marchant-Forde (New York: Springer Science & Business Media, 2009), 20.

29 Lyall Watson, *The Whole Hog: Exploring the Extraordinary Potential of Pigs* (Washington, D.C.: Smithsonian Books, 2004), 164.

30 Emma Roe and Terry Marsden, "Analysis of Retail Survey of Products That Carry Welfare Claims and of Non-Retailer Assurance Schemes Whose Logos Accompany Welfare Claims," in *Attitudes of Consumers, Retailers and Producers to Animal Welfare*, edited by Unni Kjærnes, Mara Miele, & Joek Roex (Cardiff: Cardiff University Press, 2007), 15–16; quoted in Mara Miele, "The Taste of Happiness: Free Range Chicken," *Environment and Planning A* 43 (2011), 2079.

31 In the wild, chickens commonly live for several years. Miele, "The Taste of Happiness," 2081.

32 For example, heritage turkey hens used for breeding are commonly productive for 5–7 years and breeding toms for 3–5 years. Livestock Conservancy, "Definition of a Heritage Turkey," accessed 12 November 2018, https://livestockconservancy.org/index.php/resources/internal/heritage-turkey.

33 Accessed 5 February 2020, http://stories.renewingthecountryside.org/2012/06/the-willis-farm/.

34 Orwell, *Animal Farm*, 5–6.

35   The natural life span of breeds raised for beef is about 15–20 years. Accessed 5 February 2020, https://www.aussiefarms.org.au/kb/48-age-animals-slaughtered.

36   Orwell, *Animal Farm*, 6.

37   John Webster, *Animal Welfare: A Cool Eye Towards Eden* (Oxford: Blackwell Publishing, 1994), 170.

38   I. Bazzoli et al., "Factors Associated with Age at Slaughter and Carcass Weight, Price, and Value of Dairy Cull Cows," *Journal of Dairy Science* 97 (2) (2014), 1087.

39   M. A. von Keyserlingk and Daniel M. Weary, "Maternal Behavior in Cattle," *Hormones and Behavior* 52 (2007), 106.

40   Jonathan Balcombe, *Second Nature: The Inner Lives of Animals* (New York: Palgrave Macmillan, 2010), 203.

41   Neville G. Gregory, *Animal Welfare and Meat Production* (Wallingford, Oxfordshire: CABI Publishing, 2007), 122.

42   Webster, *A Cool Eye Towards Eden*, 157.

43   Temple Grandin, "Corporations Can Be Agents of Great Improvements in Animal Welfare and Food Safety and the Need for Minimum Decent Standards," (4 April 2001), accessed 16 December 2018, https://www.grandin.com/welfare/corporation.agents.html.

44   For our purposes, "fish" will refer to bony fishes (or teleosts) because they have been the subjects of the pain-related research to be discussed and include almost all commercially significant fishes.

45   Neville G. Gregory, "Can Fish Experience Pain?" *ANZCCART News* 12 (4) (1999), 1; quoted in K. P. Chandroo, I. J. H. Duncan, and R. D. Moccia, "Can Fish Suffer? Perspectives on Sentience, Pain, Fear and Stress," *Applied Animal Welfare Science* 86 (2004), 233.

46   Gregory, "Can Fish Experience Pain?," 3.

47   Lynne U. Sneddon, Victoria A. Braithwaite, and Michael J. Gentle, "Do Fishes Have Nociceptors? Evidence for the Evolution of a Vertebrate Sensory System," *Proceedings of the Royal Society London B* 270 (2003), 117–118.

48   Lynne U. Sneddon, "The Evidence for Pain in Fish: The Use of Morphine as an Analgesic." *Applied Animal Behaviour Science* 83 (2) (2003), 153.

49   Lynne U. Sneddon, "Do Painful Sensations and Fear Exist in Fish?" in *From Science to Law*, edited by T. A. Van der Kemp and M. Lachance (Toronto: Carswell, 2013), 99.

50   James D. Rose, "The Neurobehavioral Nature of Fishes and the Question of Awareness and Pain," *Reviews in Fisheries Science* 10 (1) (2002), 24.

51 Daniel M. Weary et al., "Identifying and Preventing Pain in Animals," *Applied Animal Behavior Science* 100 (1) (2006), 73.

52 Webster, *Limping Towards Eden*, 69.

53 Jonathan Balcombe, *What a Fish Knows* (New York: Farrar, Straus and Giroux, 2016), 219.

54 Neville G. Gregory, *Animal Welfare and Meat Science* (Wallingford, Oxfordshire: CABI Publishing, 1998), 198.

55 Balcombe, *What a Fish Knows*, 219.

56 Gregory, *Animal Welfare and Meat Science*, 199.

57 B. K. Diggles et al., "Ecology and Welfare of Aquatic Animals in Wild Capture Fisheries," *Reviews in Fish Biology and Fisheries* 21 (2011), 753.

58 D. H. F. Robb and S. C. Kestin, "Methods to Kill Fish: Field Observations and Literature Reviewed," *Animal Welfare* 11 (2002), 270.

59 Ibid., 272.

60 Ibid., 274.

61 D. H. F. Robb et al., "Commercial Slaughter Methods Used on Atlantic Salmon: The Determination of the Onset of Brain Failure by Electroencephalography," *Veterinary Record* 147 (2000), 300.

62 Björn Kok et al., "Fish as Feed: Using Economic Allocation to Quantify the Fish In : Fish Out Ratio of Major Fed Aquaculture Species," *Aquaculture* 528 (2020), 8.

63 Victoria Braithwaite, *Do Fish Feel Pain?*, (Oxford: Oxford University Press, 2010), 18.

64 As Albert Bandura noted, harming others is easier when their suffering is not visible. Bandura, *Moral Disengagement: How People Do Harm and Live with Themselves*, (New York: Worth Publishers, 2016), 64; cited in Hank Rothgerber, "Efforts to Overcome Vegetarian-Induced Dissonance Among Meat Eaters," *Appetite* 79 (2014), 33.

65 Daniel Imhoff, "What the Industry Doesn't Want Us to Know," in *The CAFO Reader: The Tragedy of Industrial Animal Factories*, edited by Daniel Imhoff. Berkeley (California: Watershed Media, 2010), 89.

66 Joan Dunayer, *Animal Equality: Language and Liberation* (Derwood, Maryland: Ryce Publishing, 2001), 137; *cited* in Les Mitchell, "Moral Disengagement and Support for Nonhuman Animal Farming," *Society & Animals* 19 (2011), 50.

67 Brock Bastian and Steve Loughnan, "Resolving the Meat Paradox: A Motivational Account of Morally Troubling Behavior and Its Maintenance," *Personality and Social Psychology Review* 21 (2017), 281.

68 Helen Proctor, "Animal Sentience: Where Are We and Where Are We Heading?," 2 *Animals* (2012), 629.

69 Orwell, *Animal Farm*, 118.

70 Melanie Joy, *Why We Love Dogs, Eat Pigs, and Wear Cows: An Introduction to Carnism, the Belief System That Enables Us to Eat Some Animals and Not Others* (San Francisco: Conan Press, 2011).

71 Kristof Dhont, et al., "Rethinking Human–Animal Relations: The Critical Role of Social Psychology," *Group Processes and Intergroup Relations* 22(6) (2019), 770.

72 Ian J. H. Duncan, "The Changing Concept of Animal Sentience," *Applied Animal Behaviour Science* 100 (2006), 17.

73 Bastian and Loughnan, "Resolving the Meat Paradox: A Motivational Account of Morally Troubling Behavior and Its Maintenance," 281.

74 Boyka Bratanova, Steve Loughnan, and Brock Bastian, "The Effect of Categorization as Food on Perceived Moral Standing of Animals," *Appetite* 57 (2011), 195. Rather than deal with the uncomfortable realization that a sentient being is suffering, a person may unburden his or her conscience by denying that the victim has the capacity to suffer. Steve Loughnan, Nick Haslam, and Brock Bastian, "The Role of Meat Consumption in the Denial of Moral Status and Mind to Meat Animals," *Appetite* 55 (2010), 157.

75 Ohio Revised Code 959.13.

76 Scott Plous, "Is There Such a Thing as Prejudice Toward Animals?," in *Understanding Prejudice and Discrimination*, edited by Scott Plous (Boston: McGraw-Hill, 2003), 510.

VIII. Overcoming Supremacism

1   Carl Sagan, *Pale Blue Dot: A Vision of the Human Future in Space* (New York: Random House, 1994), 14.

2   Roger Manvell and Heinrich Fraenkel, *Heinrich Himmler: The Sinister Life of the Head of the SS and Gestapo* (New York: Skyhorse Publishing, 2007), 196–197.

3   Robert Rochefort, *Robert Schuman* (Paris: Éditions du Cerf, 1968), 128; quoted in R. C. Mowat, *Creating the European Community* (New York: Harper & Row, 1973), 44.

4   Robert Schuman, *For Europe* (Geneva: Nagel Editions, 2010), 112–113.

5   Mowat, *Creating the European Community*, 208.

6   Margriet Krijtenburg, *Schuman's Europe: His Frame of Reference*, (2011), accessed 2 March 2019, https://openaccess.leidenuniv.nl/bitstream/handle/1887/19767/fulltext.pdf?sequence=17, 67.

7 Schuman, *For Europe*, 104.

8 For our purposes, "nationalism" will be defined as a belief that a country is superior and should be dominant. *See* Rick Kosterman and Seymour Feshbach, "Toward a Measure of Patriotic and Nationalistic Attitudes," *Political Psychology* 10 (2) (1989), 261.

9 Theodore Brameld, *Minority Problems in the Public Schools: A Study of Administrative Policies and Practices in Seven School Systems* (New York: Harper and Brothers, 1946), 245; cited in John F. Dovidio, Samuel L. Gaertner, and Kerry Kawakami, "Intergroup Contact: The Past, Present, and the Future," *Group Processes & Intergroup Relations* 6 (5) (2003), 6.

10 Gordon Allport, *The Nature of Prejudice* (Reading, Massachusetts: Addison-Wesley Publishing, 1979), 7.

11 Ibid., 281.

12 Thomas F. Pettigrew and Linda R. Tropp, "A Meta-Analytic Test of Intergroup Contact Theory," *Journal of Personality and Social Psychology* 90 (5) (2006), 751–783.

13 Thomas Fraser Pettigrew and Linda R. Tropp, "How Does Intergroup Contact Reduce Prejudice? Meta-Analytic Tests of Three Mediators," *European Journal of Social Psychology* 38 (2008), 927–928.

14 Ananthi Al Ramiah and Gordon Hewstone, "Intergroup Contact as a Tool for Reducing, Resolving, and Preventing Intergroup Conflict," *American Psychologist* 68 (7) (2013), 538.

15 Ibid., 536.

16 "Nationalist supremacists" will refer to people who believe that those from a particular country are naturally superior to those from other countries and should be able to dominate them. Some examples are state-based colonial empires and the National Socialists.

17 "Political supremacists" will refer to people who believe people in their political group are superior to those in other political groups and are entitled to dominate them. In extreme cases, they murder political opponents. Examples are the Cambodian Khmer Rouge and the Soviet Communists.

18 As President François Mitterand warned members of the European Parliament shortly before he retired, "nationalism means war!" 17 January 1995 speech to the European Parliament.

19 *A History of Franco-German Relations in Europe: From "Hereditary Enemies" to Partners*, edited by Carine Germond and Henning Turk (New York: St. Martin's Press, 2008).

20 In his May 9, 1950, Declaration, Schuman said, "The solidarity in production

thus established will make it plain that any war between France and Germany becomes not merely unthinkable, but materially impossible." Schuman, *For Europe*, 147.

21 It is not unusual for citizens to have multiple identities; for example, Spaniards may feel Catalan, Spanish, and European at the same time. Liesbet Hooghe and Gary Marks, "Calculation, Community and Cues," *European Union Politics* 6 (4), 423.

22 Standard Eurobarometer 88, "European Citizenship Report," (2017), accessed 2 March 2019, http://publications.europa.eu/resource/cellar/b02975b3-58b2-11e8-ab41-01aa75ed71a1.0001.02/DOC_1, 4.

23 Krijtenburg, *Schuman's Europe*, 26 ("C'est ma petite Lorraine où mes ancêtres ont vécu et travaillé au long des siècles. C'est là que sont mes interêts.").

24 Allport, *The Nature of Prejudice*, 281.

25 Ibid., 68.

26 Jim Sidanius and Felicia Pratto, *Social Dominance: An Intergroup Theory of Social Hierarchy and Oppression* (Cambridge: Cambridge University Press, 1999), 67.

27 Felicia Pratto et al., "Social Dominance Orientation: A Personality Variable Predicting Social and Political Attitudes," *Journal of Personality and Social Psychology* 67 (4) (1994), 742, 754–755.

28 "Nationalism" and its denigration of other groups should be distinguished from "patriotism," which signifies pride in a nation and is not necessarily associated with a desire to dominate and oppress other groups. Yesilernis Peña and Jim Sidanius, "U.S. Patriotism and Ideologies of Group Dominance: A Tale of Asymmetry," *The Journal of Social Psychology* 142(6) (2002), 783.

29 Arnold K. Ho et al., "Social Dominance Orientation: Revisiting the Structure and Function of a Variable Predicting Social and Political Attitudes," *Personality and Social Psychological Bulletin* 38 (5) (2011), 584.

30 Pratto et al., "Social Dominance Orientation: A Personality Variable Predicting Social and Political Attitudes," 754.

31 Felicia Pratto, Jim Sidanius, and Shana Levin, "Social Dominance Theory and the Dynamics of Intergroup Relations: Taking Stock and Looking Forward," *European Review of Social Psychology* 17 (2006), 281; Nour Kteily, Arnold K. Ho, and Jim Sidanius, "Hierarchy in the Mind: The Predictive Power of Social Dominance Orientation Across Social Contexts and Domains," *Journal of Experimental Social Psychology* 48 (2011), 546.

32 Ho et al., "Social Dominance Orientation: Revisiting the Structure and Function of a Variable Predicting Social and Political Attitudes," 3.

33 Kristof Dhont, Gordon Hodson, and Ana C. Leite, "Common Ideological Roots of Speciesism and Generalized Ethnic Prejudice: The Social Dominance Human-Animal Relations Model (SD-HARM)," *European Journal of Personality* 30 (2016), 516–518; Kristof Dhont et al., "The Psychology of Speciesism," in *Why We Love and Exploit Animals: Bridging Insights from Academia and Advocacy*, edited by Kristof Dhont and Gordon Hodson (New York: Routledge, 2019), 35–36.

34 Taciano Lemos Milfont et al., "Environmental Consequences of the Desire to Dominate and Be Superior," *Personality and Social Psychology Bulletin* 39 (9) (2013), 1134; Taciano L. Milfont et al., "On the Relation Between Social Dominance Orientation and Environmentalism: A 25-Nation Study," *Social Psychological and Personality Science* 9 (7) (2018), 810.

35 Dhont, Hodson, and Leite, "Common Ideological Roots," 518.

36 Brock Bastian et al., "When Closing the Human-Animal Divide Expands Moral Concern: The Importance of Framing," *Social Psychological and Personality Science* 3 (2011), 427.

37 Kimberly Costello and Gordon Hodson, "Exploring the Roots of Dehumanization: The Role of Animal–Human Similarity in Promoting Immigrant Humanization," *Group Processes & Intergroup Relations* 13 (1) (2009), 16–17.

38 The author of the study defined "prosocial behaviors" as "any act which assists, benefits, or provides support for another." William Ellery Samuels, "Nurturing Kindness Naturally: A Humane Education Program's Effect on the Prosocial Behavior of First and Second Graders Across China," *International Journal of Educational Research* 91 (2018), 49.

39 Ibid., 61.

40 Bastian et al., "When Closing the Human-Animal Divide Expands Moral Concern," 427; Lynne M. Jackson, *The Psychology of Prejudice from Attitudes to Social Action*, 2nd edition (Washington, D.C.: American Psychological Association, 2020), 201.

41 Sidanius et al., "Social Dominance Theory: Explorations in the Psychology of Oppression," in *The Cambridge Handbook of the Psychology of Prejudice*, edited by Chris G. Sibley and Fiona Kate Barlow (Cambridge: Cambridge University Press, 2016), 149.

42 According to statistics compiled by an agency of the United Nations that tracks migration patterns, the number of international migrants has increased by more than 40 percent since the turn of the century, from 173 million in 2000 to 258 million in 2017. *International Migration Report 2017 Highlights*

(New York: United Nations, Department of Economic and Social Affairs, Population Division, 2018), 4.

43 Kanta Kuman Rigaud et al., "Groundswell—Preparing for International Climate Migration" (Washington, D.C.: World Bank, 2018), accessed on 6 April 2019, http://documents.worldbank.org/curated/en/846391522306665751/pdf/124719-v2-PUB-PUBLIC-docdate-3-18-18WBG-ClimateChange-Final.pdf, xix; cited in David Wallace-Wells, *The Uninhabitable Earth: Life After Warming* (New York: Tim Duggan Books, 2019), 7.

44 Gordon Hodson, Miles Hewstone, and Hermann Swart, "Epilogue and Future Directions," in *Advances in Intergroup Contact*, edited by Gordon Hodson and Miles Hewstone (New York: Psychology Press, 2013), 297.

45 King's statement that "the moral arc of the universe is long but it bends toward justice" was from a sermon written by Theodore Parker, an American Unitarian preacher and abolitionist, in which Parker said that "I do not pretend to understand the moral universe; the arc is a long one, my eye reaches but little ways . . . And from what I see I am sure it bends towards justice." Theodore Parker, *The Collected Works of Theodore Parker*, edited by F. P. Cobbe (London: Tribner, 1879), 2:48.

46 Robert F. Kennedy, *RFK: Collected Speeches*, edited by Edwin O. Guthman and C. Richard Allen (New York: Viking, 1993), 243–244.

47 United Nations Educational, Scientific, and Cultural Organization (UNESCO) (1945).

48 Pettigrew and Tropp, "A Meta-Analytic Test of Intergroup Contact Theory," 766.

49 Kristof Dhont and Alain Van Hiel, "We Must Not Be Enemies: Interracial Contact and the Reduction of Prejudice Among Authoritarians," *Personality and Individual Differences* 46 (2009), 177; Gordon Hodson, Kimberly Costello, and Cara C. MacInnis, "Is Intergroup Contact Beneficial Among Intolerant People?" in *Advances in Intergroup Contact*, 64.

50 Pettigrew and Tropp, "A Meta-Analytic Test of Intergroup Contact Theory," 751.

51 Gordon Hodson and Miles Hewstone, "Introduction," in *Advances in Intergroup Contact*, 13.

52 Ethnic groups that are treated unequally resent and usually attempt to improve their position. Barbara Harff and Ted Robert Gurr, *Ethnic Conflict in World Politics*, Second Edition (Boulder, Colorado: Westview Press, 2004), 5.

53 *Global Trends—Forced Displacement in 2017* (Geneva: United Nations High Commissioner for Refugees, 2018), accessed on 29 April 2019, 60–64, https://www.unhcr.org/5b27be547.pdf, 7, 13.

54 David Miliband, *Rescue: Refugees and the Political Crisis of Our Time* (New York: Simon & Schuster, 2017), 29–30; *Global Trends—Forced Displacement in 2016* (Geneva: United Nations High Commissioner for Refugees, 2017), accessed on 29 April 2019, https://www.unhcr.org/globaltrends2016/.

55 *Global Trends—Forced Displacement in 2017*, 29–30.

56 Milfont et al., "Environmental Consequences of the Desire to Dominate and Be Superior," 1134; Milfont et al., "On the Relation Between Social Dominance Orientation and Environmentalism: A 25-Nation Study," 810.

57 Samuels, "Nurturing Kindness Naturally," 49–64.

58 Nik Taylor and Tania D. Signal, "Empathy and Attitudes to Animals," *Anthrozoös* 18 (1), 810.

59 Comparing animals to humans can expand children's moral concern, while comparing humans to animals does not seem to have the same beneficial effect, so it is important to approach the issue from that perspective. *See* Bastian et al., "When Closing the Human-Animal Divide Expands Moral Concern: The Importance of Framing," 426.

60 Dhont et al., "The Psychology of Speciesism," 44.

61 Donald Trump was an exception when he urged governors in the United States to "dominate" people who were protesting police brutality directed against African Americans in June of 2020. See Katie Rogers, Jonathan Martin, and Maggie Haberman, "As Trump *Calls Protestors 'Terrorists,'* Tear Gas Clears a Path for His Walk to a Church," *New York Times*, June 1, 2020.

62 Martin Backstrom and Frederik Björklund, "Structural Modeling of Generalized Prejudice," *Journal of Individual Differences* 28 (1) (2007), 12.

63 Ibid.

64 Milfont et. al., "Environmental Consequences of the Desire to Dominate and Be Superior," 1127.

65 Ibid., 1134; Kirsti Jylhä and Nazar Akrami, "Social Dominance and Climate Change Denial: The Role of Dominance and System Justification," *Personality and Individual Differences* 86 (2015), 110.

66 Sidanius et al., "Social Dominance Theory: Explorations in the Psychology of Oppression," in *The Cambridge Handbook of the Psychology of Prejudice*, 149.

67 Jylhä and Akrami, "Social Dominance and Climate Change Denial," 111.

68 See Wallace-Wells, *The Uninhabitable Earth*, 118.

69 Michael Pollan, accessed on 20 February 2019, https://www.nourishlife. org/2011/03/vote-with-your-fork/.

Afterword: Beyond Supremacism

1 Edward O. Wilson, *The Meaning of Human Existence* (New York: Liveright Publishing Corporation, 2014), 176–177.

2 Richard Dawkins, *The Magic of Reality: How We Know What's Really True*, with illustrations by Dave McKean (New York: Simon & Schuster, 2012), 51.

3 Richard Dawkins, *The Ancestor's Tale: A Pilgrimage to the Dawn of Evolution* (New York: Houghton Mifflin, 2004), 192.

4 Ibid., 293.

5 Neil Shubin, *Your Inner Fish: A Journey into the 3.5 Billion Year History of the Human Body* (New York: Pantheon Books, 2008), 41.

6 Henry Beston, *The Outermost House: A Year of Life on the Great Beach of Cape Cod* (New York: St. Martin's, 2003), 25.

7 Stephen Jay Gould, *The Mismeasure of Man* (New York: W. W. Norton, 1984), 324.

8 Carl Sagan, *Cosmos* (New York: Random House, 1980), 196.

9 Carl Sagan, *Pale Blue Dot: A Vision of the Human Future in Space* (New York: Random House, 1994), 52.

References and Bibliography

Akrami, Nazar, Bo Ekehammar, and Robin Bergh. "Generalized Prejudice: Common and Specific Components." *Psychological Science* 22, no. 1 (2010).

Aldrovandi, Ulisse. *Aldrovandi on Chickens: The Ornithology of Ulisse Aldrovandi.* Translated by L.R. Lind. Norman, OK: University of Oklahoma Press, 2012.

Allport, Gordon. *The Nature of Prejudice.* Reading, MA: Addison-Wesley Publishing, 1979.

Al Ramiah, Ananthi, and Gordon Hewstone. "Intergroup Contact as a Tool for Reducing, Resolving, and Preventing Intergroup Conflict." *American Psychologist* 68, no. 7 (2013).

Anger, Per. *With Raoul Wallenberg in Budapest: Memories of the War Years in Hungary.* Translated by David Mel Paul and Margareta Paul. Washington, DC: Holocaust Library, 1981.

Appleby, Paul N., M. Thorogood, J. I. Mann, and T. J. Key. "The Oxford Vegetarian Study: An Overview," supplement. *American Journal of Clinical Nutrition* 70 (1999).

Ascherson, Neal. *The King Incorporated: Leopold the Second and the Congo.* London: Granta Books, 1963.

Atkinson, Diane. *Votes for Women.* Cambridge: Cambridge University Press, 1988.

Bäckström, Martin, and Fredrik Björklund. "Structural Modeling of Generalized Prejudice." *Journal of Individual Differences* 28, no. 1 (2007).

Balcombe, Jonathan. *Second Nature: The Inner Lives of Animals.* New York: Palgrave Macmillan, 2010.

Bandura, Albert. *Moral Disengagement: How People Do Harm and Live with Themselves.* New York: Worth Publishers, 2016.

———. "Moral Disengagement in the Perpetration of Inhumanities." *Personality and Social Psychology Review* 3, no. 3 (1999).

———. "Selective Moral Disengagement in the Exercise of Moral Agency." *Journal of Moral Education* 31, no. 2 (2002).

Bartley, Paula. *Votes for Women 1860–1928*. Abington, Oxfordshire: Hodder and Stoughton, 1978.

Bastian, Brock, Kimberly Costello, Steve Loughnan, and Gordon Hodson. "When Closing the Human-Animal Divide Expands Moral Concern: The Importance of Framing." *Social Psychological and Personality Science* 3 (2011).

Bazzoli, I., M. De Marchi, A. Cecchinato, D. P. Berry, and G. Bittante. "Factors Associated with Age at Slaughter and Carcass Weight, Price, and Value of Dairy Cull Cows." *Journal of Dairy Science* 97, no. 2 (2014).

Bennett, Daphne. *Emily Davies and the Liberation of Women 1830–1921*. London: Andre Deutsch, 1990.

Bentham, Jeremy. *An Introduction to the Principles of Morals and Legislation*. Oxford: Clarendon Press, 1823.

Beutler, Bernhard, ed. *Réflexions sur Europe*. Paris: Éditions Complexe, 1993.

Bierman, John. *Righteous Gentile: The Story of Raoul Wallenberg, Missing Hero of the Holocaust*. New York: Viking Press, 1981.

Blackstone, William. *The American Students' Blackstone: Commentaries on the Laws of England*. Edited by George Chase. New York: Banks & Brothers, 1884.

Boesch, Christophe, and Hedwige Boesch. "Optimization of Nut-Cracking with Natural Hammers by Wild Chimpanzees." *Behaviour* 83, no. 3 (1988).

Boesch, Christophe, Josephine S. Head, and Martha M. Robbins. "Complex Tool Sets for Honey Extraction in Loango National Park, Gabon." *Journal of Human Evolution* 56 (2009).

Bouissou, Marie-France, Alain Boissy, Pierre Le Neindre, and Isabelle Veissier. "The Social Behaviour of Cattle." In *Social Behaviour in Farm Animals*. Edited by Linda J. Keeling and H. W. Gonyou. Wallingford, Oxfordshire: CABI International, 2001.

Boulger, Demetrius Charles. *The Congo State Is NOT a Slave State: A Reply to Mr. E. D. Morel's Pamphlet Entitled "The Congo Slave State."* London: Sampson, Low, Marston & Co., 1903.

Braham, Randolph L. *Eichmann and the Destruction of Hungarian Jewry*. New York: Twayne Publishers, 1961.

––––––. *The Politics of Genocide: The Holocaust in Hungary*. 3rd ed. New York: Columbia University Press, 2016.

Braham, Randolph L., and Scott Miller, eds. *The Nazis' Last Victims: The Holocaust in Hungary*. Detroit: Wayne State University Press, 1998.

Braham, Randolph L., and William J. vanden Heuvel, eds. *The Auschwitz Reports and the Holocaust in Hungary*. New York: Columbia University Press, 2011.

Braithwaite, Victoria. *Do Fish Feel Pain?* Oxford: Oxford University Press, 2010.

Brameld, Theodore. *Minority Problems in the Public Schools: A Study of Administrative Policies and Practices in Seven School Systems*. New York: Harper and Brothers, 1946.

Broom, Donald M. "Sentience." In *Encyclopedia of Animal Behavior*. Edited by Jae C. Choe. 2nd ed. Cambridge, MA: Academic Press, 2019.

Brosnan, Sarah F., and Frans B. M. de Waal. "Evolution of Responses to (Un)Fairness." *Science* 346, no. 6207 (2014).

Brown, Culum. "Familiarity with the Test Environment Improves Escape Responses with the Crimson Spotted Rainbowfish, *Melanotaenia duboulayi*." *Animal Cognition* 4, no. 2 (2001).

————. "Fish Intelligence, Sentience and Ethics." *Animal Cognition* 18, no. 1 (2015).

Browning, Christopher. *The Path to Genocide: Essays on Launching the Final Solution*. Cambridge: Cambridge University Press, 1992.

Buchwalder, T., and B. Huber-Eicher. "Effect of the Analgesic Butorphanol on Activity Behavior in Turkeys." *Research in Veterinary Science* 79 (2005).

Carlberg, Ingrid. *Raoul Wallenberg: The Heroic Life and Mysterious Disappearance of the Man Who Saved Thousands of Hungarian Jews from the Holocaust*. Translated by Ebba Segerberg. New York: MacLehose Press, 2015.

Cattier, Félicien. *Étude sur La Situation de l'État Indépendant du Congo*. Brussels: Larcier, 1906.

Cavalieri, Paola, and Peter Singer, eds. *The Great Ape Project: Equality Beyond Humanity*. New York: St. Martin's Press, 1993.

Caviola, Lucius, Jim A. C. Everett, and Nadira S. Faber. "The Moral Standing of Animals: Towards a Psychology of Speciesism." *Journal of Personality and Social Psychology* 116 (2019).

Cesarani, David. *Becoming Eichmann: Rethinking the Life, Crimes, and Trial of a "Desk Murderer."* New York: Da Capo Press, 2004.

Chedzoy, Alan. *A Scandalous Woman: The Story of Caroline Norton*. London: Allison & Busby, 1992.

Chignell, Andrew. "Can We Really Vote with Our Forks? Opportunism and the Threshold Chicken." In *Philosophy Comes to Dinner: Arguments about the Ethics of Eating*, edited by Andrew Chignell, Terence Cuneo, and Matthew C. Halteman. New York: Routledge, 2016.

Chignell, Andrew, Terence Cuneo, and Matthew C. Halteman, eds. *Philosophy Comes to Dinner: Arguments about the Ethics of Eating*. New York: Routledge, 2016.

Cline, Catherine. *E. D. Morel 1873–1924: The Strategies of Protest*. Belfast: Blackstaff Press, 1980.

Cobbe, Frances Power. "Our Policy: An Address to Women Concerning the Suffrage." In *Before the Vote Was Won: Arguments For and Against Women's Suffrage 1864–1896*, edited by Jane Lewis. London: Routledge & Kegan Paul, 1987.

————. "Criminals, Idiots, Women, and Minors." In *Criminals, Idiots, Women, and Minors: Victorian Writing on Women by Women*. Edited by Susan Hamilton. Peterborough, Ontario: Broadview Press, 2004.

Cocks, Frederick Seymour. *E. D. Morel: The Man and His Work*. London: George Allen & Unwin, Ltd., 1920.

Conrad, Joseph. *Collected Letters of Joseph Conrad: 1903–1907*. Edited by Frederick R. Karl and Laurence Davies. Vol. 3. Cambridge: Cambridge University Press, 1988.

————. *Heart of Darkness*. Edited by Paul B. Armstrong. New York: W.W. Norton, 2006.

Cornelius, Deborah S. *Hungary in World War II: Caught in the Cauldron*. New York: Fordham University Press, 2011.

Costello, Kimberly, and Gordon Hodson. "Explaining Dehumanization among Children: The Interspecies Model of Prejudice." *British Journal of Social Psychology* 53 (2012).

————. "Exploring the Roots of Dehumanization: The Role of Animal–Human Similarity in Promoting Immigrant Humanization." *Group Processes & Intergroup Relations* 13, no. 1 (2009).

Crawford, Elizabeth. *The Women's Suffrage Movement: A Reference Guide 1866–1928*. London: Routledge, 1999.

Danbury, T. C., C. A. Weeks, J. P. Chambers, A. E. Waterman-Pearson, and S. C. Kestin. "Self-Selection of the Analgesic Drug Carprofen by Lame Broiler Chickens." *Veterinary Record* 146 (2000).

Darwin, Charles. *The Descent of Man and Selection in Relation to Sex: The Concise Edition*. Edited by Carl Zimmer. New York: Penguin Group, 2007.

Dauchet, Luc, Philippe Amouyel, Serge Hercberg, and Jean Dallongeville. "Fruit and Vegetable Consumption and Risk of Coronary Heart Disease: A Meta-Analysis of Cohort Studies." *The Journal of Nutrition* 136 (2006).

Dawkins, Richard. *The Ancestor's Tale: A Pilgrimage to the Dawn of Evolution*. New York: Houghton Mifflin, 2004.

————. *The Magic of Reality: How We Know What's Really True,* illustrated by Dave McKean. New York: Simon & Schuster, 2012.

DeGrazia, David. *Taking Animals Seriously: Mental Life and Moral Status*. Cambridge: Cambridge University Press, 1996.

De la Torre, Victoria Martín. *Europe, a Leap into the Unknown: A Journey Back in Time to Meet the Founders of the European Union.* Brussels: Peter Lang, 2014.

de Waal, Frans B. M. *The Ape and the Sushi Master: Cultural Reflections of a Primatologist.* New York: Basic Books, 2001.

————. *Are We Smart Enough to Know How Smart Animals Are?* New York: W. W. Norton, 2016.

————. "The Chimpanzees' Service Economy: Food for Grooming." *Evolution and Human Behavior* 18 (1987).

————. *Good Natured: The Origins of Right and Wrong in Humans and Other Animals.* Cambridge, MA: Harvard University Press, 1996.

————. *Our Inner Ape: A Leading Primatologist Explains Why We Are Who We Are.* New York: Riverhead Books, 2005.

de Waal, Frans B. M., and Kristin E. Bonnie. "In Tune with Others: The Social Side of Primate Culture." In *The Question of Animal Culture*, edited by Kevin N. Laland and Bennett G. Galef. Cambridge, MA: Harvard University Press, 2009.

de Waal, Frans B. M., and Sarah F. Brosnan. "Simple and Complex Reciprocity in Primates." In *Cooperation in Primates and Humans: Mechanisms and Evolution*, edited by Peter M. Kappeler and Carel P. Van Schalk. Heidelberg, Germany: Springer, 2005.

Dewey, John. *Reconstruction in Philosophy.* New York: Henry Holt, 1920.

Dhont, Kristof, and Alain Van Hiel. "We Must Not Be Enemies: Interracial Contact and the Reduction of Prejudice among Authoritarians." *Personality and Individual Differences* 46 (2009).

Dhont, Kristof, Alain Van Hiel, and Gordon Hewstone. "Changing the Ideological Roots of Prejudice: Longitudinal Effects of Intergroup Contact on Social Dominance Orientation." *Group Processes & Intergroup Relations* 17 (2014).

Dhont, Kristof, and Gordon Hodson. "Why Do Right-Wing Adherents Engage in More Animal Exploitation and Meat Consumption?" *Personality and Individual Differences* 64 (2014).

Dhont, Kristof, and Gordon Hodson, eds. *Why We Love and Exploit Animals: Bridging Insights from Academia and Advocacy.* New York: Routledge, 2019.

Dhont, Kristof, Gordon Hodson, and Ana C. Leite. "Common Ideological Roots of Speciesism and Generalized Ethnic Prejudice: The Social Dominance Human-Animal Relations Model (SD-HARM)." *European Journal of Personality* 30 (2016).

Dhont, Kristof, Gordon Hodson, Ana C. Leite, and Alina Salmen. "The Psychology of Speciesism." In *Why We Love and Exploit Animals: Bridging Insights from*

Academia and Advocacy, edited by Kristof Dhont and Gordon Hodson. New York: Routledge, 2019.

Dickson, James G., ed. *The Wild Turkey: Biology and Management.* Mechanicsburg, PA: Stackpole Books, 1992.

Doyle, Arthur Conan. *Crime of the Congo.* London: Hutchinson, 1909.

Duncan, I. J. H. "Animal Welfare Issues in the Poultry Industry: Is There a Lesson to Be Learned?" *Journal of Applied Animal Welfare Science* 4, no. 3 (2001).

Duncan, I. J. H., E. R. Beatty, P. M. Hocking, and S. R. I. Duff. "Assessment of Pain Associated with Degenerative Hip Disorders in Adult Male Turkeys." *Research in Veterinary Science* 50, no. 2 (1991).

Dwork, Debórah, and Robert Jan van Pelt. *Holocaust: A History.* New York: W.W. Norton, 2002.

Edgar, J. L., J. C. Lowe, E. S. Paul, and C. J. Nicol. "Avian Maternal Response to Chick Distress." *Proceedings of the Royal Society B* 278 (2011).

Edgerton, Robert B. *The Troubled Heart of Africa: A History of the Congo.* New York: St. Martin's Press, 2002.

Emerson, Barbara. *Leopold II of the Belgians: King of Colonialism.* London: Weidenfeld & Nicolson, 1979.

Ewans, Martin. *European Atrocity, African Catastrophe: The Congo Free State and Its Aftermath.* London: RoutledgeCurzon, 2002.

Faulkner, D. B., T. Eurell, W. J. Tranquilli, R. S. Ott, M. W. Ohl, G. F. Cmarik, and G. Zinn. "Performance and Health of Weanling Bulls after Butorphanol and Xylazine Administration at Castration." *Journal of Animal Science* 70, no. 10 (1992).

Fawcett, Millicent Garrett. "Electoral Disabilities of Women." In *Before the Vote Was Won: Arguments For and Against Women's Suffrage 1864–1896.* Edited by Jane Lewis. London: Routledge & Kegan Paul, 1987.

————. *What I Remember.* Honolulu: University Press of the Pacific, 2004.

————. *Women's Suffrage: A Short History of a Great Movement.* New York: Dodge Publishing, 2005.

————. *The Women's Victory—and After: Personal Reminiscences, 1911–1918.* London: Sidgwick & Jackson, 1920.

Flack, Jessica C., and Frans B. M. de Waal. "'Any Animal Whatever': Darwinian Building Blocks of Morality in Monkeys and Apes." *Journal of Consciousness Studies* 7 (2000).

Flörcke, Cornelia, Terry E. Engle, Temple Grandin, and Mark J. Deesing. "Individual Differences in Calf Defence Patterns in Red Angus Beef Cows." *Applied Animal Behaviour Science* 139, no. 3–4 (2012).

Florence, Ronald. *Emissary of the Doomed: Bargaining for Lives in the Holocaust.* New York: Viking Press, 2010.

Food and Agriculture Organization of the United Nations. *The State of Food Security and Nutrition in the World: Safeguarding Against Economic Slowdowns and Downturns.* Rome: Food and Agriculture Organization of the United Nations, 2019.

Fouts, Roger S., and Deborah H. Fouts. "Chimpanzees' Use of Sign Language." In *The Great Ape Project: Equality Beyond Humanity,* edited by Paola Cavalieri and Peter Singer. New York: St. Martin's Press, 1993.

Fouts, Roger S., Deborah H. Fouts, and Thomas E. Van Confort. "The Infant Loulis Learns Signs from Cross-Fostered Chimpanzees." In *Teaching Sign Language to Chimpanzees,* edited by R. Allen Gardner, Beatrice T. Gardner, and Thomas E. Van Confort. Albany: University of New York Press, 1989.

Fouts, Roger S., and Stephen Tukel Mills. *Next of Kin: What Chimpanzees Have Taught Me About Who We Are.* New York: William Morrow, 1997.

Franklin, Benjamin. *Autobiography of Benjamin Franklin.* Edited by John Bigelow. Philadelphia: J. P. Lippincott, 1868.

Fulford, Roger. *Votes for Women: The Story of a Struggle.* London: Faber and Faber, 1958.

Gallup, Gordon. "Self-Recognition in Primates: A Comparative Approach to the Bi-Directional Properties of Consciousness." *American Psychologist* 32 (1977).

Gardner, R. Allen, Beatrice T. Gardner, and Thomas E. Van Confort, eds. *Teaching Sign Language to Chimpanzees.* Albany: University of New York Press, 1989.

Gerber, Pierre J., H. Steinfeld, B. Henderson, A. Mottet, C. Opio, J. Dijkman, A. Falcucci, and G. Tempio. *Tackling Climate Change Through Livestock—A Global Assessment of Emissions and Mitigation Opportunities.* Rome: Food and Agriculture Organization of the United Nations, 2013.

Germond, Carine, and Henning Turk, eds. *A History of Franco-German Relations in Europe: From "Hereditary Enemies" to Partners.* New York: St. Martin's Press, 2008.

Gilbert, Martin. *Auschwitz and the Allies.* New York: Holt, Rinehart, and Winston, 1981.

———. *The Holocaust: A History of the Jews of Europe During the Second World War.* New York: Henry Holt, 1985.

———. *The Routledge Atlas of the Second World War.* New York: Routledge, 2009.

———. "What Was Known and When." In *Anatomy of the Auschwitz Death Camp,* edited by Yisrael Gutman and Michael Berenbaum. Indianapolis: Indiana University Press, 1994.

Goldstone, Jack, Ted R. Gurr, Barbara Harff, and Marc A. Levy. "State Failure Task Force Report: Phase III Findings." *Environmental Change & Security Project Report* no. 5 (1999).

Gondola, Ch. Didier. *The History of Congo.* Westport, CT: Greenwood Publishing Group, 2002.

Goodall, Jane. *In the Shadow of Man.* London: Collins, 1971.

_____. "Learning from the Chimpanzees: A Message Humans Can Understand." *Science* 282 (1998).

_____. *My Friends the Wild Chimpanzees.* Washington, DC: National Geographic Society, 1967.

Goonewardene, L. A., H. Pang, R. T. Berg, and M. A. Price. "A Comparison of Reproductive and Growth Traits of Horned and Polled Cattle in Three Synthetic Beef Lines." *Canadian Journal of Animal Science* 79, no. 2 (1999).

Gould, Stephen Jay. *The Mismeasure of Man.* New York: W. W. Norton, 1984.

Grandin, Temple, and Catherine Johnson. *Animals Make Us Human: Creating the Best Life for Animals.* New York: Houghton-Mifflin Harcourt, 2009.

Gregory, Neville G. *Animal Welfare and Meat Production.* Wallingford, Oxfordshire: CABI Publishing, 2007.

_____. *Animal Welfare and Meat Science.* Wallingford, Oxfordshire: CABI Publishing, 1998.

_____. "Can Fish Experience Pain?" *ANZCCART News* 12, no. 4 (1999).

Gutman, Yisrael, and Michael Berenbaum, eds. *Anatomy of the Auschwitz Death Camp.* Indianapolis: Indiana University Press, 1994.

Hagen, Kristin, and Donald M. Broom. "Emotional Reaction to Learning in Cattle." *Applied Animal Behaviour Science* 85 (2004).

Hamilton, Susan, ed. *Criminals, Idiots, Women, and Minors: Victorian Writing on Women by Women.* Peterborough, Ontario: Broadview Press, 2004.

Harrison, Brian. *Separate Spheres: The Opposition to Women's Suffrage in Britain.* New York: Holmes & Meier, 1978.

Hausner, Gideon. *Justice in Jerusalem.* New York: Shocken Books, 1968.

Healy, William M. "Behavior." In *The Wild Turkey: Biology and Management*, edited by James G. Dickson. Mechanicsburg, PA: Stackpole Books, 1992.

Held, Suzanne, Jonathan J. Cooper, and Michael Mendl. "Advances in the Study of Cognition, Behavioural Priorities and Emotions." In *The Welfare of Pigs*, edited by Jeremy N. Marchant-Forde. New York: Springer, 2009.

Hertwich, Edgar, Ester van der Voet, Mark Huijbregts, and Sangwon Suh. *Assessing the Environmental Impacts of Consumption and Production: Priority Products and Materials.* New York: United Nations Environmental Programme, 2010.

Hilberg, Raul. "Confronting the Moral Implications of the Holocaust." *Social Education* 42 (1961).

_____. *The Destruction of the European Jews.* Chicago: Quadrangle Books, 1967.

_____. *The Destruction of the European Jews.* 3rd ed. New Haven, CT: Yale University Press, 2003.

_____. "The Destruction of the European Jews: Dehumanization and Concealment." In *Understanding Prejudice and Discrimination*, edited by Scott Plous. New York: McGraw-Hill, 2003.

Hixson, Michael D. "Ape Language Research: A Review and Behavioral Perspective." *The Analysis of Verbal Behavior* 15 (1998).

Hochschild, Adam. *King Leopold's Ghost: A Story of Greed, Terror, and Heroism in Colonial Africa.* New York: Mariner Books, 1999.

Hodson, Gordon, and Miles Hewstone, eds. *Advances in Intergroup Contact.* New York: Psychology Press, 2013.

Hodson, Gordon, Kimberly Costello, and Cara C. MacInnis. "Is Intergroup Contact Beneficial Among Intolerant People?" In *Advances in Intergroup Contact*, edited by Gordon Hodson and Miles Hewstone. New York: Psychology Press, 2013.

Hogue, Michèle-E., Jacques Beaugrand, and Paul C. Lagüe. "Coherent Use of Information by Hens Observing Their Former Dominant Defeating or Being Defeated by a Stranger." *Behavioural Processes* 38, no. 3 (1996).

Hollis, Patricia. *Ladies Elect: Women in English Local Government 1865–1914.* Oxford: Oxford University Press, 1987.

Holton, Sandra. *Feminism and Democracy: Women's Suffrage and Reform Politics in Britain, 1900–1918.* Cambridge: Cambridge University Press, 2003.

Höss, Rudolf. *Death Dealer: The Memoirs of the SS Kommandant at Auschwitz.* Edited by Steven Paskuly. Translated by Andrew Pollinger. New York: Da Capo Press, 1996.

Hume, Lesley Parker. *The National Union of Women's Suffrage Societies 1897–1914.* New York: Garland Publishing, 1982.

Hunt, Gavin R. "Manufacture and Use of Hook Tools by New Caledonian Crows." *Nature* 249 (1996).

Inoue, Sana, and Tetsuro Matsuzawa. "Working Memory of Numerals in Chimpanzees." *Current Biology* 17, no. 23 (2007).

Jackson, Lynne M. *The Psychology of Prejudice: From Attitudes to Social Action*, 2nd Edition. Washington, DC: American Psychological Association, 2020.

Jacobs, Frank. "A Boot Fit for a King." *New York Times*, February 6, 2012.

Jangfeldt, Bengt. *The Hero of Budapest: The Triumph and Tragedy of Raoul Wallenberg.*

Translated by Harry D. Watson and Bengt Jangfeldt. London: I. B. Tauris, 2014.

Jenkins, Lindsey. *Lady Constance Lytton: Aristocrat, Suffragette, Martyr.* London: Biteback Publishing, 2005.

Jylhä, Kirsti, and Nazar Akrami. "Social Dominance and Climate Change Denial: The Role of Dominance and System Justification." *Personality and Individual Differences* 86 (2015).

Kádár, Gábor, and Zoltán Vági. *Self-Financing Genocide.* Budapest: Central European University Press, 2001.

Kawai, Masao. "Newly-Acquired Pre-Cultural Behavior of the Natural Troop of Japanese Monkeys in Koshima Islet." *Primates* 6, no. 1 (1965).

Keeling, Linda J., and H. W. Gonyou, eds. *Social Behaviour in Farm Animals.* Wallingford, Oxfordshire: CABI International, 2001.

Keir, David Lindsay. *The Constitutional History of Modern Britain 1485–1937.* London: A & C Black, 1948.

Keith, Arthur B. *The Belgian Congo and the Berlin Act.* London: Oxford University Press, 1919.

Kennedy, Robert F. *RFK: Collected Speeches.* Edited by Edwin O. Guthman and C. Richard Allen. New York: Viking, 1993.

Kershaw, Alex. *The Envoy: The Epic Rescue of the Last Jews of Europe in the Desperate Closing Months of World War II.* Cambridge, MA: Da Capo Press, 2010.

Kestin, S. C., T. G. Knowles, A. E. Tinch, and N. G. Gregory. "Prevalence of Leg Weakness in Broiler Chickens and Its Relationship with Genotype." *Veterinary Record* 131 (1992).

Key, Timothy, and Gwyneth Davey. "Prevalence of Obesity Is Low in People Who Do Not Eat Meat." *British Medical Journal* 313 (1996).

Key, Timothy, G. E. Fraser, M. Thorogood, P. N. Appleby, V. Beral, G. Reeves, M. L. Burr, J. Chang-Claude, R. Frentzel-Beyme, J. W. Kuzma, J. Mann, and K. McPherson. "Mortality in Vegetarians and Non-Vegetarians: A Collaborative Analysis of 8,300 Deaths among 76,000 Men and Women in Five Prospective Studies." *Public Health Nutrition* 1, no. 1 (1998).

Kinzer, Bruce L., Ann P. Robson, and John M. Robson. *A Moralist in and out of Parliament: John Stuart Mill at Westminster 1865–1868.* Toronto: University of Toronto Press, 1992.

Kluivers-Poodt, Marion, B. B. Houx, S. R. M. Robben, G. Koop, E. Lambooij, and L. J. Hellebrekers. "Effects of a Local Anesthetic and NSAID in Castration of Piglets, on the Acute Pain Responses, Growth, and Mortality." *Animal* 6, no. 9 (2012).

Knopp, Guido. *Hitler's Hitmen*. Translated by Angus McGeoch. Gloucestershire: Sutton Publishing, 2006.

Knowles, Toby G., Steve C. Kestin, Susan M. Haslam, Steven N. Brown, Laura E. Green, Andrew Butterworth, Stuart J. Pope, Dirk Pfeiffer, and Christine J. Nicol. "Leg Disorders in Broiler Chickens: Prevalence, Risk Factors and Prevention." *PLoS One* 3, no. 2 (2008).

Kosterman, Rick, and Seymour Feshbach. "Toward a Measure of Patriotic and Nationalistic Attitudes." *Political Psychology* 10, no. 2 (1989).

Krijtenburg, Margriet. "Schuman's Europe: His Frame of Reference." PhD diss., Universiteit Leiden, 2012. https://openaccess.leidenuniv.nl/bitstream/handle/1887/19767/fulltext.pdf?sequence=17.

Kteily, Nour, Arnold K. Ho, and Jim Sidanius. "Hierarchy in the Mind: The Predictive Power of Social Dominance Orientation Across Social Contexts and Domains." *Journal of Experimental Social Psychology* 48 (2011).

Laland, Kevin N., and Bennett G. Galef, eds. *The Question of Animal Culture*. Cambridge, MA: Harvard University Press, 2009.

Laland, Kevin N., Culum Brown, and Jens Krause. "Learning in Fishes: From Three-Second Memory to Culture." *Fish and Fisheries* 4 (2003).

Laland, Kevin N., and Kerry Williams. "Shoaling Generates Social Learning of Foraging Information in Guppies." *Animal Behaviour* 53 (1997).

Lawrence, D. H. "Love Was Once a Little Boy." In *Reflections on the Death of a Porcupine and Other Essays*. Bloomington: Indiana University Press, 1963.

Leakey, Louis Seymour Bazette. *The Progress and Evolution of Man in Africa*. London: Oxford University Press, 1961.

Leite, Ana C., Kristof Dhont, and Gordon Hodson. "Longitudinal Effects of Human Supremacy Beliefs and Vegetarianism Threat on Moral Exclusion (vs. Inclusion) of Animals." *European Journal of Social Psychology* 49 (2018).

Lester, Elenore. *Wallenberg: The Man in the Iron Web*. Englewood Cliffs, NJ: Prentice-Hall, 1982.

Levai, Jeno. *Black Book on the Martyrdom of Hungarian Jewry*. Zurich: Central European Times Publishing Co., 1948.

_____. *Raoul Wallenberg: His Remarkable Life, Heroic Battles, and the Secret of His Mysterious Disappearance*. Translated by Frank Vajda. Melbourne: White Ant Occasional Publishing, 1988.

_____, ed. *Eichmann in Hungary: Documents*. Budapest: Panama Press, 1961.

Levine, Paul A. *Raoul Wallenberg in Budapest: Myth, History and Holocaust*. London: Vallentine Mitchell, 2010.

Lewis, Jane, ed. *Before the Vote Was Won: Arguments For and Against Women's Suffrage 1864–1896.* London: Routledge & Kegan Paul, 1987.

Lieberman, Philip. *The Unpredictable Species: What Makes Humans Unique.* Princeton: Princeton University Press, 2013.

Lifton, Robert Jay. *The Nazi Doctors: Medical Killing and the Psychology of Genocide.* New York: Basic Books, 1986.

Linnéa, Sharon. *Raoul Wallenberg: The Man Who Stopped Death.* Philadelphia: The Jewish Publication Society, 1993.

Lippi, Guiseppi, Camilla Mattiuzzi, and Gianfranco Cervellin. "Meat Consumption and Cancer Risk: A Critical Review of Published Meta-Analyses." *Critical Reviews in Oncology/Hematology* 97 (2015).

Longerich, Peter. *Heinrich Himmler.* Translated by Jeremy Noakes and Lesley Sharpe. Oxford: Oxford University Press, 2012.

Loughnan, Steve, Brock Bastian, and Nick Haslam. "The Psychology of Eating Animals." *Current Directions in Psychological Science* 23, no. 2 (2014).

Loughnan, Steve, Nick Haslam, and Brock Bastian. "The Role of Meat Consumption in the Denial of Moral Status to Meat Animals," *Appetite* 55 (2010).

Louis, Wm. Roger. *Ends of British Imperialism.* London: I.B. Tauris, 2007.

Louis, Wm. Roger, and Jean Stengers. *E. D. Morel's History of the Congo Reform Movement.* Oxford: Clarendon Press, 1968.

Lowe, Dan. "Common Arguments for the Moral Acceptability of Eating Meat: A Discussion for Students." *Between the Species* 19, no. 1 (2016).

Lowther, James William. *A Speaker's Commentaries.* London: Edward Arnold, 1925.

Lytton, Constance. *Letters of Constance Lytton.* Edited by Betty Balfour. Cambridge: Cambridge University Press, 1925.

_____. *No Votes for Women: A Reply to Some Recent Anti-Suffrage Publications.* London: A.C. Fifield, 1909.

_____. *Prisons and Prisoners.* Edited by Jason Haslam. Peterborough, Ontario: Broadview Press, 2008.

Macartney, C. A. *October Fifteenth: A History of Modern Hungary, 1929–1945.* Edinburgh: Edinburgh University Press, 1956.

Manton, Jo. *Elizabeth Garrett Anderson.* New York: E.P. Dutton, 1965.

Manvell, Roger, and Heinrich Fraenkel. *Heinrich Himmler: The Sinister Life of the Head of the SS and Gestapo.* New York: Skyhorse Publishing, 2007.

Marchant-Forde, Jeremy N., ed. *The Welfare of Pigs.* New York: Springer, 2009.

Marino, Lori. "Thinking Chickens: A Review of Cognition, Emotion, and Behavior in the Domestic Chicken." *Animal Behavior and Cognition* 20 (2017).

Marino, Lori, and Kristin Allen. "The Psychology of Cows." *Animal Behavior and Cognition* 4, no. 4 (2017).

Marlow, Joyce, ed. *Suffragettes: The Fight for Votes for Women*. London: Virago Press, 2013.

Martelli, George. *Leopold to Lumumba: A History of the Belgian Congo 1877–1960*. London: Chapman & Hall, 1962.

Marx, G., T. Horn, J. Thielebein, B. Knubel, and E. von Borell. "Analysis of Pain-Related Vocalization in Young Pigs." *Journal of Sound and Vibration* 266 (2003).

Marzluff, John M., Jeff Walls, Heather N. Cornell, John C. Withey, and David P. Craig. "Lasting Recognition of Threatening People by Wild American Crows." *Animal Behavior* 79 (2010).

Masserman, Jules H., Stanley Wechkin, and William Terris. "'Altruistic' Behavior in Rhesus Monkeys." *American Journal of Psychiatry* 121 (1964).

Matsuzawa, Tetsuro. "Symbolic Representation of Number in Chimpanzees." *Current Opinion in Neurobiology* 19 (2009).

McGeown, D., T. C. Danbury, A. E. Waterman-Pearson, and S. C. Kestin. "Effect of Carprofen on Lameness in Broiler Chickens." *Veterinary Record* 144 (1999).

McMullen, Steven. *Animals and the Economy*. London: Palgrave Macmillan, 2016.

Meltzer, Milton. *Slavery: A World History*. New York: Da Capo Press, 1992.

Mendl, Michael, Suzanne Held, and Richard W. Byrne. "Pig Cognition." *Current Biology* 20, no. 18 (2010).

Mesaroş, Claudiu Marius. "Aristotle and Animal Mind." *Procedia – Social and Behavioral Sciences* 163 (2014).

Messina, V. K., and K. I. Burke. "Position Statement of the American Dietetic Association: Vegetarian Diets." *Journal of the American Dietetic Association* 97, no. 11 (1997).

Midgley, Mary. *Beast and Man: The Roots of Human Nature*. London: Routledge, 2002.

Miele, Mara. "The Taste of Happiness: Free-Range Chicken." *Environment and Planning A* 43 (2011).

Milfont, Taciano Lemos, Isabel Richter, Chris G. Sibley, Marc S. Wilson, and Ronald Fischer. "Environmental Consequences of the Desire to Dominate and Be Superior." *Personality and Social Psychology Bulletin* 39, no. 9 (2013).

————. "On the Relation Between Social Dominance Orientation and Environmentalism: A 25-Nation Study." *Social Psychology and Personality Science* 9, no. 7 (2018).

Mill, John Stuart. "On Nature." In *The Utility of Religion and Theism*. London: Watts, 1904.

_____. *The Subjection of Women.* Mineola, NY: Dover Publications, 1997.

Mitchell, Donald. *The Politics of Dissent: A Biography of E. D. Morel.* Bristol: SilverWood Books, 2014.

Mitchell, Sally. *Frances Power Cobbe: Victorian Feminist, Journalist, Reformer.* Charlottesville: University of Virginia Press, 2004.

Molony, V., and J. E. Kent. "Assessment of Acute Pain in Farm Animals Using Behavioral and Physiological Measurements." *Journal of Animal Science* 75 (1997).

Morel, E. D. *The Future of the Congo: An Analysis and Criticism of the Belgian Government's Proposals for a Reform of the Conditions in the Congo Submitted to His Majesty's Government on Behalf of the Congo Reform Association.* London: Smith Elder, 1909.

_____. *King Leopold's Rule in Africa.* London: William Heineman, 1904.

_____. *Red Rubber: The Story of the Rubber Slave Trade Which Flourished in the Congo for Twenty Years, 1890–1910.* 2nd rev. ed. London: The National Labour Press, 1920.

_____, trans. *Verbatim Report of the Five Days' Congo Debate in the Belgian House of Representatives: February 20, 27, 28; March 1, 2, 1906.* Liverpool: John Richardson & Sons, 1906.

Morley, John. *The Life of William Ewart Gladstone.* London: Macmillan, 1903.

Müller, Friedrich Max. *Lectures on the Science of Language Delivered at the Royal Institution of Great Britain.* 3rd ed. London: Longman, Green, Longman, & Roberts, 1862.

Nazi Conspiracy and Aggression. National Archives and Records Administration, Washington, DC.

Naylor, Rosamond L., Ronald W. Hardy, Dominique P. Bureau, Alice Chiu, Matthew Elliott, Anthony P. Farrell, Ian Forster et al. "Feeding Aquaculture in an Era of Finite Resources." *PNAS* 106, no. 36 (2009).

North, M. O. "Some Tips on Floor Space and Profits." *Broiler Industry*, December 1975.

Oderberg, David S. "The Illusion of Animal Rights." *Human Life Review* 26, no. 2/3 (2000).

Orwell, George. *Animal Farm.* New York: Houghton Mifflin Harcourt, 1990.

Pakenham, Thomas. *The Scramble for Africa: The White Man's Conquest of the Dark Continent from 1876 to 1912.* New York: Random House, 1991.

Pankhurst, Emmeline. *My Own Story.* London: Eveleigh Nash, 1914.

Pankhurst, Sylvia. *The Suffragette: The History of the Women's Militant Suffrage Movement.* Mineola, NY: Dover Publications, 1911.

Parker, Theodore. *The Collected Works of Theodore Parker*. Edited by F. P. Cobbe. London: Trübner, 1879.

Pavlakis, Dean. *British Humanitarianism and the Congo Reform Movement 1896–1913*. Surrey: Ashgate Publishing, 2015.

Pethick-Lawrence, F. W. *Fate Has Been Kind*. London: Hutchinson, 1943.

Pettigrew, Thomas F., and Linda R. Tropp. "How Does Intergroup Contact Reduce Prejudice? Meta-Analytic Tests of Three Mediators." *European Journal of Social Psychology* 38 (2008).

———. "A Meta-Analytic Test of Intergroup Contact Theory." *Journal of Personality and Social Psychology* 90, no. 5 (2006).

Piazza, Jared, Matthew B. Ruby, Steve Loughnan, Mischel Luong, Juliana Kulik, Hanne M. Watkins, and Mirra Seigerman. "Rationalizing Meat Consumption: The 4 Ns." *Appetite* 91 (2015).

Pimentel, David, and Marcia Pimentel. "Sustainability of Meat-Based and Plant-Based Diets and the Environment," suppl. *American Journal of Clinical Nutrition* 78 (2003).

Piper, Franciszek. "The System of Prisoner Exploitation." In *Anatomy of the Auschwitz Death Camp*, edited by Yisrael Gutman and Michael Berenbaum. Indianapolis: Indiana University Press, 1994.

Pratto, Felicia, James Sidanius, Lisa M. Stallworth, and Bertram F. Malle. "Social Dominance Orientation: A Personality Variable Predicting Social and Political Attitudes." *Journal of Personality and Social Psychology* 67, no. 4 (1994).

Pratto, Felicia, Jim Sidanius, and Shana Levin. "Social Dominance Theory and the Dynamics of Intergroup Relations: Taking Stock and Looking Forward." *European Review of Social Psychology* 17 (2006).

Price, David Heilbron. *Schuman's Warning of the Nazi Destruction of the Jews*. Brussels: Bron Communications, 2014.

Prunier, A., A. M. Mounier, and M. Hay. "Effects of Castration, Tooth Resection, or Tail Docking on Plasma Metabolites and Stress Hormones in Pigs." *Journal of Animal Science* 83 (2005).

Pugh, Martin. *Electoral Reform in War and Peace 1906–1918*. London: Routledge & Kegan Paul, 1978.

———. *The March of the Women: A Revisionist Analysis of the Campaign for Women's Suffrage, 1866–1914*. Oxford: Oxford University Press, 2000.

———. *The Pankhursts: The History of One Radical Family*. London: Vintage Books, 2008.

Rachels, James. "The Basic Argument for Vegetarianism." In *The Legacy of Socrates:*

Essays in Moral Philosophy, edited by Stuart Rachels. New York: Columbia University Press, 2007.

————. *Created from Animals: The Moral Implications of Darwinism*. Oxford: Oxford University Press, 1990.

————. *The Elements of Moral Philosophy*. Edited by Stuart Rachels. New York: McGraw-Hill, 2018.

————. "The Moral Argument for Vegetarianism." In *Can Ethics Provide Answers? And Other Essays in Moral Philosophy*. Lanham, MD: Rowan & Littlefield, 1997.

————. "Reflections on the Idea of Equality." In *Can Ethics Provide Answers? And Other Essays in Moral Philosophy*. Lanham, MD: Rowan & Littlefield, 1997.

Rees, Lawrence. *Auschwitz: A New History*. New York: Public Affairs, 2005.

Reid, B. L. "A Good Man Has Had Fever: Casement in the Congo." *Sewanee Review* 82, no. 3 (1974).

Reijnders, Lucas, and Sam Soret. "Quantification of the Environmental Impact of Different Dietary Protein Choices," suppl. *American Journal of Clinical Nutrition* 78 (2003).

Robb, D. H. F., S. B. Wotton, J. L. McKinstry, N. K. Sørensen, S. C. Kestin, ,and N. K. Sørensen. "Commercial Slaughter Methods Used on Atlantic Salmon: The Determination of the Onset of Brain Failure by Electroencephalography." *Veterinary Record* 147 (2000).

Robinson, Jane. *Hearts and Minds: The Untold Story of the Great Pilgrimage and How Women Won the Vote*. London: Doubleday, 2018.

Robson, John M. "Mill in Parliament: The View from the Comic Papers." *Utilitas* 2, no. 1 (1990).

Rochefort, Robert. *Robert Schuman*. Paris: Éditions du Cerf, 1968.

Roe, Emma, and Terry Marsden. "Analysis of Retail Survey of Products that Carry Welfare Claims and of Non-Retailer Assurance Schemes Whose Logos Accompany Welfare Claims." In *Attitudes of Consumers, Retailers and Producers to Animal Welfare*, edited by Unni Kjærnes, Mara Miele, and Joek Roex. Cardiff: Cardiff University Press, 2007.

Rolf, David. "Origins of Mr. Speaker's Conference During the First World War." *History* 64, no. 210 (1979).

Rose, James D. "The Neurobehavioral Nature of Fishes and the Question of Awareness and Pain." *Reviews in Fisheries Science* 10, no. 1 (2002).

Roseman, Mark. *The Villa. The Lake. The Meeting: Wannsee and the Final Solution*. London: Allen Lane, 2002.

Rosen, Andrew. *Rise Up, Women! The Militant Campaign of the Women's Social and Political Union 1903–1914*. London: Routledge, 2013.

Rothgerber, Hank. "Efforts to Overcome Vegetarian-Induced Dissonance among Meat-Eaters." *Appetite* 79 (2014).

Rubinstein, David. *A Different World for Women: The Life of Millicent Garrett Fawcett.* Athens: Ohio University Press, 1991.

Sabaté, Joan. "The Contribution of Vegetarian Diets to Health and Disease: A Paradigm Shift?" suppl. *American Journal of Clinical Nutrition* 78 (2003).

Sabaté, Joan, and Sam Soret. "Sustainability of Plant-Based Diets: Back to the Future," suppl. *American Journal of Clinical Nutrition* 100 (2014).

Sagan, Carl, and Ann Druyan. *Shadows of Forgotten Ancestors: A Search for Who We Are.* New York: Random House, 1992.

_____. *Pale Blue Dot: A Vision of the Human Future in Space.* New York: Random House, 1994.

_____. *The Varieties of Scientific Experience: A Personal View of the Search for God.* New York: Penguin Press, 2006.

Sakmyster, Thomas L. *Hungary's Admiral on Horseback: Miklós Horthy, 1918–1944.* Boulder, CO: East European Monographs, 1994.

Samuels, William Ellery. "Nurturing Kindness Naturally: A Humane Education Program's Effect on the Prosocial Behavior of First and Second Graders across China." *International Journal of Educational Research* 91 (2018).

Sanotra, Gurbakhsh Singh, Lartey G. Lawson, Klaus S. Vestergaard, and Martin G. Thomsen. "Influence of Stocking Density on Tonic Immobility, Lameness, and Tibial Dyschondroplasia in Broilers." *Journal of Applied Animal Welfare Science* 4, no. 1 (2001).

Scarborough, Peter, Paul N. Appleby, Anja Mizdrak, Adam D. M. Briggs, Ruth C. Travis, Kathryn E. Bradbury, and Timothy J. Key. "Dietary Greenhouse Gas Emissions of Meat-Eaters, Fish-Eaters, Vegetarians and Vegans in the UK." *Climatic Change* 125 (2014).

Schlottman, Christopher, and Jeff Sebo. *Food, Animals and the Environment.* New York: Routledge, 2019.

Schuman, Robert. *For Europe.* Geneva: Nagel Editions, 2010.

Shanley, Mary Lyndon. *Feminism, Marriage, and the Law in Victorian England.* Princeton: Princeton University Press, 1989.

Shubin, Neil. *Your Inner Fish: A Journey into the 3.5 Billion Year History of the Human Body.* New York: Pantheon Books, 2008.

Sibley, Chris G., and Fiona Kate Barlow, eds. *The Cambridge Handbook of the Psychology of Prejudice,* Cambridge: Cambridge University Press, 2016.

Sidanius, Jim, and Felicia Pratto. *Social Dominance: An Intergroup Theory of Social Hierarchy and Oppression.* Cambridge: Cambridge University Press, 1999.

Sidanius, Jim, Sarah Cotterill, Jennifer Sheehy-Skeffington, Nour Kteily, and Héctor Carvacho. "Social Dominance Theory: Explorations in the Psychology of Oppression." In *The Cambridge Handbook of the Psychology of Prejudice*, edited by Chris G. Sibley and Fiona Kate Barlow. Cambridge: Cambridge University Press, 2016.

Singer, Peter, and Jim Mason. *The Ethics of What We Eat: Why Our Food Choices Matter.* Emmaus, PA: Rodale, 2006.

Sinha, Rashmi, Amanda J. Cross, Barry I. Graubard, Michael F. Leitzmann, and Arthur Schatzkin. "Meat Intake and Mortality: A Prospective Study of over Half a Million People." *Archives of Internal Medicine* 169, no. 6 (2009).

Síocháin, Séamas, and Michael O'Sullivan. *The Eyes of Another Race: Roger Casement's Congo Report and 1903 Diary.* Dublin: University College Dublin Press, 2003.

Smith, Carolyn L., and Jane Johnson. "The Chicken Challenge: What Contemporary Studies of Fowl Mean for Science and Ethics." *Between the Species* 15, no. 1 (2012).

Smith, David Livingstone. *Less Than Human: Why We Demean, Enslave, and Exterminate Others.* New York: St. Martin's Press, 2011.

Smith, F. B. *The Making of the Second Reform Bill.* Cambridge: Cambridge University Press, 1966.

Smith, Jane A., and Kenneth M. Boyd, eds. *Lives in the Balance: The Ethics of Using Animals in Biomedical Research.* Oxford: Oxford University Press, 1991.

Smith, Wesley J. *A Rat Is a Pig Is a Dog Is a Boy: The Human Cost of the Animal Rights Movement.* New York: Encounter Books, 2010.

Sneddon, Lynne U. "Do Painful Sensations and Fear Exist in Fish?" In *From Science to Law*, edited by T. A. Van der Kemp and M. Lachance. Toronto: Carswell, 2013.

————. "The Evidence for Pain in Fish: The Use of Morphine as an Analgesic." *Applied Animal Behaviour Science* 83, no. 2 (2003).

Sneddon, Lynne U., and Michael J. Gentle. "Pain in Farm Animals." In *Animal Welfare and Animal Health: Proceedings of Workshop 5 on Sustainable Animal Production*, edited by Franz Ellendorff, Volker Moennia, Jan Ladewig, and Lorne A. Babink. Braunschweig, Germany: FAL Agricultural Research, 2000.

Sneddon, Lynne U., Victoria A. Braithwaite, and Michael J. Gentle. "Do Fishes Have Nociceptors? Evidence for the Evolution of a Vertebrate Sensory System." *Proceedings of the Royal Society London B* 270 (2003).

Snowdon, David A., and Roland L. Phillips. "Does a Vegetarian Diet Reduce the Occurrence of Diabetes?" *American Journal of Public Health* 75 (1985).

Snyder, Timothy. *Black Earth: The Holocaust as History and Warning*. New York: Tim Duggan Books, 2015.

Sørensen, P., G. Su, and S. C. Kestin. "Effects of Age and Stocking Density on Leg Weakness in Broiler Chickens." *Poultry Science* 79 (2000).

Stangneth, Bettina. *Eichmann before Jerusalem: The Unexamined Life of a Mass Murderer*. Translated by Ruth Martin. New York: Alfred A. Knopf, 2014.

Steinfeld, Henning, Pierre Gerber, Tom Wassenaar, Vincent Castel, Mauricio Rosales, and Cees de Haan. *Livestock's Long Shadow: Environmental Issues and Options*. Rome: Food and Agriculture Organization of the United Nations, 2006.

Stolba, A., and D. G. M. Wood-Gush. "The Identification of Behavioural Key Features and Their Incorporation into a Housing Design for Pigs." *Annals of Veterinary Research* 15, no. 2 (1984).

Strachey, Ray. *The Cause: A Short History of the Women's Movement in Great Britain*. Middletown, Delaware: Endeavour Press, 2016.

_____. *Millicent Garrett Fawcett*. London: John Murray, 1931.

Suddendorf, Thomas. *The Gap: The Science of What Separates Us from Other Animals*. New York: Basic Books, 2013.

Swanick, Helena. *I Have Been Young*. London: V. Gollancz, 1935.

Świebocki, Henryk. "Auschwitz: What Did the World Know During the War?" In *London Has Been Informed: Reports by Auschwitz Escapees*, edited by Henryk Świebocki. Oświęcim: The Auschwitz-Birkenau State Museum, 1997.

_____. "Prisoner Escapes." In *Anatomy of the Auschwitz Death Camp*, edited by Yisrael Gutman and Michael Berenbaum. Indianapolis: Indiana University Press, 1994.

_____, ed. *London Has Been Informed: Reports by Auschwitz Escapees*. Oświęcim: The Auschwitz-Birkenau State Museum, 1997.

Szabó, Zoltán. "The Auschwitz Reports: Who Got Them and When?" In *The Auschwitz Reports and the Holocaust in Hungary*, edited by Randolph L. Braham and William J. vanden Heuvel. New York: Columbia University Press, 2011.

Taylor, Alex H., Douglas M. Elliffe, Gavin R. Hunt, Nathan J. Emery, Nicola S. Clayton, and Russell D. Gray. "New Caledonian Crows Learn the Functional Properties of Novel Tool Types." *PLoS One* 6, no. 12 (2011).

Taylor, Alex H., Gavin R. Hunt, Jennifer C. Holzhaider, and Russell D. Gray. "Spontaneous Metatool Use by New Caledonian Crows." *Current Biology* 17, no. 17 (2007).

Taylor, Nik, and Tania D. Signal. "Empathy and Attitudes to Animals." *Anthrozoös* 18, no. 1 (2005).

Teleki, Geza. "Chimpanzee Subsistence Techniques: Materials and Technology." *Journal of Human Evolution* 3, no. 6 (1974).

Terrace, Herbert S., L. A. Petitto, R. J. Sanders, and Thomas Bever. "Can an Ape Create a Sentence?" *Science* 206 (1979).

Tomback, Diana F. "How Nutcrackers Find Their Food Stores." *Condor* 82 (1980).

Twain, Mark. "Hunting the Deceitful Turkey." In *Mark Twain: Collected Tales, Sketches, Speeches and Essays 1891–1910*, edited by Louis J. Budd. New York: Library of America, 1992.

Ungváry, Kristián. *The Siege of Budapest: 100 Days in World War II*. Translated by Ladislaus Löb. New Haven, CT: Yale University Press, 2002.

United Nations, Department of Economic and Social Affairs. *World Population Prospects: The 2012 Revision*. New York: United Nations, 2013.

————. *International Migration Report 2017: Highlights*. New York: United Nations, 2017.

United Nations High Commissioner for Refugees. *Global Trends: Forced Displacement in 2016*. Geneva: United Nations High Commissioner for Refugees, 2017.

————. *Global Trends: Forced Displacement in 2017*. Geneva: United Nations High Commissioner for Refugees. 2018.

Vági, Zoltán, László Csősz, and Gábor Kádár. *The Holocaust in Hungary: Evolution of a Genocide*. Lanham, MD: AltiMira Press, 2013.

Van Reybrouck, David. *Congo: The Epic History of a People*. Translated by Sam Garrett. New York: HarperCollins, 2014.

Varner, Gary E. *In Nature's Interests? Interests, Animal Rights and Environmental Ethics*. New York: Oxford University Press, 1998.

Vermeersch, Arthur. *La Question Congolaise*. Brussels: Imprimerie Scientifique, 1906.

Von Keyserlingk, M. A., and Daniel M. Weary. "Maternal Behavior in Cattle." *Hormones and Behavior* 52 (2007).

Vrba, Rudolf. "The Preparations for the Holocaust in Hungary: An Eyewitness Account." In *The Nazis' Last Victims: The Holocaust in Hungary*, edited by Randolph L. Braham and Scott Miller. Detroit: Wayne State University Press, 1998.

Vrba, Rudolf, and Alan Bestic. *I Cannot Forgive*. New York: Grove Press, 1964.

Vrba, Rudolf, and Alfréd Wetzler. "Report of Rudolf Vrba and Alfréd Wetzler." In *London Has Been Informed: Reports by Auschwitz Escapees*, edited by Henryk Świebocki. Oświęcim: The Auschwitz-Birkenau State Museum, 1997.

Waddock, Sandra, and Pietra Rivoli. "'First They Fight You . . .': The Time–Context Dynamic and Corporate Responsibility." *California Management Review* 53, no. 2 (2011).

Wallace-Wells, David. *The Uninhabitable Earth: Life after Warming.* New York: Tim Duggan Books, 2019.

Wallenberg, Raoul. *Letters and Dispatches 1924–1944.* Translated by Kjersti Board. New York: Arcade Publishing, 1987.

Watson, Lyall. *The Whole Hog: Exploring the Extraordinary Potential of Pigs.* Washington, DC: Smithsonian Books, 2004.

Weary, Daniel M., and David Fraser. "Calling by Domestic Piglets: Reliable Signals of Need?" *Animal Behaviour* 50, no. 4 (1995).

Weary, Daniel M., Lee Niel, Frances C. Flower, and David Fraser. "Identifying and Preventing Pain in Animals." *Applied Animal Behavior Science* 100, no. 1 (2006).

Webster, John. *Animal Husbandry Regained: The Place of Farm Animals in Sustainable Agriculture.* New York: Routledge, 2013.

———. *Animal Welfare: A Cool Eye Towards Eden.* Oxford: Blackwell Publishing, 1994.

———. *Animal Welfare: Limping Towards Eden.* Oxford: Blackwell Publishing, 2005.

Weir, Alex A. S., Jackie Chapell, and Alex Kacelnik. "Shaping of Hooks in New Caledonian Crows," *Science* 297 (2002).

Werbell, Frederick E., and Thurston Clarke. *Lost Hero: The Mystery of Raoul Wallenberg.* New York: New American Library, 1985.

Whiten, Andrew, J. Goodall, W. C. McGrew, T. Nishida, V. Reynolds, Y. Sugiyama, C. E. G. Tutin, R. W. Wrangham, and C. Boesch. "Cultures in Chimpanzees." *Nature* 399 (1999).

Wilson, Edward O. *The Meaning of Human Existence.* New York: Liveright Publishing Corporation, 2014.

Yerkes, Robert M., and Ada W. Yerkes. *The Great Apes.* New Haven, CT: Yale University Press, 1929.

Zuidhof, M. J., B. L. Schneider, V. L. Carney, D. R. Korver, and F. E. Robinson. "Growth, Efficiency, and Yield of Commercial Broilers from 1957, 1978, and 2005." *Poultry Science* 93, no. 12 (2014).

Index

About the Author

Peter Marsh received a bachelor's degree in psychology from Wesleyan University in 1976. Since receiving a law degree four years later, he has represented people with disabilities and organizations that provide services to them. Peter lives with his wife in a small New Hampshire town.

About the Publisher

LANTERN PUBLISHING & MEDIA was founded in 2020 to follow and expand on the legacy of Lantern Books—a publishing company started in 1999 on the principles of living with a greater depth and commitment to the preservation of the natural world. Like its predecessor, Lantern Publishing & Media produces books on animal advocacy, veganism, religion, social justice, and psychology and family therapy. Lantern is dedicated to printing in the United States on recycled paper and saving resources in our day-to-day operations. Our titles are also available as ebooks and audiobooks.

To catch up on Lantern's publishing program, visit us at www.lanternpm.org.

 facebook.com/lanternpm
instagram.com/lanternpm
twitter.com/lanternpm